An Everlasting
LOVE(R)

Susan Mason Joiner

Moonstruck ◯ Publishers
Santa Rosa, CA

AN EVERLASTING LOVE(R)

How One Couple Learns the Secret of A Multi-Orgasmic Man

By Susan Mason Joiner

Published by: Moonstruck ◯ Publishers
5299 Hall Road
Santa Rosa, CA 95401-5566

Copyright © 1997 by Susan Mason Joiner
Printed and bound in the United States of America

10 9 8 7 6 5 4 3 2 1

Publisher's Cataloging-in-Publication
(Provided by Quality Books, Inc.)

Joiner, Susan Mason
    An everlasting love(r): how one couple learns the secret of a multi-orgasmic man/ by Susan Mason Joiner
    p.cm.
    Includes bibliographical references.
    ISBN 0-9656958-4-0

    1. Sex. 2. Sex instruction. 3. Man-woman relationships. 4. Male orgasm I. Title. II. Title: Everlasting lover.

HQ31.E84 1998   613.9'6
                  QB197-40371

To my husband Marty,
a warrior and a lover

And to my parents,
James Homer Joiner and Gene Mary Mason Joiner,
for giving me their love and values

A Note From the Publisher

This book was written to help men and women improve their sexual relationships and develop a more loving bond through the mastery of multiple male orgasms. The techniques described in Part II are not a gimmick, a fad, or a trick. They are based on ancient Eastern principles that have been practiced over thousands of years of history and recently proven through modern medical research. The exercises are effective, but they aren't magic. Discipline and persistence are required in learning these techniques, but the rewards are well worth the investment.

Because sexual activity requires a certain amount of physical effort, readers must consider their general condition before beginning this practice. If you have heart disease, high blood pressure, or another physical condition of some consequence, or have generally poor health, consult your doctor and proceed slowly.

The material in this book is based on recent research and was written as completely and accurately as possible. In spite of thorough editing, content or typographical errors may be found. Therefore, this book should be read and used as a general guide only, and not as the ultimate source of information on multiple male orgasms.

This book was written for the reader's entertainment as well as education. The author and Moonstruck Publishers shall have neither responsibility nor liability to any reader or entity with respect to any damage or loss caused, or alleged to be caused, directly or indirectly by any information contained in this book.

Please return this book to the publisher for a complete refund if you do not wish to be bound by the above stipulations.

Table of Contents

Preface   7

Introduction   8

Part I: The Story

Chapter 1   13
   In The (Very) Beginning...

Chapter 2   15
   Thank You, Mr. President

Chapter 3   25
   "It Ain't Fact, But It's True"

Chapter 4   35
   Mustang Sally

Chapter 5   48
   Man To Man

Chapter 6   59
   A Thousand Repetitions and The Four-Minute Mile

Chapter 7   70
   Acting on Instinct

Chapter 8   78
   Jesse Loves Clare

Chapter 9   86
   Everlasting Love(rs)

Part II: The Guide

Chapter 10   93
   Getting Started
      Three Major Principles of Multiple Male Orgasms   93
      General Guidelines for Mastering Multi-Orgasmic Skills   94

Chapter 11   97
   Preliminary Conditioning
      Illustration: Male Sexual Anatomy   98
      Exercise #1: PC Power   98
      Exercise #2: PC Power Plus   99

Chapter 12   100
   Sensory Awareness
      Exercise #3: Know Thyself   101
      Exercise #4: Controlled Peaks   102
      Exercise #5: The Squeeze Play   104
      Exercise #6: Surfing A Plateau   105

Chapter 13   107
   Putting It All Together
      Exercise #7: Eyes Wide Open   107
      Exercise #8: The Majority Method   108

Chapter 14   111
   The Main Event
      Working As A Team   111
      A Few Helpful Tips   112
      Going From Good To *Better* To *GREAT!*   114

Chapter 15
   Riding Into The Sunset   116

Bibliography

Preface

"La vida está corta, pero está ancha."

This Spanish proverb is one of my favorite rules-to-live-by: "Life is short, but it's wide." It gently reminds me of two facets of human life that are perhaps most significant—brevity and potential. Life *is* short, and we are well-advised to follow the wisdom of a popular bumper sticker: *Enjoy your life—this is not a dress rehearsal.* At the same time, a lifelong commitment to broaden our horizons will provide a rich cornucopia of experiences during the brief time that we have.

This book was written to broaden the horizons of my life. For twenty years I pursued a career which was extremely fulfilling in many ways. Yet over time a new awareness gradually dawned within me. Like a sunrise in my consciousness, it gave increasing light and became harder to shield against as it rose higher and higher. Under this bright new light, I saw that a significant part of who I am was not being expressed, and I knew it was time to check the charts and adjust the course of my life.

This book is a result of my new direction. It is written for lovers everywhere who seek a wider *love* life.

Introduction

In the last half of the twentieth century, a great deal of research has been done investigating female sexuality. As a result of learning more about the process, problems, and potential of female sexual response, scientists discovered almost fifty years ago that women have the capacity for multiple orgasms. But only in the last twenty years have most of the leading researchers acknowledged that, like women, *men are also capable of multiple orgasms*.

Clinical studies of human sexuality have shown that there are actually more similarities than differences in the sexual response of males and females. Researchers William Hartman and Marilyn Fithian, in their book *Any Man Can*, state that when measuring physiological changes during orgasm in both sexes, "unless we looked at the name of the subject, we could not tell whether a chart we studied was that of a male or female... " These similarities led scientists to this question: if women are capable of multiple orgasms, do men have the same capacity? The answer they found was *yes*. In other words, *men are capable of having two, three or more orgasms in a single lovemaking session,* without *losing their erection or needing any "recovery time" in between*.

Actually, as early as the 1940's researchers in the West were slowly becoming aware of the male potential for multiple orgasms. However, at that time it was typically considered to be somewhat dysfunctional, or outside the norm of a "natural" sexual response. Eastern cultures are a different story. More than three thousand years ago the Chinese realized the male's capacity for multiple orgasms, and have throughout history cultivated sexual practices to develop that capability for increased sexual pleasure as well as improved health.

For most Westerners the idea of multiple male orgasms is still a new—and often very surprising—concept. Yet thousands of men in our culture have already developed the skills necessary for multiple orgasms, and *as a result of learning a few simple techniques, multi-orgasmic men dramatically increase the pleasure of intercourse not only for themselves but for their partners as well.* Whether young or old, fit or flabby, movie star or truck driver, a multi-orgasmic man can easily maintain his erection to continue intercourse for much longer periods. For his partner, the endurance of a multi-orgasmic man will often enable a non-orgasmic woman to experience orgasms. Or, if a woman already has orgasms, with a multi-orgasmic partner she will often become multi-orgasmic as well. Increasing pleasure and fulfillment for both partners helps to eliminate any feelings of resentment, frustration, or exploitation that can result from an unsatisfying sexual relationship, and *increased pleasure and satisfaction naturally lead to greater intimacy and a deeper, more loving bond between partners.* These are just a few of the possible benefits of an Everlasting Love(r).

Although the heart of this book is a complete guide to teach men the skills to become multi-orgasmic, *this book is written for women as well as men.* The guide, found in Part II, provides step-by-step exercises for men to learn these skills, but the story tells how the physical satisfaction and increased intimacy made possible by an Everlasting Love(r) contribute to the bond of love between partners. To get the most benefit from this book, it is best if both you and your partner read the story and the "how-to" guide. But many women may prefer to just curl up with the love story, and many men may want to "cut to the chase" and just read the guide. That's fine, too. But you'll probably have better success learning the techniques (and more fun!) if you share the whole book together.

One final point. This love story is like the title of Chapter Three: It ain't fact, but it's true. In the story, Sam helps his younger brother, Jesse, learn the secret of an Everlasting Love(r). The characters in this book are fictional, but the story is based on actual people and events. This book was written to show that, just like the characters in the story, with patience and a consistent effort *any couple can experience more exciting, satisfying sex, and develop a stronger, more loving relationship, by learning the secret of an Everlasting Love(r).*

Part I: The Story

Chapter 1

In the (Very) Beginning...

It just doesn't make sense.

Most of us give sex a pretty high rating on the scale of human experiences. We know that one of the great peaks in life is the love between a man and a woman, and that sex is a natural, beautiful expression of that love. But the words we use to describe sex are nothing but u-g-l-y! If we truly believe sex to be natural and beautiful, why did we give the principal parts in this passionate play—the body parts—such *un*attractive names?

For example: penis. Go ahead, say it out loud. (You might want to skip that part if you're reading this, say, in a crowded airport.) Sounds sort of like spitting that turns into hissing, doesn't it? Not very sexy, at any rate. His leading lady—vagina—is even worse. This could be the name of a prudish spinster from a wealthy family: Miss Vagina Doolittle. And the worst offender of all: mammary gland. Perhaps a paleontologist's term for the scent gland of a woolly mammoth...? Yes, a skunk-like organ that would emit a foul odor when the hairy beast was threatened by enemies. C'mon. Think of the soft, smooth, scented bosoms you have known. Does mammary gland do them justice?

Shouldn't we have more poetic names for this cast of characters? Something that rolls off the tongue with enticing images? Better to follow the lead of the Chinese, who refer to His and Her sex apparatus with the likes of *Jade Stem* and *Jade Gate*. Even some New Age terms like *Wand of Light* and *Valley of Heaven* would be an improvement.

And how about giving those bit players in this whole drama (actually itty, bitty players—the sperm and egg) some sexy names to spice things up a bit at the moment of conception? Spike and Kitty, perhaps? Imagine how much more interesting high school biology could be:

> *Spike plunges in and begins his journey. His Olympian physique reveals the grace and strength of a natural athlete. Broad at the top and tapering to a narrow end, he is built for endurance swimming. With each forceful contraction he thrusts forward toward his destination, blindly swimming with only one purpose: to reach her in spite of all odds. As he steadily moves closer and closer, Kitty waits in the darkness, her round, ripe form floating freely in a sea of warmth and wetness. Finally, he arrives. At last they are together! In one joyful moment of union, they become one...*

And SHAZAM! We have a zygote.

Let's name her Sally...

Chapter 2

Thank You, Mr. President

Sally smiled as she stepped out onto the wide veranda, wrapped around the gracious old hotel like a welcoming friend. White-paned windows yawned open on three sides, and French doors swung idly on their hinges. Sheer curtains floated on the gentle breeze, brushing against the potted ferns like a gauzy summer skirt against a woman's ankles. The roomy wicker chairs beckoned to her with their bright, ample cushions and she smiled again as she imagined the small, crackly sound of settling into one. And the flowers, the flowers... everywhere there were flowers. In potted groups, in window boxes, in vases on the wicker tables, they displayed a palette of vibrant colors and delicate fragrance.

But it was the sunshine, like tiny golden spotlights streaming in through the open windows, that made Sally feel carefree and relaxed. Drawn by its bright, seductive power, she picked a chair bathed in light and sank down into it, slowly closing her eyes as she leaned back and tipped her face towards the warmth. She sat without moving, and immediately began to feel the strength of the sun seeping into her body. It was the cure she had sought, a physical and spiritual tonic melting her malaise.

But something was wrong. A sound, far away but growing closer, intruded on her quiet reverie. What was that sound? A ringing, a persistent ringing... *Why doesn't somebody take care of it?*

Oh shit, Sally thought, as she woke to the alarm and realized she was only dreaming. Lying on her side, face pressed into the sheet, the soothing scene had instantly faded as the noise intruded on her subconscious and her Dream Director yelled, "Cut!" But the feeling remained, leaving her even more frustrated when she opened her eyes and, raising her head, realized that outside it was raining. Again.

Sally reached out to silence the clock, then rolled onto her back as she stretched her legs and put one hand behind her head. Looking out the large window next to the bed, she watched the rain pelting the earth outside. Record rainfall that winter had reduced most of the citizens of Potter Creek, their small, northern California town, to borderline hysteria, fed up with gray skies, soggy ground, and housebound kids. *Is it ever going to stop?* she wondered wearily.

Across their land between the front porch and the road into town, Sally could see the cherry trees flanking their long driveway. Each winter she looked forward to their glorious display of blossoms, and now it was showtime. Like huge bundles of cotton candy, the trees formed delicate pink clouds in startling contrast to the turbulent gray skies. But Sally knew a few days of hard rain would strip the trees of their pastel glory and, depressed by the thought, she reached over to the night stand and clicked on the radio. Emmy Lou Harris was singing one of Sally's favorite oldies, and her feet began to dance beneath the quilt to the rhythm of the fiddle solo. For a few moments, it was enough to block the miserable, unrelenting weather out of her mind.

Downstairs, she heard her husband open the door on the back porch and call the dog. She remembered then that it was a holiday, and their son, Danny, who usually let the dog out in the morning, was sleeping over at a friend's house. When she heard the sound of Jake's paws bounding up the back steps, then scrambling across the wooden floor, Sally knew her husband had thrown a towel over the old dog and was giving him a vigorous rubdown.

"Good dog, Jake. Yes, you're a good boy," he said, slapping his hand with a loud thump against the dog's body. She pictured him standing over the hound, stroking Jake's fur, man and dog looking into each other's eyes in a statement of mutual regard and affection.

Sally's husband called up the stairs, "Are you ready for some coffee, Sal?"

"Yeah," she answered loudly, thinking, *Maybe some strong coffee will chase these blues.* "I'll be right down." Sally lay still for another minute, then slowly swung her legs out of bed and sat up. Nude except for bright red socks bunched at her ankles, she stretched up on long, shapely legs as she stood to her full height of five feet, seven inches. After thirty-six years and one child, Sally's hips and waist were just beginning to thicken with age. Her breasts were full and well-shaped and her straight blonde hair fell past her shoulders with simple bangs framing her face. She wasn't a woman to constantly fuss with her appearance. But even in blue jeans and cowboy boots, when she strode through town with the proud, long-legged gait of a racehorse, her fresh, wholesome sexiness still turned heads.

Feeling the morning chill, Sally grabbed a silk kimono from the bedpost and pulled it on. As she tightened the robe's sash around her waist, her fingers lingered over its intricate embroidery, and she smiled remembering her husband's gift. Sam had brought it to the hospital when Danny was born, and knelt by the bed saying "Happy Mother's Day" as she nursed their new son. Now frayed and fading, the rich purple silk with white cranes stitched across a red sun had quickly moved the robe onto Sally's Top-Ten-All-Time-Favorite-Clothes List.

Sally grabbed a clip as she passed the dresser and twisted her hair into a topknot on her way down the stairs. When she reached the last step, she could see her husband in front of the kitchen counter, his back turned, absorbed with the task in front of him. *What is he up to?* she wondered. Realizing he was oblivious to her, she sat down on the bottom step and, leaning forward, propped her elbows on her knees and rested her chin on her hands to watch in silence.

In his entire thirty-eight years, Sam Bennett had never done a job halfway. He approached any task with the calm, deliberate concentration of a Zen monk. As a paperboy earning money on his own for the first time, he made sure his papers hit their mark even if it meant retrieving them from the bushes when his aim was off. He brought the same commitment to his work as a carpenter. To Sam, work was a form of meditation, to be completed with care, skill, and thoughtful attention to detail.

This morning while Sally watched, he tidied the kitchen and wiped down the counters, then poured two mugs of freshly brewed coffee. Finally he turned, calling, "Hey, Sal, are you—," and trailed off when he saw her sitting on the stairs.

"Hi. Want some breakfast?" he asked. Then, folding his arms across his chest, he leaned back against the counter, crossed his feet, and smiled at her.

Sam was a man with that cowboy look. Lean and easy, at five-nine and a hundred and sixty pounds he moved with a strength and casual confidence born of hard physical work. He valued practicality in most things and there was little difference between his work and leisure wardrobe. This morning he wore hiking boots, jeans, and a plaid flannel shirt with the sleeves rolled up to his elbows. His shirt tucked into his pants over flat, hard muscle and even under the cover of denim his thighs showed the tone and shape of a much younger man. Thick, straight hair, blue-black and now touched with silver, fell over his eyes, and his face had begun to show the first few lines of age. But his smile held the same charm it did when he and Sally first met fourteen

18

years ago. Mysterious and magnetic, when Sam smiled at Sally she always felt he was hiding a secret... perhaps something to surprise her when it was revealed.

Sally stood, stretched, and walked into the kitchen. Standing in front of Sam, arms limp at her side, she dropped her forehead onto his shoulder and murmured, "I am so tired of this rain. I just had a dream about sunshine." He placed his hand under her chin, lifted her face toward his, and kissed her softly. "Well, I have something that should make you feel better," he said. He picked up the coffee mugs and handed one to Sally, saying, "Come on." Taking her hand, he led her into the front room.

Built in 1910, at one time the Bennett home had been surrounded by orchards. Sam and Sally had bought it ten years before with the help of a small inheritance from Sam's grandfather. A run-down old farmhouse with firewood providing the only heat, it was just what they had dreamed of—a place in the country where they could invest their time and labor to make a good home. They sometimes missed the convenience of city utilities and a corner market. But just minutes away, the homes in nearby suburbs, with enormous RV pads, tiny yards, and gaping garage doors like insatiable jaws, seemed to them a nightmare of "the good life" built more for vehicles and possessions than people.

The Bennett home had a different feel. After a decade of renovation, it had new roofing, wiring, sheetrock, and other modern amenities, but the original design and character had been carefully preserved. Behind the rail fence that ran along the two-lane country road, a long, gravel driveway led to their modest home on six acres. In front a covered porch ran the width of the house, with ample space for the kind of activities that become the best memories of life—reading to children in the rocking chair, carving a jack-o-lantern on a crisp October afternoon, or sitting with friends on warm summer nights, telling stories, drinking beer and laughing out loud. In back the old barn, a seasonal creek, and climbing trees that remained from the orchards provided a stage for Danny's playtime imagination.

Inside, the home had its original wood floors, big bedrooms with dormered windows overlooking the land, and a wide wooden staircase. The big country kitchen, with its long pine table and window seat, was a place for sharing hot homemade soup or lingering over a bottle of wine with friends and family. Sally's casual housekeeping put family activities ahead of the Better Homes and Gardens look and the coffee table in the living room was more likely to display a jigsaw-puzzle-in-progress than carefully arranged magazines. But the home's best feature was the large fireplace, built with field stones collected from the property. Flanked by overloaded bookcases and windowseats crowded with cushions, it was like the grand matriarch of the home, dispensing warmth and comfort to all in need.

This morning Sam led Sally to the fireplace, where a fire was crackling and the cat was curled in his favorite spot on the windowseat. There, spread out between the hearth and the sofa, was a thick sleeping bag, with three or four large cushions tossed on top. Next to it, on a low table, were a basket of muffins, a plate with sliced fruit, and a vase of lilies from the garden. The scene was just like their early days, before they had central heating, when they often slept in front of the fire, and Sally smiled broadly at the memory.

Lightly kissing her hand, Sam asked, "Ma'am, would you care for a fireside brunch?"

"I knew you were up to something," Sally said as she sank down onto a cushion, folding her legs underneath her. "Breakfast in bed... and flowers even. I feel better already." Looking up at her husband, she took his hand and pulled him down next to her.

Sam smiled that smile and leaned his back against the sofa. "Come here," he said, pulling Sally up against him as she sighed and leaned back against his chest. With his cheek next to hers, he kissed her lightly and wrapped one arm across the front of her shoulders. She reached up to stroke his forearm and for a time they sat without speaking, sipping their coffee and alternately watching the fire and the driving rain against the windows.

After a few minutes, Sam opened the clasp at the back of Sally's head and let her long, silky hair fall across her shoulders. He began to stroke it slowly and gently, pulling it away from her face and behind her ears and, closing his eyes, he pressed his face against her hair, inhaling its fragrance. Then he pulled it to one side over her shoulder, and bent to kiss her neck.

Watching the fire, Sally had begun to feel relaxed and self-indulgent, and with Sam's kiss her awareness quickly narrowed to focus on his touch. Anticipating what she knew was to come, she closed her eyes and with one hand reached over her shoulder to caress Sam's cheek as his lips traveled up her neck and slowly, slowly moved toward her ear, where he whispered, "I love you." Then, gently sucking her earlobe, he reached around in front and loosened the sash of her robe. Sliding one hand underneath the folds of silk, he cupped her breast, slowly moving around its contour, then brushed lightly across the nipple. Sally arched back, then turned to face Sam and began kissing him. As he caressed her breasts, she put her hands on both sides of his face, stroking the sweet-smelling, clean-shaven smoothness, then spread her fingers and combed through his thick hair, slowly moving to the back of his head.

After a few moments, Sam gently lowered Sally down on her back, and, pulling the front of her robe open, began to kiss her shoulders and breasts. He lay beside her, propped on one elbow, and slid one hand tenderly across her belly, then gradually down the side of her hips and across her leg to find the soft, smooth flesh on the inside of her thighs. It was not long before they stirred and sat up, helping each other out of their clothes, to continue unencumbered in front of the dancing shadows of the fire.

Sally never felt more *natural* than when she and Sam made love. His attentiveness and endurance were the foundation for her thorough satisfaction, and sex had become so effortless for them that she felt the most relaxed and free when they were making love. This morning was no different, as their unhurried movements in front of the flickering fire gradually led them to the passionate, satisfying crescendos of their love tango.

Afterwards they lay together quietly watching the fire. Suddenly grateful to the country's illustrious forefathers who made their rendezvous possible, Sally kissed Sam and said, "Happy Presidents Day." Then she described her dream to him and they idly fantasized about escaping to an island paradise for the rest of the rainy season. Finally they rose, went to the kitchen for the morning paper and more coffee, and had just settled down for their simple fireside meal when the phone rang.

"I'll get it," Sally said, climbing on top of the sofa and pulling the phone off the table behind it. Settling back down on the floor with the phone on her lap, she lifted the receiver and said "Howdy" as she draped one leg across Sam's lap.

At the other end of the line Sam's brother replied, "Howdy yourself. It's me, Jesse."

Sam's younger brother lived in Sunrise, just outside of Sacramento. Physically, the two brothers bore a striking resemblance to each other, but there the similarities stopped. "Like the difference between Sunday afternoon and Monday morning" was the way their mother described her two sons: Sam, the calm, easy-going one, and Jesse The Ambitious. While still in high school, Jesse set goals to own his own home and business before he reached thirty. Now twenty-eight years old, he had opened a bicycle shop three years before, and was making plans for a second location. The family figured he had a bead on his future.

"Oh, hi, Jesse," Sally answered.

"What are you guys doin' today?" Hearing running water and a microwave beep in the background, Sally knew Jesse was using his speaker phone while he had breakfast.

"Oh, we're just hanging around the house. Danny slept over at a friend's and Sam just fixed a romantic breakfast in front of the fire."

"What a guy," Jesse said.

"Yeah, he's a keeper. What are you guys up to? How's Clare?" Jesse and his fiancé Clare, a music student, had announced their engagement with the New Year and were planning a fall wedding.

"She's good. She had the flu last week but she's over it now," he answered.

"Uh-oh. Are you next?"

"No, no," Jesse replied with a short laugh, "I'm afraid I'm the one who gave it to her. Anyway, I'm just calling to see if I should make the reservation for Memorial Day. Is that going to happen this year?"

In the years since Sam had left home, the two brothers had met on Memorial Day weekends for camping at Clearwater Lake in the Sierra foothills. As the years passed, they were joined by their sister, spouses, and children until it had become a family tradition.

"Yeah, sure," Sally said.

"OK, I'll talk to Sis and reserve our usual three sites if it's a go with her," he replied. "How are Sam and Danny doing?"

"They're good. Danny still loves karate. He just got his green belt and he's so proud. Do you want to talk to your brother?" she asked.

"Nah, I'll catch him later. I'm going to meet Clare and I'm running late. Say hi to Danny for me?"

"You bet. Take care, you guys."

"You too. Talk to you later. 'Bye."

Sally pushed the phone aside and said, "Clearwater Lake for Memorial Day. Jesse's going to reserve the campsite."

"Sounds good," Sam said, dropping the newspaper in his lap as he gazed out the window at the turbulent sky. Then, cocking his head to one side, he slid his eyes toward Sally in a sideways glance and asked, "Think it'll stop rainin' before then?"

She threw a pillow at him. ♡

Chapter 3

"It Ain't Fact, But It's True"

It did stop raining before Memorial Day. Exactly one week before. After a winter of back-to-back rainstorms, flooding, and power failures, Mother Nature had written early spring as a theme on cool, overcast weather, punctuated with days of rain. But on Monday before the Annual Bennett Family Camping Trip, the skies cleared, and as it often happens in that part of California, it seemed that overnight the season changed from winter to summer.

"For those of you heading out for the weekend after work today, we've got a little message from the weatherman." Sally froze, listening to the radio forecast: "Weather-wise, we'll have a southern California weekend for Memorial Day... blue skies and temperatures climbing to the mid-80's and the low 90's inland. Hey, don't forget your sunscreen, people, and stay tuned to KKIZ for all your favorite country hits... " The DJ slid seamlessly into a Garth Brooks tune as Sally yelped and thrust both fists into the air. It was going to be a good weekend.

Swaying to the seductive beat, Sally sang along, lamenting rodeo life, as she rounded up the family camping gear. The food and cooking utensils she had packed that morning were ready to go and she pushed the boxes out of the kitchen and up near the front door, then went to the back porch to find the cooler. Hauling it out from under their antique ice cream freezer, she rinsed it clean and added it to the growing pile at the front door. Sally had gone back to the porch for Jake's dog food as Sam came in from loading the truck and asked, "Hey, Sal, how long before you'll be ready to go?"

"Fifteen, twenty minutes," Sally hollered from the porch. "We need to stop for ice, too."

"We'd better get a move on, then, if we're going to miss the traffic."

"Okay, let me check on Danny." Sally headed up the stairs, taking them two at a time, as she called out to her son. "Danny, how you doing? We want to leave in about twenty minutes."

Ouside his room, she could see through the half-open door that her ten-year-old son had abandoned his packing. He was in the middle of the floor, going through a series of karate moves, kicking and punching as he moved in different directions. This, she had learned, was *kata*, a dance-like exercise for learning defense against multiple attackers. Danny had just learned a new kata, and had been practicing it all week. Not wanting to interrupt, Sally leaned against the door frame and waited as she watched in silence.

When he finished, Danny gave a small bow and only then brushed away the lock of dark brown hair that had fallen into his eyes. He turned and looked at his mother.

Sally smiled and brought her hands together in quiet applause. "Lookin' pretty good, kiddo. Keep it up." Then she added, "But hey, we want to hit the road soon so we'll miss most of the traffic. Are you about packed? We want to leave in fifteen minutes."

"Okay, Mom... but I can't find my blue sweatshirt."

"I saw it by the fireplace, under the newspaper," she answered, and turned to leave. "And don't forget to pack your swimsuit and towel," she called over her shoulder as she headed back down the stairs.

They reached the campsite in time to join the rest of the family for supper. Jesse, Clare and Sam's sister and her two children had arrived earlier, and they waited for the late-comers before dishing up chili amidst the welcoming chatter. As they ate, both children and adults buzzed with excitement, sharing recent news from their lives and anticipation for the coming weekend.

The campfire danced and crackled as the family settled in after their evening meal. Like pioneers circling the wagons, they formed a ring around the fire, adults with their coffee in speckled porcelain mugs and the kids with marshmallows speared on sticks. Mesmerized by the hypnotic flames, for a fleeting moment there was silence, each person lost in thought yet feeling the powerful bond with each other through the fireside circle and its shared ritual.

Sam broke the silence with a mysterious query. "Do any of you kids know how Lucky Ned got his name?"

Lucky Ned Baker was a colorful figure in Potter Creek. A seventy-year-old multi-millionaire with a sixty-acre vineyard outside of town, he cruised the county backroads in his mint-condition vintage cars. He spent most of his energy following local politics, and he was the most frequent contributor of letters to the editor of their small, rural paper. An impeccable gentleman, he always came to town wearing a hat and suit with candy-filled pockets. The town's children flocked to him, knowing they would earn a sweet reward if they could answer his questions about history, science or literature. They were all curious about the two missing fingers on his left hand, but whenever one of them asked what happened, he would just wink and say, "My parachute didn't open." Ned had passed away the year before, leaving the bulk of his estate to the school district, and the whole town mourned the loss of the kindly, courteous old gentleman.

"Oh, Dad, everybody knows they called him Lucky Ned 'cause he won the lottery," Danny answered with an exasperated sigh.

"That's what a lot of people think," Sam responded. "But that's not quite right. He won that fortune only five or six years ago, but he got his name long before that. He got that name the day he lost his fingers."

With that, the kids exploded with questions. "How could he be lucky 'cause he lost his fingers?" and "What *really* happened to his hand?"

"Well," Sam began, "Before he won the lottery, Lucky Ned used to be a teacher. He was pretty quiet, kept to himself most of the time. He was married, never had any children, but he was devoted to his wife, Dora. He thought the sun rose and set for that woman, and he would have done anything for her.

"Folks think that Dora, on the other hand, was never in love with Ned. She always had dreams of living in Florida, on the beach, with palm trees in her front yard and seagulls flying overhead. Well, one day a traveling salesman came to town—this was sometime in the fifties—and he filled her head with all kinds of stories about what he would do for her if she would run away with him. And darned if that's not exactly what she did. Just up and left. One day Ned came home and she had packed a suitcase, left him a note, and disappeared.

"Well, Ned took this pretty hard. But folks had no idea he was so broke up about it to do what he did then.

"Ned went to his closet and pulled out an old revolver that his father had given him. He loaded it, then rummaged around under the kitchen sink until he found some rat poison, and finally went to the garage and got some rope. He took all of this and

28

walked down to the creek. It was early spring then and the creek was running high and fast.

"He walked over to a tree that was right by the water's edge and threw the rope over a big branch that was hanging out over the water. He tied one end of the rope around the trunk, and made a noose on the other end. Then, with the gun and the poison, he walked out on some rocks underneath that overhanging branch."

Just then Sam yawned and reached his arms high overhead, stretching his back. "You know, it's getting kind of late," he said, slipping a wink to the grown-ups. "Maybe we should call it a night and finish this story tomorrow."

The kids snapped to life. "Noo-o-o!" they chorused, "you can't stop now. Tell us what happened!"

"Well, okay, if you're not tired yet... " Sam replied, and then continued his tale. "So, Ned was ready. He swallowed the rat poison and put the noose over his head. He was holding onto the rope with his left hand, just over his head, to keep some slack in it," Sam explained, reaching his hand overhead to clutch an imaginary rope as the kids sat wide-eyed. "Then he put the gun to the side of his head and got ready to pull the trigger." With the deft timing of a natural-born storyteller, Sam paused with the index finger of his right hand pointed toward his temple.

"Well, just then Ned shifted his foot onto another rock and that rock rolled underneath his weight *just* as he was pulling the trigger. He slipped on the rock and missed his target but shot clean through the rope, and unfortunately got two of his fingers at the same time. Then he fell into the water and was thrashing around trying to get the rope off his head and keep from drowning. He took in some water, started choking and threw up the rat poison. By this time he had been pulled downstream some, but next thing he knew his clothes caught on a branch underwater, and he was able to haul himself over to a rock and out of the water.

"Well, Ned figured his grand failure must be a divine omen, and he pulled himself out of the water and went straight to the town doctor. He told the doctor his story while he got fixed up, and from then on folks around town called him Lucky Ned."

For a moment the kids were quiet, absorbing the impact of the tale. Then they clamored for answers. "Did anybody ever find his fingers?" "Did his wife ever come back?" and finally "Did that really happen?" they asked. "Yeah, is that really true?"

With a sly grin, Sam gave the traditional storyteller's reply. "It ain't *fact*, but it's true." Then he stood and shook out his legs, announcing, "Well, I'm headed for bed. Anybody who's going fishing tomorrow morning had better do the same, 'cause we'll be on the water by daybreak." Looking at Jesse, he asked, "You up for that?"

"Sure," Jesse answered, tossing the dregs from his coffee into the fire.

All three kids jumped up saying, "We want to go! We want to go! Will you wake us up?"

Sam replied, "You bet... but only once. If you want to go, you'd better shake a leg in the morning, 'cause we won't wait around for any sleepyheads."

Sam looked down at Sally, sitting in a lawn chair as she hugged her knees to her chest. He gave her a kiss and said, "I'll get the kids to bed."

She squeezed his hand and said softly, "I'll be along soon."

After a chorus of "good night" the kids followed Sam and Jesse as they disappeared into the darkness outside the ring of firelight, flashlights bobbing on the trail to the tents while their voices floated on the soft night air.

Sally and Clare sat staring into the fire with Sam's sister, who suddenly asked, "Is there any of that wine left from supper?" She walked to the boxes near the picnic table and began to dig through them in the dark, feeling for the bottle. "I can never sleep on a full moon and a little wine might help me drop off. Ah, here it is," she exclaimed, pulling half a bottle of red wine from the supplies. "Either of you two want to join me for a little night-cap?"

Roberta Louise was named after both her grandmothers, but the family had always called her by her childhood name: Bobby Lou. Born three years to the day after Sam, she was a robust, generous woman with Sam's thoughtful, easygoing nature. She had thick, glossy black hair, like her brothers, that she usually wore in a long, heavy braid down her back. Since her husband's death in an auto accident four years before, she had earned her teaching credential and become a popular fifth-grade teacher, finding a new life as she shared her natural curiosity and love for learning with her young charges.

Sally and Clare looked at each other and shrugged. "Why not?" they answered. Bobby Lou found plastic cups and brought them to the fire with the bottle. After the wine was poured and passed around, she asked, "Okay, who has a toast?" They were all quiet for a moment before Clare said, "I've got one," and together they raised their rustic goblets. "'What you are is a gift that God gives to you. What you do with yourself is your gift to God.'" Smiling at the gentle thought, they said "cheers" across the fire and sipped from their cups.

From the warmth of the wine, the fire, and their friendship, before long the conversation evolved into the shared intimacies among women that are not possible in the company of men. Giggling like schoolgirls discussing their first crush, they told jokes and reminisced about coming of age and discovering the mystery of sex.

"When I was about ten or eleven," Bobby Lou said, wiping a tear from her eye after the last joke, "my best friend, Maria Mendoza, asked me if I wanted to be pointed or round when I grew up. Well, I had no idea what she was talking about. She was really exasperated that I could be so dense about female issues and finally explained that she was talking about *breasts*." Sally and Clare laughed as she continued. "I just remember thinking, *Is this really something important?* I mean, did it make any difference if my boobs were round or pointed? Was one better than the other and was it really something I should worry about?"

"Well," Sally chimed in, "when I was in junior high school, my best friend was a cheerleader and I thought she had the best figure in the whole school. Now I realize that actually, she was really short-waisted and had a square butt, but her chest was well-endowed, and from all the clues I got that was the definition of a good figure."

Clare broke in, asking, "Yeah, but was she pointed or round?" as they giggled again and poured the last of the wine.

"I was really naive when I started dating in high school," Bobby Lou confessed. "In my senior year, I would go on double dates with my girlfriend and we would go parking at the lake. One night we stopped at a drugstore on the way to the lake and the guys went in. I asked Lisa what they were buying and she said, 'Rubbers.' Well, I wasn't *that* naive; I mean, this was before AIDS and all that, but at least I knew that rubbers were for birth control. Still, I panicked because I had to admit to Lisa, 'I've never used one!'"

Bobby Lou and Sally burst into loud laughter, and Sally noticed a quick blush of color flood Clare's face as she ducked her head and covered her mouth. Suddenly realizing they could be disturbing other campers, Sally brought her finger to her lips, saying between suppressed giggles, "Shh-h-h... we'd better keep it down or they'll have the park rangers after us."

"Oops," Bobby Lou added, looking around over her shoulder, "I guess we might be getting a little noisy." The women reined in their high spirits and sat for a moment in silence, smiling as they gazed at the waning fire.

"Well," Sally finally said, "I wonder if boys are as confused as girls are when they're growing up. I mean, when you think about it, with all the *mis*information we get, in a way it's pretty amazing that we can actually be sexually compatible as adults!" Then, giving her companions a quick grin, she added, "Anyway, when you're ready for bed, men are pretty nice to have around, aren't they?"

"Amen," Bobby Lou responded.

"Yes, they are," Clare mused. Then, after a pause, she added softly, "Even if they do get the better end of the deal." Her afterthought was murmured so quietly that only Sally heard it, and she glanced quickly at her future sister-in-law. Clare was leaning forward in her chair, elbows propped on her knees, as she idly poked the glowing embers with a long stick. Sally felt a tiny shock of surprise seeing her expression. Like a woman trapped in a loveless marriage, her face was a mask of resignation.

Bobby Lou rose and said, "Well, I think this bit of wine was just what I needed to drop off to sleep. I'm going to call it a night. See you two in the morning."

"Good night," called the other two women as Bobby Lou headed for her tent. Soon Sally and Clare stood and scattered the coals, and then they, too, headed down the trail, finding their way through the darkness to the tents and their sleeping lovers.

The long weekend passed in a blur of activity. The family spent the cool morning hours fishing or hiking and by early afternoon it was hot enough for the kids to don their swimsuits and race for the lake. Jesse taught Danny and his cousins how to dive from the long wooden dock while the other grown-ups watched, interrupting their novels and idle conversation to applaud and cheer from their post on the beach. Around the evening campfire they entertained themselves with family stories, charades, and old folk songs, relishing the moments that would become fond memories as part of the Bennett family history.

As they began the drive home, Sally settled back in the truck and reached across the back of the seat to pat Sam's shoulder. Danny sat between them, chattering about the highlights of the weekend, and Sam and Sally exchanged smiles over the top of his head, enjoying their son's happiness. But they both knew that within thirty minutes he would be sound asleep, and Sally would feel the sweet weight of her child's head against her shoulder. When sleep gently overtook him, they drove on in silence to avoid waking him.

Time passed quickly as they watched twilight spread across the rolling California hills. Still green from the late spring rains, the softly curved contours of the rural terrain were splashed with native oak and patches of golden poppies. Their drive took them through a changing panorama of orchards, vineyards and dairies, and the pastoral scenery lulled them into quiet meditation on their own thoughts.

Sally felt a satisfied contentment from the weekend events but it was marred by her thoughts of Clare. Like a foxtail working its way into her sock, Clare's melancholy on Friday night stuck in Sally's mind. What was going on between her and Jesse? Were they happy together? From Clare's comment, Sally guessed that their sex life was probably less than ideal. She mulled over the nagging thoughts in her mind, and by the time Sam turned onto their long driveway, Sally had made her decision. She would talk to Clare, and she would tell her about Sam's secret. ♡

Chapter 4

Mustang Sally

Clare Maguire lay in bed and looked up at the ceiling. Feeling wide awake, she turned her head to read the numbers on the nightstand clock: 6:51. She crossed, then uncrossed, her legs, then rolled onto her stomach, and finally turned on her side and pulled her knees up, and with her arms folded under the pillow, closed her eyes tight, trying to force her way back into slumber.

But it was hopeless. The restless yearning she felt inside was like a tiger pacing his cage, and she knew sleep would not come. Relenting, she opened her eyes and looked at Jesse sleeping next to her, bare-chested, with one arm flung wide across the bed. She watched his slow, even breathing as he slept with the innocent surrender of a child, oblivious to her fitful movements. A lock of ebony hair fell over his eyes and for a moment she thought of leaning over him to brush it aside, her nipples lightly touching his chest, then covering his mouth with a slow kiss. Instead, she rolled out of bed and got dressed.

It was a beautiful day in June, and the gentle rays of an early morning sun were just beginning to slip through the glass doors that opened onto the patio outside their bedroom. She had awakened earlier when Jesse's warm hand slid between her legs. She turned to him eagerly, her excitement growing as his slow caress chased the sleep from her mind. As he stroked and licked her skin, her mounting pleasure aroused him quickly. In one move, he threw the sheets off them, then began to cover her body with kisses, lingering over the soft, smooth skin of her belly and thighs. Clare felt her desire sharpen, and reached both hands down to stroke Jesse's tousled hair. Her whole body ached for the wave of contractions that would release her from this exquisite tension.

But in the next moment everything changed.

Soon, too soon, Jesse entered her and immediately his desire shot skyward. Feeling the excitement in his body and its urgent cry to be answered, Clare felt her own arousal begin to ebb as she realized instantly that their union was doomed to derail. Predictably, Jesse continued only briefly before his body tensed with the pleasure in his groin. Then, kissing her cheek, he rolled to one side and soon lay sound asleep after murmuring "I love you."

Jesse was still sleeping when Clare left for her morning run. She walked quietly to the doorway of their bedroom, pausing to look back at her fiancé before heading for the front door. She had enough time for a good, long run before Sam and Sally picked them up.

Stepping out into the cool morning air, Clare closed her eyes and inhaled deeply. The jasmine vine climbing their garage wall was in full bloom, and she filled her lungs with its potent fragrance. Wearing a T-shirt and jogging shorts, she walked to the driveway and began to stretch. Her shoulder-length, wavy, auburn hair was pulled into a ponytail, and her jade green eyes and fine facial features were enhanced by flawless skin as fair and smooth as porcelain. A small woman, her petite waist separating the soft curves of her bosom and hips gave her body the kind of proportions that men fantasize and women envy. Together with her fair coloring and small frame, Clare's figure gave an impression of classic feminine innocence and frailty.

But looks can be deceiving. For in spite of her delicate appearance, Clare's passion was running. In the seventh grade, when she began to join her father for his daily jog, she discovered the cleansing high of the simple, repetitive movements. She had stored a treasure of fond memories from those morning runs, enjoying her father's attention and the beauty of their lakeside route. Now twenty-four years old, Clare saw her daily habit as a ritual of moving meditation, the physical equivalent of the passion and release she felt in music. She loved the sense of well-being that running produced, and she had learned to use it as a dependable cure for the blues.

This morning it felt especially good. With the morning sun at her back, she watched her shadow moving steadily with a hypnotic, soothing tempo, and finding her rhythm, she felt as though she could run forever. Her feet pounded the streets, relieving her restlessness with each step, and she ran easily for several miles before sprinting the last hundred yards and returning home to shower and wake Jesse.

Tucking his tray underneath one arm, the waiter stopped in front of their table and asked, "Are you two ladies ready to order?"

"Yes, we are," Clare replied. "I'll have the Chicken Caesar Salad with some iced tea."

"The Southwest Sandwich for me," Sally added. "And make it two iced teas." Then, having sudden doubts about her mission for the day, she said, "On second thought, change that tea to a Budweiser."

They were seated in the dappled sunlight of the arbor at Carmella's, a small sidewalk cafe in San Francisco. Sam and Jesse had taken Danny and his best friend to a ballgame while Sally and Clare had lunch and shopped in the city. With the long stretch of uninterrupted time Sally hoped for an opportunity to explain Sam's secret to Clare. They lingered over their lunch, and when the waiter came to clear their dishes, the last of the other diners had left. *This is perfect*, Sally thought.

"Can I get you anything else?" the waiter asked. "How about another beer?" he suggested, picking up the empty bottle.

Sally looked at Clare. "Well, we're not in any hurry. I think I will have another," she replied. "How about you, Clare?"

"Sure... " Clare said, looking at the waiter. "But make mine a glass of chardonnay."

The waiter left and Clare excused herself for a trip to the ladies room. Grateful for a few minutes alone, Sally turned to watch the passing traffic as she considered what she would say. Although she was close to Clare, she felt a sudden panic realizing that she had only known her less than a year. Ay, Caramba! Would Clare feel comfortable talking about sex with her? At family gatherings, she was usually a little shy... maybe demure was a better word. Yes, well-mannered and demure. *Not like me*, Sally mused, thinking of her own casual, direct nature. Still, Sally sensed a passion that lay dormant in Clare. She knew Clare liked and respected her, and Clare was intelligent and open to new ideas. Sally took a deep breath and decided to take the plunge just as Clare returned to the table and the waiter brought their drinks. Pouring beer into the frosty mug, Sally said, "Maybe it's because of all the practice I got in college, but I still haven't outgrown my taste for beer... "

"According to Sam, you were quite the party girl," Clare laughed and leaned forward, taking Sally's bait as the lead-in for her story.

Sally looked up in mock horror. "Hey, don't believe everything he tells you!" Then she continued. "But, yeah, I confess, I was. Before I met Sam, before I was a wife, and a mother, and the town bookkeeper, and the person who feeds the dog, I did my share of hellraising. When I was in college my nickname was 'Mustang Sally'—you know why my friends called me that?"

"Well, it's just a wild guess—because you drove a Mustang?"

"Nope. Because my maiden name is Ford... " Then, with a comic's timing, she added, "...and because I drove a Mustang!

"It was my first car, and it was red, with those big, fat back tires. The paint job was all faded and there were holes in all the seats. I bought it from my roommate—five hundred bucks—and it took me to rock concerts, camping in the desert, trips to the beach... " Sally smiled at the memories. "We did some crazy things with that car. One summer night—God it was hot that night—we'd been out partying and around two in the morning we drove onto the athletic field. The sprinklers were on, and we rolled down all the windows and drove around in centerfield with the horn blaring until the campus cops chased us off!"

Clare was wide-eyed. "You didn't get caught?"

"Nah," Sally answered. "The campus cops were mostly just kids like us. They would catch us picking avocados from the college groves and we would just share the loot with them and they'd let us go." Sally laughed at the memory then suddenly grew more serious. "Some things we did could have gotten us nailed by the real police, though. One time we went out to a turkey farm and two of the guys cut a wire fence, snuck in, and killed a turkey for our Thanksgiving dinner. I was driving the getaway car, and now I feel kind of bad about it. But you know, we were just a bunch of hungry kids, with no money for anything, and we just wanted to have a good Thanksgiving dinner. But if I knew who that farmer was today, I'd pay him back," she said. "Anyway," she added, lowering her voice, "it was a damn good turkey!"

Sally sat back and began idly peeling the label from her beer bottle. Nostalgia had settled over her like a warm blanket. "I made some really good friends in those days. Some crazy friends, to be sure. Just some of their names were a dead giveaway: Wild Bill, Roach, Candy...and also Joe and Helen, Debbie, Fritz... We had some wild parties, lots of drinking, every kind of drug... " Suddenly she paused and looked up at Clare. "But you understand, it was different then. Those were the days of, 'Oh, far out, man, groovy, love and peace,'" Sally played like she was stoned and waved the peace sign with both hands. "I mean, that's what the youth culture was then—sex, drugs, and rock 'n' roll! Things are different now."

"Anyway," she continued, leaning forward on her elbows, "let me tell you about Skip Hawkins. I met him when I was twenty. I was on the commons at school and he came up and started talking to me. He had a cast on his foot and when I asked him what happened, he said he fell out of an airplane. *Yeah, right*, I thought, but he said, 'No, really,' with this totally enchanting, seductive smile and I knew he was telling the truth and being playful at the same time. Anyway, he wasn't much to look at... "

"Wait," Clare interrupted, "so how did he break his foot?"

"Oh, well, those were the early days of hang gliders and he was really into that. He and his friends would build these gliders and test them on a nearby hill—with lots of strawberry wine for courage—and he broke his foot when he crashed one of them.

"So anyway, Skip was about five-six, a hundred and thirty pounds, with narrow shoulders and skinny legs. He had kind of scraggly, shoulder-length brown hair and a droopy mustache. Not the kind of guy who would win 'Best Looking' in his high school Hall of Fame, right? But there was something about him that was just so... oh, what's the right word... so... *irresistible*. Yeah, irrresistible. He wasn't real handsome—but he was definitely sexy." Sally poured the rest of her beer, then looked at Clare and grinned, "*Very* sexy."

"The day we met he invited me to a barbecue and after the party we went back to his place. He was almost twenty-seven then, and I felt sort of daring being out with 'an older man.' Anyway, when we got around to it, he started kissing me and all I remember thinking was—swear to God—I was thinking, *I wonder if anyone has ever had an orgasm just from kissing!* Because I had never kissed anybody like this guy. I knew right away he was no ordinary lover."

Sally sat back, teasing Clare with a slow, blissful smile. Clare was leaning forward on her elbows. *She doesn't look shy now*, Sally thought.

"Well... ?" Clare prodded her on.

Now we're getting to the nitty gritty, Sally thought. *Well, here goes.* She leaned over the table again and lowered her voice, although no one was within earshot of their table. "I'll never forget that night,"she said. "We were lying on his waterbed kissing for a while and pretty soon he took his shirt off, and lo and behold, on one shoulder he had a small tattoo of the Cheshire Cat and underneath it said, 'We're all mad, you know.' Well, it so happens I'm a big fan of *Alice in Wonderland*, and that tattoo just won my heart. I was his!" she exclaimed, throwing her arms open and falling back against her chair as they both laughed.

Sally took another sip of beer. "Now I was only twenty then—and I wasn't a virgin—but still I didn't have much experience, and guys I had been with were too young to have much skill at pleasing women. At the time, I had probably never had an orgasm during intercourse before," Sally said, glancing at Clare for any clues that she was uncomfortable. But Clare was intent on Sally, following every word. Sally knew she had struck a chord as she continued. "Hell, the only times I'd ever come were probably just the times I, ah... 'pleased myself,' if you know what I mean." Blushing, Clare smiled and nodded.

"But Skip was different. For starters... um-m... well, his tongue could win a talent contest, if you know I mean, and I came that way for the first time. Then when we got around to intercourse, it was amazing—he could just go on forever! I mean we'd change positions half a dozen times and he would keep going for several minutes with each switch! Well, that was really different from any sex I'd ever had before, you know—'wham, bam, thank you, ma'am.' I'm telling you, Skip was no ordinary lover. All the gals in our crowd knew it and they would always be jealous of Skip's current flame. And the guys just couldn't understand what the big deal was with this one, skinny guy that all the gals fought over!"

"So," Clare interuppted. "What was his secret?"

"Well, okay, here's the clincher," Sally answered. "The reason he could go so long was because," and Sally threw her hands up in front of her "—believe it or not—he had orgasms *without* ejaculating."

Clare was silent for a moment. Then, incredulous, she cried, "What? That's not possible... is it?"

"That's what most people think," Sally said.

"And is it healthy?" Clare protested. "I mean, I've always heard that guys need to come when they get that aroused or else it's really painful, and the semen can sometimes—I don't know—back up into their system and cause, um-m, some kind of illness, or... or *something*. Anyway, aside from that, if a guy doesn't come, how can sex be any fun for him?"

"Whoa, wait, slow down," Sally said. "One thing at a time. The answer to your first question, whether it's healthy, is a definite yes. Okay, now, part two—whether sex like this is any fun for a guy. Well, Skip Hawkins was the undisputed Don Juan in my college crowd. He could please any woman in bed and if you asked any of his lovers back then—including me—they'd tell you he was having just as much fun as they were!

42

"But let me come back to that in a minute. Anyway, Skip was the love of my young life and after we split I pined for him big time." Laughing, she added, "I mean, who wouldn't, right? But, even though he was a great lover and incredibly sexy, he was also incredibly lazy and I knew for sure I didn't need that in a long-term relationship!

"So, we went our separate ways, and I met Sam, fell in love, got married and lived happily ever after," Sally said, and her voice softened as she spoke of her husband. "Sam is one in a million and I can't imagine being married to anyone else. He's always been a gentle, attentive lover and I was never unhappy with our sex life.

"But then one day we were cleaning out the attic and we found a little book I bought used when I was in school. It was by this Chinese guy and it was about something called the tao of love. Sam asked me what it was about. I had never gotten around to reading it so he started to read it, and after a few days he wanted to tell me all about it. He said it talked about how men can make love and have orgasms without ejaculating, and WHAM—it hit me!" Sally said, slapping the table. "I realized this book was talking about Skip's technique! All those years I had thought he just had this unusual, unique talent, but here this little book was saying *it's something guys can learn!*

"Well, you know Sam," Sally continued with a smile. "He's like a dog with a bone—once he grabs ahold of something, he's not gonna' let go! He read that little book and then studied it until he learned the secret that Skip Hawkins knew a long time ago."

As Sally sat back with a satisfied smile, Clare tilted her head to one side and asked, "You mean now Sam has orgasms without ejaculating?"

"That's right."

"Well," she continued slowly, "doesn't that confuse things a little when you make love? I mean, if he doesn't come, how do you know when you're, um... finished?"

Sally stifled a laugh as she answered. "Well, we're 'finished' when we're *both* satisfied." She knew from Clare's puzzled look that she needed to explain a little more. "See, when a guy learns this, he can easily control his ejaculation long enough for his partner to have an orgasm. And beyond that, if he continues the control, the woman can have several more—no sweat."

"Do you?" Clare asked, still absorbing the whole concept.

"You bet," Sally replied. "Three or four is probably about average, but six or seven is not uncommon if we're really hot that night! Here," Sally said, as she dug a pen out of her purse, "let me draw a diaphram." They laughed at Sally's slip before she corrected herself. "I mean, a *diagram*." On the paper placemat in front of her, she drew a chart like this:

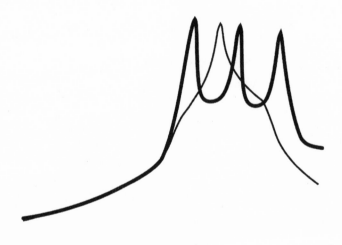

"That's pretty close," she said, examining her finished product. "See, for the gals, this skinny line is the typical, single orgasm pattern of your average, garden variety sex, and the peak at the top is—what else—'the Big O.' The fat black line shows what sex can be like when your man has learned to have orgasms without ejaculating—the same kind of build up, but then lots of peaks before you come back down. Now, for the guy it's more like this," she said, and she turned the placemat over and drew this:

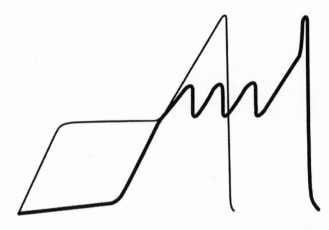

"Again," she said, "the skinny line is mainstream sex." Starting at the left side, she traced its path. "The guy is aroused quickly, hits the peak—and ejaculates—then drops like a shooting star into Dreamland, right? When he learns to have orgasms without ejaculating, his arousal is about the same, but then he has a plateau of peaks, and after he has satisfied his partner and himself, then his arousal drops off—usually *without* putting him to sleep."

"And the guy *never* comes... " Clare said.

"Well, actually," Sally replied, "Sam still does maybe a third of the time. But the point is, because he can control it, he can go as long as he wants, until we're both happy, and then ejaculate if he wants to, without sabotaging our sex by doing it

45

too soon. But most of the time he doesn't want to ejaculate because it just drains too much of his energy."

"Wow," Clare said, sitting back and shaking her head. "This sure puts a new twist on things. I guess I've just always heard about how intense ejaculation is for guys that it's hard to imagine sex would be satisfying for them without it."

"Hey, I thought the same thing when Sam was learning this. I kept asking him if it was okay for him, 'cause I thought maybe he was just trying to make me happy. But he used a good example to explain it. He said our old way of having sex was kind of like when you go to one of those parks with the water slides. If you climb up the biggest, monster slide and then go down—WHOOSH!—and SPLASH into the water, that's what one-act sex with an ejaculation is like—pretty exciting, but over too quick. On the other hand, when he controls his ejaculation, and has that plateau of peaks, he says it's more like white water rafting, and he can enjoy a longer ride and more thrills of different degrees along the way.

"And for the woman," Sally continued, raising her eyebrows, "it's the same story. This method puts sex in a whole different league. I mean, I think with most people making love this first way," she said, tapping the skinny line, "a lot of times it can turn out to be kind of a tense struggle, you know, to time things just right and make both partners happy. But let me tell you, since Sam has learned this, our sex is so effortless. At first, Sam had to work at it a little to get the hang of it, but now when we make love, I have that first orgasm—and everything after that is just gravy! And fat-free, too!"

Sally laughed at her joke and put the pen back in her purse, then sat still and silent watching her future sister-in-law. Clare stared at the drawing while she fingered the rim of her wine glass, then finally looked up.

"I think I'd like to get a copy of that book," she said. "You know, I only slept with one guy before Jesse, so I don't have much experience. I've thought that's probably why a lot of times we haven't hit it off very good in bed." Clare stopped as tears suddenly filled her eyes. She looked down at her lap for a moment, then continued. "I really love Jesse and I know he's the right man for me. I don't want to hurt him but sometimes I just feel so *frustrated*. Anyway, we both know we need to work on this, and maybe reading this book would be a good start."

"If you think it would help," Sally suggested, "I could ask Sam to talk with him."

"Would you? I mean, if you think Sam would feel comfortable talking about sex with him, I think Jesse would really listen to what he had to say."

"Well, okay," Sally said. "I'll talk to Sam about it." Suddenly she remembered the time, and looking at her watch, she said, "Oh my God, how did it get so late? We'd better get out of here if we're going to get our shopping done and meet the guys on time."

They rose and found the waiter to pay the bill, then watched him as he turned and retreated to the register. Sally had just begun thinking about what she would say to Sam when Clare suddenly nudged her elbow, and, nodding in the waiter's direction, murmured quietly, "Nice butt." ♡

Chapter 5

Man to Man

"Are you sure?" Sam asked. "If they're having problems, it could be something else. Maybe finances, or whether they want children... "

Sam and Sally sat on the tailgate of their blue Chevy pickup, parked in front of the house. Between them were two mugs of coffee steaming in the cool air. It was Saturday morning, a time when they rose early for breakfast and quiet conversation together while Danny was still sleeping. Soon Jesse would arrive to help Sam fell a dead oak behind the barn, and Sally knew this was her chance to ask Sam about talking to his brother.

"No, it's not that, Sam. When we went camping—after you guys went to bed that first night—me and Clare and Bobby Lou were giggling and telling jokes and stories. Anyway, when the talk got around to sex, Clare made a comment, something about 'guys have it a lot better' and it surprised me 'cause she had this really... um-m... *hopeless* expression on her face. Then last week when we had lunch we talked about it."

"Does Jesse know about this?" Sam asked.

"I don't know if Clare has told him about our talk at lunch. But she did say they'd had some problems with sex and they both knew it was something they needed to work on, so I know they've talked about it before," Sally replied. Looking down, she saw Mr. Mouser, their gray tabby, crouching below them, ready to jump. Sally patted her leg and he sprang onto her lap, then purred loudly as he moved back and forth, rubbing against them while they scratched his head and back. "Anyway, when I told her about Skip Hawkins, and what you learned from that little book, and how good sex is for us now, she was definitely interested. She said she really loves Jesse—and we both know she does—but she was obviously frustrated, Sam, almost to the point of tears. When I told her I would ask you to talk to Jesse, she seemed relieved."

Sam crossed his arms and sat silently staring at the ground. Sally had learned long ago to expect these long pauses as her husband carefully sorted his thoughts during the course of their discussions. But sometimes her patience ended before his mental analysis. This morning she waited a full minute before she sought an answer. "So," she began, "what are you thinking... ?"

Sam looked up at her and said, "I wonder if I need gas for the chainsaw... "

"Oh, Sam!" Sally cried, scowling, as she gave his shoulder a good push. Sam brought his hands up for cover and ducked his head, laughing, then draped one arm across her shoulder and kissed her cheek. "Sure, I'll talk to him, Sal. I guess it can't hurt."

"I knew I could count on you," she said, and dropped her head on his shoulder. Sally reached behind Sam and slowly stroked his back for a moment, then picked up the coffee mugs and hopped off the tailgate. "Want a refill?"

"No, not now. I'm going down to the barn to check the gear. Holler when Jesse gets here, okay?"

"You got it."

From the kitchen window, Sally saw Jesse's shiny black sports coupe pull into the drive. He drove slowly toward the house, coming to a stop in front just as Sally stepped onto the porch, drying her hands with the kitchen towel, and waved. Jesse waved back, and Sally could hear one of his business tapes playing as he opened the car door. She threw the towel over her shoulder and stood waiting with her arms folded across her chest. Jesse listened for another fifteen seconds, then stopped the tape and stepped out of the car.

"Hey, dude, don't you ever take a day off?" she called out, starting their familiar tango of friendly teasing.

"'Carpe diem,' Sal." Translating his favorite philosophy-to-live-by, he repeated loudly, "Seize the day!" with exaggerated gusto. Taking a deep breath, his eyes scanned the wispy threads of fog that were beginning to lift off the oak-studded hills beyond the house, and he added softly, "And don't we have a beautiful one today... " Jesse reached behind him to close the car door, then started toward the house as Sally walked to the end of the porch and yelled down to the barn, "Sa-a-am-m! Jesse's here!"

Jesse had always been the family celebrity. Even as a young child, he attracted attention. He won the awards, his picture was in the paper, he was the star athlete. Handsome and charismatic, he had the poise of a movie star, not the type of superficial facade molded by an agent, but innate and unaffected. He bore a strong resemblance to Sam but Jesse was a more sophisticated, superlative version of his brother—bigger, more handsome, more polished. Six feet tall, Jesse's body was strong and sleek, the product of carefully planned exercise and nutrition. His thick, wavy black hair, whether neatly combed back for business or falling into his eyes during a workout at the gym, provoked women's fantasies of stroking it. Deep-set, dark eyes, alert and intelligent, peered over his prominent cheekbones, and tanned, smooth skin enhanced a dazzling smile. Wearing blue jeans and a workshirt with the casual elegance of a fashion model, he began to climb the stairs to the front porch, reaching the top step just as Sally noted the faint wash of fatigue across his face.

"How was the drive? You look a little tired."

He stepped onto the porch and gave her a hug, then ran both hands through his hair. "Oh, it was fine," he answered. "I just didn't get much sleep last night."

"Want some coffee?"

"Nah, I had some on the way over."

"How's the store?" Sally asked.

Always ready to talk business, Jesse replied quickly, "It's doing good. I've found a location for the second shop. It's not ideal, but it's pretty close."

Sally sat down in the rocker and Jesse leaned back against the porch railing just as Sam rounded the corner of the house and called out, "Hey, Jesse. How's everything going?" Jesse looked over his shoulder to watch his brother climb the steps, saying, "Can't complain, bro', can't complain," then stood to shake his hand as Sam stepped onto the porch. The two brothers smiled with affection and for a moment stood silently regarding each other.

"Say, did you get breakfast? Sally could fix you something to eat before we start... " Sam offered.

"No thanks, I ate before I left home. Anyway," he added, "we've got a lot of work ahead of us, right? I'm ready if you are, so let's do it."

"Well, all right," Sam replied.

Together they turned and headed down the stairs. Sally watched from the end of the porch as they walked toward the barn to begin their day's work.

By mid-morning the big old oak was down, lying in the field like a fallen sentry, and the men had begun to cut and split the branches. From the house Sally could hear their shouts over the chainsaw as they worked. She knew they had taken a break when it suddenly became quiet, and she walked down to them with coffee and banana bread still warm from the oven. The early fog had burned off, and although the morning air was still cool, the two men had already shed their shirts. While they rested, Sally enjoyed the secret pleasure of watching the muscle movement in their arms and chest. Since waking to the buzz of the saw, Danny had been beside his father and uncle, relishing his temporary place in the world of men's work, and he proudly related to Sally how he had been helping. When the break was over, Danny howled his protest at having to abandon his field duties for household chores.

The men fell to their work again and by noon the bulk of the task was behind them. They began loading the truck with the split wood and hauling it up to the barn, where they stacked it neatly inside. They had just brought the last truckload up when Sally delivered some cold lemonade.

"When will you guys be ready to eat?" she asked.

Sam replied, "Soon as we empty this load."

"Okay," Sally answered. "I'll have lunch ready in half an hour."

Soon they were all sitting down to eat at the long kitchen table. Turkey sandwiches, homemade potato salad, big, juicy, sliced tomatoes from the garden and chilled, sweet cherries from their trees disappeared quickly, washed down with tall glasses of iced tea. When they had finished, they sang a medley of oldies while they cleaned up, and afterwards Sam and Jesse moved to the rocking chairs on the front porch. Sally was headed to town for shopping and errands while Danny went to a birthday party, and as she kissed Sam good-bye he gave her a wink.

Sam and Jesse settled into their chairs, feeling the fatigue in their backs and grateful for the simple, satisfying reward of rest after labor. Their eyes followed Sally and Danny as the truck moved down the long driveway, and they waved when Sally pulled out onto the country road. When the truck disappeared around the first bend in the road, Jesse said, "Danny's a good kid."

Sam had pulled off his boots and socks and was wiggling his toes in the fresh air. "Aah-h-h-h... " he said, taking a deep breath and exhaling with a satisfied smile before responding to his brother. "Yep, Danny is a good kid. He has his days, like all of us, but a man couldn't ask for a better son." Then he laughed and said, "Say, did Sally tell you about the rabbits?"

"The rabbits? No."

"Well, we've been thinking about getting some rabbits—not for pets, but as a little project on the side. We figured to butcher some and sell the others."

"Is that right?" Jesse asked. "What do they sell for?"

"Oh, not much, around six or seven bucks a piece when they're about eight weeks old. We wouldn't be doing it for the money, but we figured it would be a good experience for Danny. He could help with the rabbits—earn a little, save a little, and learn something about business at the same time. But we weren't quite sure how he would take to the idea of raising some to eat, so we thought about what we should say to him, and finally sat him down for a little talk.

"Well, anyway," Sam continued, punching his brother lightly on the shoulder, "he must have a little of your business sense, because after we finished our talk—you know, after we explained about family responsibilities, and saving for a rainy day, and the whole bit—he only had one question: 'Dad,' he says, 'can I have the feet?'"

They laughed together as they imagined Danny selling a rabbit's foot to each of his friends.

"Kids," Sam said. Planting one foot on the porch railing, he crossed the other on top.

Jesse leaned back and studied his older brother. With an age difference of ten years, they lived in different worlds growing up. Sam had left home about the time Jesse started school, so their contact during Jesse's childhood was limited to holiday

53

visits and summer trips. With widely different interests, they had seemingly little in common. But like everyone who knew Sam, Jesse had great respect for that ineffable quality that was the basis of Sam's nature, a steadfast dependability and common-sense wisdom.

Sam broke the silence asking, "So, do you and Clare plan to have any?"

"Rabbits?" Jesse replied playfully. "Oh, you mean *kids*. Well, sure, but not anytime soon. I know I'm not ready yet, and Clare wants to finish school before we start a family. But we've talked about it, and yeah, a couple of kids are part of the future game plan."

"So how are you two doing, anyway?" Sam said, then looked evenly at his brother.

Jesse felt a small wave of discomfort under Sam's steady gaze. "We're doing good. We've got a couple of things to work on... but who doesn't?" As he talked, Jesse turned his eyes away from Sam and looked out toward the cars passing by on the distant road. Sam's gaze followed his, and for a long moment they sat without speaking.

"Well, Jesse... " Sam began, then stopped and suddenly swung his legs down from the railing as he turned to face his brother. "Look, I'm not great with words and I don't quite know how to say this, but I'm not one for beating around the bush, so I guess I'll just come right out and say it. How's your sex life?" Sam asked, then, before Jesse could answer—or object—he continued. "Now before you answer, let me say I understand if you don't want to talk about this, and if you think it's none of my damn business just say so. But, if you're willing to hear me out, I think you'll be interested in what I have to say."

"Wait a minute, wait a minute," Jesse protested. "What makes you think we're having a problem with sex? I mean, we have our bad times, but I don't think it's any more than anyone else."

"Well," Sam replied, "Clare has been talking to Sally about it—you know, just 'girltalk' that gets around to talking about sex—and according to Sally, Clare is a little frustrated. Anyway, Sally told Clare that I would talk to you if she wanted me to... and she did, pal... "

Jesse was silent for a moment. Then he slowly asked, "Well... if our sex life is less than perfect... what can you do that would make any difference?"

"That's what Sally talked to Clare about when they had lunch last week," Sam replied. Then he sat forward in his chair, resting his elbows on his knees and leaning in toward Jesse as he continued. "We've learned something that a lot of people don't know anything about, but let me tell you, Jess, it makes great sex easy if you pick up on a couple of simple techniques."

Jesse suddenly felt a little uneasy as he regarded his brother with faint suspicion and thought, *Just what has he gotten into?* "What are you talking about?" he asked slowly. "Is this something weird? Some goofy yoga-stand-on-your-head thing or a Swappin' Swingers Club?"

"Right, Jesse, like me and Sally are really the 'swinging couple' type," Sam laughed. "No, it's nothing like that—" he said, then added thoughtfully, "—although now that you mention it, I guess some people could consider it kind of strange because it's definitely different from the way people typically make love."

Jesse was beginning to feel his early skepticism start to crumble under a growing curiosity, but Sam's slow response was exasperating. "Well, just tell me, Sam! What the hell is it?"

"Okay, okay, here it is: it's a way to make love *without ejaculating*."

I was wrong, Jesse thought, gazing intently at his brother. *This is beyond strange—it's just plain crazy!* After a pause, he answered with a mild scoff, "Come on, Sam. You're kidding, right? How could having sex without coming possibly improve things?"

Sam settled back in the big rocking chair with both palms resting flat on the wide armrests. In spite of Jesse's dubious response, Sam knew he had his full attention.

"Well," Sam began, "let me explain a few things. First, let's forget about using the term 'come.' It will just confuse things because people use it to mean both 'ejaculate' and 'have an orgasm.' And that's because most people think the two are always a package deal. But, Jesse, I can tell you from my own experience that men can learn to separate the two and actually have orgasms without ejaculating. And that is the whole idea behind this other way of making love."

"So you're saying you've learned how to do that?" Jesse asked. "And when you and Sally make love, you don't come? Okay, I mean, ejaculate."

"That's right—most of the time, anyway. But I do have orgasms—usually two or three, and sometimes more.That's the beauty of it! Instead of a one-shot deal—where you ejaculate and it's all over—when you gain control of your ejaculation, you can have several orgasms instead of just one. And when you can do that, you're a multi-orgasmic man."

Jesse just sat and looked at Sam before he finally asked, "But what does this have to do with Clare? I mean, whether I have orgasms with or without ejaculating, how does that make it any better for her?"

"Well, you've got to look at the big picture," Sam answered. "And think about the difference between men and women. I mean, when it comes to sex, most people would probably agree that men usually respond faster than women, right? You could say we're sort of like... a microwave," he said, and laughed. "And women... well, women are more like building a fire. If you start small and go through the right steps, you'll end up with a roaring blaze, but if you don't, it just sort of fizzles, right?"

"Yeah," Jesse mused, "that's pretty accurate."

"Well," Sam continued, "once a guy learns how to have orgasms without ejaculating, he doesn't have a problem lasting long enough for his partner to have an orgasm, and he can basically just keep going as long as he wants. As a matter of fact, because of the guy's increased endurance, what often happens is that his lover becomes multi-orgasmic. And Jess, believe me, making love this way puts sex in a whole different league.

"Let me think of something to compare it to," he said, and sat staring at the floor, scratching his chin, before he looked up and said, "I've got it. Let's compare it to food. What's that great burrito place near your apartment? The one with those big, fat super-size jobs?"

"Oh. Felipe's."

"That's right. Okay, say you work late one night, you're hungry and stressed out, and when you finally get home there's nothing to eat. So you head over to Felipe's for one of their world deluxe burritos and a cold beer. It's quick and it tastes great—it really hits the spot, right?"

"It sure does," Jesse conceded.

"Well, okay, that's traditional sex with an ejaculation. And hey, I'm not knocking it, sometimes it's just the right thing. But now imagine... let's say you're just back from a vacation, and... we'll say it's Clare's birthday, okay? You're taking her someplace really special for dinner—what's the best restaurant in Sacramento?"

"Probably Sommerset."

"Okay, so you're rested and relaxed, and you have this big date you've been looking forward to. Clare looks great in this little black number and you go to Sommerset. You have a relaxing five-course dinner with candlelight, a private conversation, champagne, great food, a fancy dessert—the works. Well, that's what this 'alternative' sex is like."

After a long pause, Jesse looked at his brother and threw his hands up. "Okay, Sam, you sold me. So how do I find out more about this? How did you learn it?"

"Well, the first I heard of it was from a little book Sally had in school. Just a minute, I'll go and find it." Sam rose and retreated to the bookshelves by the fireplace, then returned with a tattered paperback book.[1]

Handing the book to Jesse, Sam said, "This'll give you a pretty good idea of the whole concept. Give me a call when you've read the book and we'll go from there." As Jesse sat thumbing through the book, Sam suddenly changed the subject. "Hey, why don't you stay around for dinner? We're going to barbecue and then go into town for a bluegrass concert."

"Thanks, but not this trip. I've still got some things to do at home. Actually," he said, rising from his chair, "I should probably hit the road now."

"Well," Sam replied, "You know I appreciate your help today. Let me know when I can return the favor."

"You bet. I'm sure the new shop will need some work before we open. I'll give you a call then."

"You got it."

The two brothers walked down the steps to Jesse's car, and after a quick handshake, Jesse slid behind the wheel, then waved as he turned the car and started down the driveway. In the rearview mirror, he could see Sam standing in front of the house, watching him pull away. Jesse looked down at the borrowed book tossed on the passenger's seat and, considering the drive ahead, thought to himself, *Too bad that book's not on tape.* ♡

---

[1] *The Tao of Love and Sex*, by Jolan Chang

Chapter 6

A Thousand Repetitions
and the Four-Minute Mile

It was late August, mid-afternoon on a sizzling day in the Sacramento Valley, and Sam and Sally were invited for a barbecue to celebrate Jesse's 29th birthday. Sam rang the bell and dropped down on one knee as Sally quickly sat on the other, placing the brightly wrapped gift on her lap. Their timing was perfect. When Jesse opened the front door they had struck a pose with their arms flung wide as they sang out "Happy Birthday!"

Jesse shook his head and laughed, then pulled Sally to her feet. "Thank you, thank you. Come on in." He ushered them in as Clare stepped out from the kitchen, with a knife in one hand and mushrooms in the other, and waved a welcome. "Hi, you guys. How's it going?"

The four of them stood talking in the living room for a few minutes before the inevitable gender split, when Sally followed Clare into the kitchen with an offer of help and the two men went to the patio to clean the grill.

"Do you want something to drink?" Clare asked, raising a wine glass to her lips.

"Mm-m-m... maybe a little later," Sally said as she began rinsing lettuce. Together they finished making the salad, then shucked corn and skewered meat and vegetables for the barbecue. When everything was finished, Clare suggested, "Let's go in the other room. Jesse can start the coals in a little while."

Jesse's apartment was furnished with chrome, glass and leather in a statement of contemporary, sophisticated efficiency. The dark sofa and chairs and gleaming tables were arranged to create the illusion of space, with the TV and sound system hidden in a sleek cabinet of smoked glass. Even the light fixtures, traditionally humble, utilitarian objects, were more like unusual works of art, looking over the shoulder of an armchair or casting a dramatic glow across the wall.

Clare dropped cross-legged into a wide leather swivel chair and Sally sat on the floor with her back against the sofa as they settled in for their chat. Their conversation wandered from Danny, to the wedding plans, and then to Clare's music before they were interrupted by Sam and Jesse coming through the room.

"We're going down to the new shop to talk about the remodel," Jesse announced as they headed out the front door. "We won't be long. I'll start the coals when we get back, okay?"

Clare was silent for a moment before she answered. "All right, but don't be late, Jesse—we're getting hungry."

"An hour, tops."

"Yeah, okay," Clare said. She waved him off and turned back to Sally.

The men closed the door behind them, and Sally watched Clare as she dropped her eyes and idly twirled the stem of her empty wine glass between her thumb and forefinger. It was obvious that something was bothering her. Finally she looked up at Sally, and breaking away from her thoughts, remembered her responsibility as a hostess. With a distracted glance, she asked quickly, "Are you sure you don't want something to drink? Iced tea? A beer?"

"No, I'm fine for now," Sally replied. Then after a pause, she said, "Seems like you've got something on your mind." She waited a moment before asking softly, "Do you want to talk about it?"

Clare smiled weakly, then slumped back in her chair with a deep sigh. "Yeah, Sally, I do... I do... " She thought for a moment and said, "God, yeah—the thing is, I'm supposed to say those two words to Jesse in a couple of months, and Sally, I think I'm getting cold feet or something. I don't know, I just—something just feels *wrong*." Their eyes met and Clare shrugged her shoulders, feeling frustrated and confused.

"What happened? Did you have a fight about something?"

"No. Well, not really. I mean, it's not like I just discovered he's still interested in an old girlfriend or anything like that. It's just that so much of the time Jesse seems like he's not really... there... you know what I mean? Sometimes I feel sort of... lonely when I'm with him. And I hate that! I mean, that's not the way it should be with someone you're planning to spend the rest of your life with, right? Jesse just works too hard—and so much of the time when he's not working, he's *thinking* about work. I really admire Jesse, I do respect him for the success he's achieved. But it's like he always has to prove himself, and he thinks that he does that by doing more, and more... " Clare brushed a lock of hair out of her eyes as her voice trailed off.

Sally was quiet for a moment before saying, "You know, I've always thought maybe Jesse feels a little jealous of his big brother. I know he respects Sam—"

"Yes, he does, he thinks the world of Sam," Clare interjected.

"—but I don't think Sam has ever encouraged any competition between them. Being ten years apart, when they were growing up they really couldn't share the same friends, or the same interests or anything. But just having a big brother who was already a man—when Jesse was still a kid—might have made Sam seem larger than life, and maybe Jesse tried to live up to that. But anyway, I also think it's just part of Jesse's personality that he's more competitive."

"Yes, I do, too. You know, he told me before that once when he was pretty little—I think he was maybe only seven or eight—he won a contest for the local kids. Somebody in town offered a new bicycle as a prize for the kid who collected the most walnuts from this guy's orchard, and Jesse collected more than twice as many as the runner-up. He told me that he clearly remembers getting that bike and the feeling of being rewarded for all his hard work, and he really liked that feeling."

Sally smiled and nodded. "I know that story. That's a classic from the Bennett family history. The next day Jesse woke up and announced that he would not be going to school. He told his mom and dad that he was just too tired because all night long he had dreamed that he was picking up walnuts!" They laughed together before Sally continued.

"Well, anyway, it sounds like you and Jesse need to talk. *Soon*. But Clare, I think it's something you can work out if you love each other. That's what you have to know in your heart, whether you truly love him."

"Yes," Clare said. "That's the easy part—I know the answer is yes. I do love Jesse. But I love *him*, not what he does, or his business, or any of that. And I just don't know if he understands that."

"Talk to him. Just talk to him and tell him everything you just told me. I know with the new shop opening it's hard to get his attention, but if you make him stop and see how important it is to you, he'll listen. He'll really listen, and he'll think hard about what you say. "

After a pause, Sally asked, "Is there anything else going on between you?" Without wanting to pry, she continued slowly, "How is Jesse doing with those exercises Sam gave him?"

Clare looked up quickly and said, "That's the second thing on my mind. Jesse's been doing the exercises—and he is making progress. He's gotten so that more often he can continue long enough for me to come. But I think it's starting to frustrate him a little that, so far, he hasn't been able to come without ejaculating. You know, most of the time Jesse picks up on things really quickly, and I think he's kind of annoyed with himself that he just can't get it yet. But honestly, I don't care about all that as much as just having him completely there with me, showing his love for me, instead of being obsessed with overcoming this challenge and proving himself. I mean, then we just get back to that same old problem! And who wants that kind of tension in bed?"

"He's probably just trying *too* hard. It's funny, but when a guy is learning this he has to learn to be really relaxed and aware before it will work. Kind of a 'less is more' thing. Hey, maybe a massage or a romantic bath together would loosen him up a little."

"There's an idea," Clare mused. Then she asked, "Did it take Sam a while to learn this ?"

"Yeah, it did, probably several months. But you know, he basically taught himself, just by trial and error. But then he found those exercises that he gave Jesse and we hoped that would make it easier for him learning it. The most important thing is that Jesse has to be patient and understand that it just takes a little time for most men to learn this." Sally paused for a moment before adding, "But Clare, if he sticks with it, he'll really be glad he did—and so will you!

"Listen, let me tell you a little bit more of what this 'new' sex is like. Remember, before Sam learned this, I really didn't have any complaints about our sex life. I almost always came having sex our old way. But now that Sam is multi-orgasmic, instead of having sex that's like a slide—you know, it's fun, but over too quick—I can have multiple orgasms, too, and that's like a giant rollercoaster! It's a much longer ride, with a lot more thrills! There are high peaks, and sometimes a bunch of little ones, one right after the other, 'til you can hardly tell where one

63

orgasm ends and the other begins. Since Sam has learned this it's so easy for me to have multiple orgasms that now when I have that first one I know it's just Act One. But for most women, if they have 'mainstream' sex, that first orgasm is like the final curtain, because their man usually comes soon after and then that's it. What gets me is that *so many couples don't even know what they're missing.* I just can't figure out why there aren't more people who know about this! I mean, if the Chinese have been doing this for thousands of years, why did it take so long to get across the ocean?"

Sally was leaning forward, her eyes wide with enthusiasm, when suddenly she threw her head back and laughed.

"I'll never forget the first time Sam was able to control his ejaculation long enough so I had several orgasms. It felt so good, it was like I was *paralyzed* with pleasure. I had this tingling feeling in my body, and—this is kind of funny—I remember feeling my nostrils and my fingertips tingling! I kept thinking it would be impossible to even move—I could do nothing but just lie there and enjoy the incredible pleasure," Sally said, then laughed again before continuing. "Anyway, all of a sudden I had this image in my mind of those laboratory mice, you know, the ones in the experiment with a wire planted in their little brains. And when the mice push on a button, it stimulates their pleasure center, and they just keep pushin' that button until they're half-dead with exhaustion! Well, right then I felt like I could identify with those little critters." They laughed together before Sally added, "Except it wasn't my *brain* that was being stimulated!"

Sally sat back against the couch and pulled her knees to her chest. Clare watched her for a few moments before she finally said, "God, you make it sound like winning the lottery, an Olympic gold medal, and a Nobel Prize all in one."

"Oh, hey," Sally replied quickly, "Don't get me wrong here. After you guys get the hang of this you'll still have to do your laundry, and make car payments, and it's not like you'll never have another argument again. But you will get a lot more satisfaction—and feel closer." For a moment they sat without speaking, then Sally slapped her thighs and got to her feet as Clare rose from her chair.

Sally stood with her hands in her hip pockets and looked long and hard at Clare. Finally she said, "I think you and Jesse will work things out. I have a feeling that you're on the verge of... something... I don't know what, exactly. But some sort of break-through. Anyway, if you feel like you want to talk, you know you can call anytime." In a spontaneous gesture, the two women reached out and hugged each other with easy affection, and as they moved apart, Sally said, "You know, I think I'm ready for that beer now."

Jesse pulled on the heavy roll-up door and sunlight flood-ed the warehouse as he stepped inside with his brother. Together they stood in the middle of the room and surveyed their surround-ings. Framed-in walls formed a skeleton that would give the finished shape to the large, open space. In one corner there were stacks of sheetrock and two-by-fours together with power saws and tool belts retired for the weekend. Wood shavings, sprinkled across the concrete floor like cake decorations, filled the air with the smell of construction.

Sam stepped over supplies and walked through the unfin-ished walls as he followed Jesse, listening to the narration of his brother's tour.

"This whole back area will be for repairs and supplies. We have a lot more room here than in the first shop, so it will be easier to work in, and the roll-up door will be better for deliver-ies. The bathroom is over here, and this room will be a small lounge and locker room. Up front where the windows are we'll have the showroom, and the office is right over here." Jesse led the way as he walked through the door frame, then turned and pointed to the opening that had been framed in for the service counter. "That's where your countertop and storage cabinets will go."

Sam walked over and placed one hand on the bottom length of wood framing the opening, and, thinking to himself, pulled a pencil and pad of paper from his pocket. Jesse joined him and together they sketched their ideas for the project as they discussed the details. When they had reached an agreement, Sam took the necessary measurements.

"I'll draw up something to scale to give you an idea of how the finished piece will be," Sam said. "Then you can look it over and make any changes before I get started on the work. How does that sound?"

"Sounds good."

"I'll have something to show you in a week or two, and it shouldn't take more than two weeks to build it. Does that fit with your schedule?"

"Sure. In the meantime the framing and sheetrock will be done, and by then I should have this permit thing settled," Jesse replied with a frown.

"What permit thing?" Sam asked.

"Remember? I mentioned it the last time we talked on the phone," Jesse pulled up two five-gallon buckets of joint compound and sat down on one as Sam took the other. "I have a hearing with the planning department next week to revise the use permit. It's a little risky because there's a small chance they'll deny the variance, and if they do I'll have to appeal it, which would cost some money," Jesse explained. "But I know people in the city departments, and I know how to handle it, so I'm not worried," he added, but Sam could see the concern etched on his brother's face.

"Well, if there's any way I can help, I'd be happy to."

"Hey, you're already helping with this carpentry work."

For a moment they sat without speaking in the sultry heat of the warehouse, gazing at the work around them as they imagined the finished product. Finally Sam said, "Well, Jesse, you're a lucky man, you know that? You have a successful business, you're about to marry a beautiful woman. Your dreams are coming true."

Jesse looked at Sam with a blank expression, almost as though it were the first time he had considered the thought, then nodded. "Yes, they are. I am a lucky man."

Again they were silent for a time before Sam asked, "So, how is everything with you and Clare? How are you doing with those exercises I gave you?"

"Well, I've had some success, but so far I haven't been able to trigger an orgasm and keep from ejaculating. It's a little frustrating. It just takes so much effort, you know, to maintain control and not go too far, and I'll admit I'm starting to wonder if it's really worth it. The old way sure seems a lot simpler—you get horny, you get laid and you get off—and it feels pretty darn good, so maybe that's enough. You know what I mean?"

"Yeah, I know what you mean," Sam said, before adding, "But you know what that reminds me of?"

Jesse had heard his brother ask that question many times, and he knew what it usually led to. "I'll bet it reminds you of a story that you're about to tell."

Sam laughed. "Not a story, exactly. I guess it's more of a joke—a joke with a moral. Did you hear the one about the two stallions?" When Jesse shook his head, he continued. "Well, there's these two stallions, a young one and an old one, and they're standing on top of a hill looking out over this big pasture with this big herd of mares grazing in it. The young stallion is really excited. He sees all those mares, and he's so excited, he's snortin' and pawin' at the ground, just rarin' to go. He says to the

67

old stallion, 'Hot damn, let's run down there and screw one of those mares!' But the old stallion just looks at the young one, and says, 'Nah-h-h... let's *walk* down there and screw 'em all... '"

Jesse laughed and said, "Okay, okay, I get it: experience and patience bring a greater reward than youthful impulsiveness."

"You catch on quick, Jess," Sam answered as he reached out and slapped his brother's back. "Anyway, it's just the same with people. The young stallion doesn't have any patience 'cause he only knows the one way. But when he learns the other way, believe me, he won't want to go back to the old way of doing things.

"You know, the Chinese have a saying: 'A thousand repetitions is a good beginning.' I'm not saying it will take you that many tries to get this, but even if it does, you won't regret it. It's worth the effort, Jess, believe me. Just keep at it and one day you'll be glad you did."

Jesse leaned forward and propped his knees on his elbows. "Well, I'm not going to give up. But I have been wondering about one thing: if this is such a great lovemaking technique, why aren't there more people who know about it?"

"I've wondered about that, too. I don't know, in places like India and China and Japan, maybe most people do know about it. But in the good ol' USA, this idea is still pretty new, and it just takes time before something new catches on. As a matter of fact, I learned something just the other day that relates to this. You know who Roger Bannister was, right?"

"Wasn't he the first guy to run a mile in less than four minutes?"

"That's right. But before he did that, all the experts thought it was humanly impossible to run a sub-four-minute mile. Runners had tried for years to break that record, and most people felt that it was just impossible. But in the first year and a half after Bannister broke that four-minute barrier, *fifty-six* other runners did, too! Just knowing that it was possible opened the door for all those runners after him to do the same thing. Anyway, right now, if you did a poll, most Americans would probably say that it's impossible for a man to have an orgasm without ejaculating, but people are slowly beginning to learn that's just not true." Sam straightened up and folded his arms across his chest before he continued. "Here's something else you can think about. You know Kinsey, the scientist? In the fifties, when Kinsey started doing his research on sex, only one out of ten women he studied had had multiple orgasms, and now it's more like fifty percent. Well, today people estimate that about one out of ten *men* have multiple orgasms. But I'd wager that thirty or forty years from now we'll probably be about even with women!"

Jesse mulled over his brother's facts before commenting, "Well, Sam, you really did your homework."

"Hey, you've got to admit, it's a pretty interesting topic," he replied.

"You bet it is, and—" Suddenly Jesse broke off. "Oh, shit! I forgot about the time. We'd better head for home pronto or *we'll* be barbecued." Sam collected his notes while Jesse locked up, and in less than three minutes they were back on the freeway heading toward home and the birthday dinner.♡

69

Chapter 7

Acting on Instinct

Clare had finished the dishes and was sweeping the floor when she heard Jesse call her from the bedroom.

"Clare! Do you know where my flight bag is?" Sam and Sally had left thirty minutes ago. Jesse would leave the next morning for a trade show in San Diego, where he hoped to find a sponsor for a bike race he had planned for the fall. It was a little before ten as he began packing for his early flight, and Clare sensed the fatigue in his voice.

"I put it in the garage," she answered loudly. When she had finished in the kitchen, Clare walked back to Jesse to offer her help.

"Did you find it?" she asked, coming into the bedroom.

"Yeah, thanks."

Clare sat on the edge of the bed, then pulled both feet under her to watch Jesse collect a few necessities for the quick trip. A light traveler, he packed his flight bag with a change of clothes and put the business materials he would need in his briefcase.

"Did you like your birthday dinner?" Clare asked.

Jesse snapped the briefcase shut and set it beside the bed. "Yeah, it was great, thanks." He looked around the room, scanning a mental checklist to make sure he hadn't forgotten anything.

"When do you think you'll be back?"

Jesse paused for a few seconds before answering with irritation in his voice. "If everything goes well I'll be back tomorrow night, otherwise it will probably be sometime Tuesday. I just can't say for sure now."

"It doesn't matter," Clare said softly. "If it takes longer that's fine."

"Then why do you ask?" he replied. "Why do I always have to explain everything to you? Why do you need to know all the details?"

Stung by Jesse's impatient response, Clare wanted only to end the conversation. "I was just wondering if I should plan dinner for tomorrow. That's all."

"Well, shit, Clare, if I get home early and there's nothing planned, we'll just go out and get something to eat!"

"Okay, fine. Just forget it." Clare rose and began to leave.

As she passed the bed, Jesse turned suddenly and caught her by the shoulders. "Look, Clare, I'm sorry. I didn't mean to... that didn't come out right, I know. It's just that I have a lot on my mind with the new shop opening, and I... " He reached out to brush the hair back from her face before continuing. "I'm sorry I snapped at you... I was actually thinking maybe we could climb into bed and really celebrate my birthday after I finish packing. How about it?"

Exasperated, Clare pulled his hands off her shoulders and said, "God, Jesse, do you really think it would be any fun when you're obviously so preoccupied?"

"What are you talking about?"

"Well, you seem to schedule sex just like you do everything else, according to the available time, without really thinking about the *timing*. I'm sure not interested in thinking about sex when *you're* thinking about work."

"What do you mean?" he asked, his voice rising. "I just want to make love to you tonight, when we have the opportunity."

"That's just what I'm talking about! You don't want to make love to me, you just want to have sex when it fits into your schedule!"

Jesse stepped back and purposely took a deep breath. Suddenly he felt weary and defeated, but in the next breath the feeling turned to anger. In his mind's eye he helplessly watched as he released his pent-up anxiety, angry with himself for losing control.

"Clare, I can't believe this. Don't you know the reason I'm working so hard is to make a future for us? I want to make sure we'll be happy and secure, and not have to worry from day to day about bills, or getting laid off, or how we'll pay for our kids' education or our retirement. Don't you know I'm doing this for you? And how can you believe I don't want to make love to you, when I've been doing so much to try to make it better for you?"

Clare listened without a word before she finally blurted, "Stop, Jesse, stop! I don't care about all that!" she exclaimed, and looked directly at him, her fair skin flushed with the heat of her anger. "I would rather we had less money and more time to-gether—I mean *real* time together— when we can relax and talk about things, and just enjoy each other's company and really be there for each other. Because right now, Jesse, I feel alone a lot of the time when I'm with you, and that makes me feel so bad. I love you Jesse, I truly love you, but I can't live like that... " She reached out to take his hand but Jesse took a step back, putting his hands up and shaking his head.

Jesse looked at Clare without speaking. Suddenly his head felt like a cauldron, with the pressure from the last several weeks boiling over inside his mind and pushing out against his skull. In careful, even tones, he said quietly, "Clare, I think I need to be alone for a little while. I'm going to go to the airport and get a hotel room for the night, and I'll call you sometime tomorrow."

Without another word, he zipped the flight bag and slung it over his shoulder, then picked up his briefcase and left.

It was ten-thirty when Jesse pulled into the parking space at the mini-market and turned off the engine. During the twenty-minute drive from home his mind had been a battlefield where anger, fatigue, stress and hurt had fought for equal attention, and he was spent from the effort of sorting through his feelings. Closing his eyes, he let his head fall back against the seat, and several minutes passed as he sat without moving. Finally, knowing he would need to be alert in the morning, he made a conscious effort to rally his energy, forcing his discipline to take command and drive the troubling thoughts from his mind. He took several deep breaths and, hoping for a decent night's sleep, pulled himself from the car with the decision to quickly buy the forgotten toothbrush and check in to a hotel.

Jesse never knew what made him duck. Like the sudden, undeniable, internal message that commands one to inexplicably walk away from a lifetime career, or run to a lover, or crawl through a burning building, he acted on a decision that is not really a decision, not a rational, mental deduction but a split-second impulse, urgent and compelling. Searching the shelves for a toothbrush, Jesse had looked up briefly and seen a mottled green van pull into the lot and park near the street. A young man dressed in blue jeans, with a half-zipped, gray hooded sweatshirt over his bare chest, emerged from the passenger side, scanned his surroundings with a quick glance, and began to move toward the store. In that instant, a fierce whisper inside Jesse's mind, saying *Do this!* caused him to drop down, motionless, behind the razor blades and the cold remedies. Hidden by the shelves as the man walked through the doorway, Jesse knew he had not been seen.

While Jesse froze in a low crouch, he heard the man ask for a pack of cigarettes. The clerk suspected nothing as she searched the display behind her for the correct brand, then turned back to see the barrel of a handgun pointed at her face.

"All right, don't do anything stupid and you won't get hurt!" Holding the gun on her, the robber yelled, "Just do what I say and do it quick!"

From the far end of the aisle, Jesse could see the robber's arms extended straight forward, both hands gripping the gun. His arms were directly over the counter next to the cash register, no more than three feet from the woman. A canvas duffle bag was thrown on the counter, and he tensely gave orders to the clerk.

"Now empty the drawer into the bag! Damn it, hurry up! Do what I say or I'll fuckin' shoot!"

A stout, middle-aged woman with kittens on her T-shirt, the clerk stammered with fear. "All- All right, I'll do whatever you want. Please, just don't hurt me." Holding the gun on her as she began to empty the register, the man shifted his weight from one foot to the other with nervous agitation, then glanced quickly toward the parking lot. In that brief moment the woman's eyes met Jesse's, and he saw in those eyes something he would never forget. He saw the cold fear of death and the powerless expectations of a victim. He saw the desperate pleading for help and the instant communion with a complete stranger, himself. In a moment's time, he saw all those things—and he also saw his mother, his fiancé, his sister, his friends.

Once Jesse knew the robber's awareness was intent on getting the canvas bag filled, he slowly started around the end of the aisle, moving on his haunches in a low crouch. When he turned-ed the corner around the row of shelves, he was directly behind the robber, perhaps twelve feet away. He knew that the hood of the man's sweatshirt limited his peripheral vision, and Jesse felt sure he could close the distance to him without being detected. As he began to make his way toward the robber, he felt oddly aware of time moving in slow motion. Alert to each detail, he observed everything in his surroundings with sudden, heightened clarity: the gum wrapper on the floor... the orange tab on the robber's Levi's... his own carefully measured breath. Moving along the floor and hoping to stay low as long as possible, Jesse realized the clerk was stalling to give him more time when suddenly the nervous thief yelled, "Get moving, bitch! Now put a carton of those cigarettes in, too!"

Jesse knew he was going to run out of time. The woman had finished filling the bag and the robber was ordering her to get down behind the counter.

"Get down there while I get out of here!" he screamed. "I'm not going to shoot you, just get down!"

Jesse didn't buy it. Knowing he had to make his move before the robber fired, he leapt up just as the trembling woman's eyes desperately darted in Jesse's direction. Instantly the robber knew someone was behind him, and he spun around, wielding the gun with his outstretched arms to confront his surprise attacker.

In one move, Jesse lunged to the side, grabbing the robber's wrist with one hand as the gun went off, shooting past him, then immediately struck hard with his free hand against the outside of the robber's elbow. With a cry of pain, the robber dropped the gun and swung wildly, catching Jesse's cheek with his fist before Jesse brought his elbow across to strike against the man's temple.

It was over. Unconscious, the robber instantly fell to the floor, limp and heavy as a wet rug. Three seconds. Just three seconds, and it was over.

As he stood over the fallen man, Jesse saw the green van hastily pull out onto the road, tires squealing as it sped away. Hearing the clerk sob with relief, he wanted to comfort her but knew it wasn't safe yet.

"Are you all right?" he asked her. When she nodded, he said, "Okay, I need your help. Give me your keys and a paper bag and then call 9-1-1." Still weeping, she pulled a set of keys and a small bag from beneath the counter before reaching for the phone.

Grasping the barrel of the gun with his fingertips, Jesse carefully put it in the bag and placed it on the counter, then quickly took the keys to the back of the store and unlocked the office. When he returned, he grabbed the robber's feet, dragged him into the office, and left him there after locking the door.

Jesse was first aware that he was cut when he began walking back to the front of the store and felt a thin trickle of blood where the robber's fist had landed. Only then did Jesse consciously understand the gravity of what had happened, and the realization brought a weak, shaky feeling to his knees. Leaning against the wall, he closed his eyes and took several deep breaths before returning to the store's checkout counter.

Having witnessed the event from across the street, a well-dressed young couple had come into the store to offer their help. They appeared almost as shaken as the clerk, but tried to comfort her with reassuring hugs. When Jesse approached, the clerk looked up and said to the young couple, "He saved my life!" Then, seeing the blood on Jesse's cheek, she cried, "Oh, you're hurt—" and dissolved into tears again.

"I'm okay, I'm okay," Jesse answered softly. "It's just a little cut. How are you?" He asked, reaching out to gently pat her shoulder. The young man had just handed Jesse a clean handkerchief when the police arrived.

As soon as the police began their questioning they heard pounding from the back of the store. "That's pretty good timing," Jesse said, nodding toward the office. "It sounds like your man just came to." The police unlocked the office to apprehend the robber, and after one cruiser left with the handcuffed suspect, the second officer questioned Jesse, the clerk and the young couple.

It was well past eleven before the investigation was finished and Jesse was free to leave. He gave the clerk a final hug, who thanked him once again, then walked out into the balmy night air and slid behind the wheel of his car. He started the engine and pulled out of the parking lot, but instead of turning in the direction of the airport hotels, he pulled onto the freeway heading back the way he had come, back to his home, and his love. ♡

Chapter 8

Jesse Loves Clare

Jesse had never felt like this. Driving his customary route home, he felt as though he were seeing the familiar landmarks for the first time. *What is this feeling?* his bewildered mind asked again and again. It was not confidence, it was not determination, it was not assertiveness—traits that Jesse knew well—it was something different. He felt alert, and he felt relaxed. He felt peaceful... he felt energized. He felt dynamic... and calm. His heart held all those feelings at the same time, a marriage of opposites that somehow interwove everything that was important into a puzzling paradox. It gave Jesse a new understanding, a new perspective, and with that new perspective, he wanted only to get back to Clare. He knew that *she* was his priority. As soon as he was on the highway, Jesse called her.

"Hi, hon'."

Clare held her breath and didn't answer.

"Listen, something came up and I cancelled my trip. I'll be home in fifteen minutes and I'll explain everything then."

Still there was no response. "Clare, are you there?"

Finally, she answered, "Yes, I'm here. I heard you... okay."

"Good, I'll be home soon. I love you, Clare."

Again a silence, then Clare replied, "I love you" and they said good-bye.

Jesse pulled into the garage and, opening the door to the apartment, found their small home filled with the brooding passion of a Beethoven sonata. He peered into the living room, expecting to find Clare at the piano, but saw instead only tiny red pinpoints of light from the CD player in the darkened room. He walked softly toward the back and stepped into the bedroom, where he found her. The glass doors to the patio were open to the night air, and Clare stood in the doorway, her back to him. Knowing he was there, she stood without moving and waited, aching for the distance between them to close.

For a long moment Jesse stood motionless as he gazed at her, intensely aware of her uncommon beauty. She wore a long, white cotton sheath that billowed gently about her legs on the soft breath of a breeze. In the moonlight, he could see the contour of her body through the sheer cover of her dressing gown and he admired the graceful line of her leg, the smooth curves of her hips and waist and breasts. Her hair was loose and free, brushing her shoulders, and as the breeze lifted it away from her face, the smooth, fair skin of her neck, almost luminous in the seductive light, beckoned him.

Jesse started across the room toward her as she turned to look over her shoulder, and their eyes met. Clare looked up at him without speaking, but as he moved into the light she saw his cheek and her breath caught. "Jesse, what—" she began, but he pulled her close and put one finger to her lips to stop her.

"Don't say anything right now," he said gently. "I'll explain everything, but first I want to tell you something." He took her hand and led her through the door and onto the patio, then tenderly pushed her down into a chair beneath the vine-covered arbor.

Clare sat still and silent, overwhelmed by his intense, yet infinitely gentle manner, as he took both her hands in his. Then, dropping down on his knees in front of her, he placed his head in her lap and sat without moving. Sensing that he needed comforting, Clare slowly began to stroke his hair, then bent to kiss the top of his head. She gently brushed her hand across his cheek and stroked his big hands, now clutching her thighs with a fervent need.

Finally, lifting his head, he looked into her eyes and spoke to her. "Clare, I love you. I know I can get carried away with things, and sometimes I neglect you. But please believe me when I say I only want to make you happy and I will do anything for you. I guess I'm not the most romantic guy, so maybe I don't express it very well, but Clare, I love you with all my heart. I love just watching you move, and I love the way you laugh when you're playing with kids... I love that goofy Bullwinkle imitation you do... and I love hearing you play Chopin as I fall asleep... I will always love you, and I don't know what I would do without you. You are more important to me than anything, and I don't want to lose you."

Clare's eyes filled with tears as she said, "Sh-h-h... it's all right, don't worry. I love you, too, Jesse. When I first met you, I knew you were the only man for me. I just want us to be happy together for the rest of our lives—"

"We will be happy, I know it," Jesse replied. Then, getting to his feet, he pulled Clare up and closed his arms around her. "Don't ever leave me, Clare," he said, as he buried his face against her neck, breathing in her essence, and clung to her so tightly he worried that he might hurt her. He began to kiss the soft curve of her neck, and as his lips moved toward her breasts, there was a hunger and passion inside him more powerful than he had ever felt. Suddenly mindful that this overwhelming desire might frighten Clare, he broke apart from her, and gently smoothed her hair back, saying softly, "I want to make love to you now. This feeling is just so strong right now, I want to show you how much

I love you. If you're not ready for that, I understand, but I need to just hold you close for a long time."

Clare didn't need to think about her answer. Pulling his head down to her, she covered his mouth with a long, slow kiss before their tongues began a dance of insistent exploration. Soon Jesse reached up to pull the straps of Clare's gown over her shoulders, then lowered his head to her breasts as the garment slid down her arms, then past her legs, and settled in a soft pool around her feet. He covered her breasts with soft kisses, tenderly pulling on her stiff nipples while stroking her arms, neck and belly with a loving caress. Knowing she was eager for more, he slid one hand down between her legs and moved across the warm, wet flesh with slow, teasing strokes. Pushing against his touch, Clare moaned with small, soft sounds of pleasure. Then Jesse's big hands slid around to cup the smooth, firm globes of her hips, and he pulled her toward him in a tight embrace.

Jesse showered kisses on her throat and shoulders as Clare arched back against his embrace and let her head fall back. Opening her eyes, she saw a canopy of stars overhead, and her senses were overwhelmed with pleasure as she drank in the cool caress of the night air and the heat of her lover's touch.

In the next moment, Jesse scooped her up in his arms and carried her in to the bed. Laying her down gently, he ran his hands slowly, teasingly down the full length of her body as he stood up and began to undress. Clare rolled luxuriantly toward him, sliding one leg slowly across the sheets and stretching her arms overhead in anticipation of his embrace.

Jesse unbuttoned his shirt while he watched Clare's languid, sensuous movements, aching to touch the perfect shape of her breasts and the soft, smooth skin of her belly and thighs. Quickly he pulled off his shirt and tossed it aside. In the dappled moonlight of the dim room Clare saw a tantalizing glimpse of Jesse's smooth, broad chest, and she longed to caress the taut power of his muscles. Next he unzipped his pants and pulled them off, then unveiled the bulge in his shorts as he shed his last piece of clothing. At last he lay down on the bed, and Clare's breath caught when she felt the warm, muscled smoothness of his body slide down beside her.

For a moment they lay together on their sides, lost in each other's eyes. Jesse reached out and touched her face, running his hand along her cheek and down her nose before tracing the outline of her lips. As his finger brushed across her lips, Clare took the tip of it in her mouth and sucked gently for a moment before it continued its travel.

When they could no longer endure the exquisite torture of postponed contact, their bodies pressed against each other with fevered urgency. Clare put both hands on the side of Jesse's head and covered his face with passionate kisses as he rolled on top of her. Clinging to each other in a tight embrace, their hands and tongues explored the landscape of their bodies with an eager insistence. It was not long before Clare begged him to enter her, and he found his way to her warm, wet center.

Teasing each other with prolonged movements, they began a rhythmic dance of passion as they gradually increased the tempo of their lovers' tango. Soon Clare felt the tension between her legs beginning to climb, surely, steadily, until her body crested over into waves of pleasure. Her arms and legs wrapped tightly around Jesse until she felt the pulsing contractions subside, yet still Jesse had not tired. He changed his movement, teasing her with gradually slower thrusts, before once more increasing the intensity of his movement. Again, Clare felt her excitement climb, and she slid into another orgasm. As her body filled with blissful spasms, Jesse stopped his movement momentarily and she sensed the pleasurable release in his groin before he continued. Again and again, and yet again she experienced the same rise of tension and satisfying release as Jesse deftly controlled the speed and intensity of his own breathing and movement. They continued their loving duet until Jesse's body tensed with the final contractions in his groin, and then rolled apart and lay without moving, limp and fully satiated.

For a long while they lay together, slowly, gently caressing each other in unspoken conversation. Finally, Clare lifted herself onto one elbow and smiled down at Jesse. With her fingers spread wide, she slowly brushed the palm of her hand across his chest and said, "You did it, Jesse, you did it!"

He turned his head toward her and grinned. "Yeah—I did."

"You were incredible! I never knew it could be like that—I must have come four or five times!" Then, still caressing the muscles of his chest, she continued. "So, how about you? How many times did you come?"

"Well—counting the last one, when I ejaculated—three."

"Did you feel okay? I mean, was it hard to keep control?"

"No, it actually wasn't. It was like everything just finally clicked tonight."

"Well, it was wonderful," she said, leaning over him to kiss his cheek. As she pulled back, she again noticed the cut just below his eye, and asked, "So, are you going to tell me how you got that cut?"

"Oh, yeah," Jesse answered, fingering the bruise, and he told her the story.

Clare lay very still as he talked. When he finished, she rolled toward him, wrapped her arms around him, and held on very tight. She was still holding on when at last she fell asleep.

When Clare awoke the next morning, she instinctively reached toward Jesse and was dismayed to find only an empty pillow in his place. On top of the pillow, beneath a single red zinnia from her flowerbed, she saw his note.

Clare,

I woke up early and couldn't get back to sleep. I've run down to the shop for a few minutes but I'll be back at nine to take you out to breakfast. Is it a date?

Love,
Jesse

P.S. I dreamed of you all night long...

Reading the last line, Clare felt a tiny flutter inside as she remembered their night of passion. She smiled and rolled on her back, stretching her arms overhead, then turned to look at the clock on the night stand. Five after eight. There was enough time for a run before Jesse came back, and she hummed a tune as she rolled out of bed.

Clare dressed quickly and made up the bed. She was heading for the kitchen when she looked out the front window and noticed their neighbor, Mrs. Peabody, standing on the side-walk in front, looking toward their apartment. *What is she doing?* Clare wondered idly as she drank a glass of water, still looking out the window. She began walking toward the front door, but stopped suddenly when she peered through the front blinds and saw Alex and Jason, two brothers from across the street. They were talking with a delivery man, who stood staring toward her apartment as well, along with a stranger on a bicycle, and an older couple in a car, parked at the curb with the engine idling. *What is going on?* Clare thought as she slowly opened the door and stepped outside. Seeing her emerge from the apartment, the bystanders smiled broadly and waved at her, then pointed in the direction of the garage door. Clare moved down the front walk and craned her neck as she turned around the corner of the garage to see what the fuss was about.

There on the garage door, painted in bright red, was a six-foot heart with the words "Jesse loves Clare" printed inside. Clare gasped with surprise, and felt a hot flush of color on her face when the group broke into applause. She stammered, "Um, thank you, thanks" as the small crowd of observers laughed and began moving away.

Clare could not stop smiling as she began to strectch out before her run. When she finally started down the street at a slow trot, she glanced over her shoulder for one more look at Jesse's love note. ♡

Chapter 9

Everlasting Love(rs)

Fidgety with anticipation, Jesse stood in the Potter Creek town square and talked quietly with his brother. It was high noon on a bright October Sunday, and his wedding was about to begin.

Hoping to distract himself, Jesse intently studied the scene around him. *It's so incredibly beautiful,* he thought, lifting his eyes to the backdrop of rolling hills beyond the town. The terrain formed soft, gently curving lines against the vivid blue of the autumn sky, and it seemed as though the town had snuggled down into the ring of surrounding hills like a child in a mother's arms, nurtured by their gentle protection.

The town square followed a traditional design. Black lamp posts lining the sidewalks and the perimeter were authentic replicas of gaslights from the early 1900's. Four wide, diagonal walkways, starting from the redwoods grouped at each of the outer corners, merged together at a white, six-sided gazebo in the center, where Jesse stood waiting for Clare's arrival. The posts and railings were entwined with tendrils of ivy, woven together with white satin ribbons and white roses, and the flower boxes surrounding the base of the structure were filled with purple and white mums. Several rows of chairs had been placed in the grass between the walkways, seating sixty of the bridal couples' closest friends and family in a circle around the gazebo. As his eyes moved over the assembled guests, Jesse met the gaze of

86

many—his mother and sister, Pete and Charlie from the shop, Clare's family—who waved and smiled in response.

The simple scene gave life to Clare's dream of an intimate, old-fashioned wedding. Jesse's suit, like the wedding site, looked like a page from history. Dressed in turn-of-the-century fashion, he wore a black and white striped sack coat with patch pockets, white pants, and white buck shoes with rubber soles. Beneath his jacket were black suspenders, and the stiff, turned-down collar of his white shirt sported a black bow tie. Standing next to him as Best Man, Sam wore black pants, a white shirt and black suspenders.

Across from the men in her role as Matron of Honor, Sally suddenly caught their eye and whispered with excitement, "Here she comes!" Together, Jesse and Sam turned to see Clare as a soft exclamation rose from the guests at their first glimpse of the bride.

She was radiant. Standing next to her father, Clare was forty feet down the walkway directly in front of Jesse, poised to begin her wedding march. Her gown was the dress a fashionable woman might have worn to a garden party almost a hundred years earlier. Made of pale ivory voile, the low, oval neckline was bordered with lace and gathered softly across her bosom and shoulders. Full sleeves were gathered into lace-trimmed bands at her elbows above a gathered, six-inch lace cuff. The folds of the bodice were pulled into a wide waistband trimmed with ribbon and lace above a full, softly gathered skirt that fell gracefully to a wide ruffle, again trimmed with ribbon and lace. Clare's auburn hair was pulled away from her face and tied in a loose bun at the crown, with curls cascading in a spiral along each cheek. Tiny white rosebuds were woven into her hair at the base of her bun, and a simple lace choker and cameo brooch accented her beautiful skin. Clasping a small bouquet of pink and white rosebuds, she began the walk toward her soon-to-be husband with graceful, measured steps.

Jesse stood transfixed. Clare's delicate beauty so over-powered him that for a moment he forgot where he was. As she approached the steps to the gazebo, her green eyes rose to meet his, and his heart filled with a boundless joy. Clare moved up the steps and took her place between Jesse and Sally, who was dressed in a rose-colored replica of Clare's gown, and handed Sally the bouquet as Jesse took her hand in his.

The ceremony began. Caught in a dreamy fog of happiness, Clare tried to memorize every detail of the simple, loving ritual. But in later years the two impressions of the day that would be etched most vividly in her memory were the dazzling autumn sunshine and the seductive pull of Jesse's scent next to her.

"I now pronounce you husband and wife," the pastor announced with a broad smile. "You may kiss." Hand in hand, the newlyweds turned to face each other. Jesse looked into Clare's eyes, glowing with joy and tenderness, and said in a whisper, "My love, my life... Clare, I am forever yours," as he raised her hands to his lips and softly kissed them.

Suddenly a teasing voice called out from among the guests, "Aw, c'mon, Jesse, can't you do any better than that?" Jesse laughed with Clare, then winked toward the guests and, pulling her into a tight embrace, gave her a real kiss as their family and friends erupted with cheers and applause.

When they finally broke apart, Jesse and Clare ran down the steps of the gazebo. Standing arm in arm, they greeted the guests mingling in the bright afternoon sunshine, then prepared to leave for their reception at the Potter Creek Grange. Together they climbed the steps of the gazebo again and called out directions to the hall. Jesse had shed his jacket in the early afternoon sun, and to everyone's surprise, Clare reached behind her and stripped off her skirt, revealing ivory bloomers with pale stockings and over-the-ankle, ivory leather lace-up boots. Sally handed Jesse a flat-brimmed straw skimmer and Clare a lace parasol as Jesse grinned and pointed up the walkway.

The guests turned to see Sam pull a vintage tandem bicycle from its hiding place among the redwoods and begin wheeling it down the path toward the newlyweds. Attached to each of the four handlebars were a cluster of white roses with white ribbon streamers. Sam parked the vehicle in front of the gazebo, and Jesse helped his bride onto the rear seat of the 1898 bike, then kissed her. Climbing onto the front seat, he called out, "Let's party!" and whooped loudly as they began pedaling toward the hall.

Suffused with the hopeful spirit of the wedding ritual and its affirmation of love, the afternoon passed amidst the relaxed camaraderie of friends and family enjoying a weekend respite from their work. Children played among the oak trees in back of the hall, running in and out as their mothers called out futile warnings to stay clean, and Clare's father, a barrel-chested man with a booming voice, led the barbershop quartet that entertained guests before the local dance band took the stage. Late in the afternoon, Jesse and Clare slipped away to change clothes and reappeared as the gleaming, black Model A Ford pulled up in front of the hall. It was part of the legacy of Lucky Ned Baker, an immaculate specimen from his collection of antique cars that had been willed to the town as a rental vehicle for special events. While the guests pushed forward to peek inside, the driver stepped out, moved to the passenger's side and opened the back door, waiting for the departing couple.

Arm in arm, Sam and Sally stood waiting their turn to bid goodbye to the newlyweds. When they had moved up to the front of the crowd, Sam gave Clare a big hug while Jesse embraced Sally. Then Sally turned to Clare, who smiled with contentment. In silent communication, Clare reached out and squeezed Sally's hand, then embraced her new sister-in-law. Stepping apart, Clare said simply, "Thanks, Sally. For everything."

"I'm so happy for you both," Sally replied, smiling and blinking back tears. "Always be good to each other."

Clare squeezed Sally's hand once more, then turned toward Jesse.

"Well, I guess we're about ready," Jesse began. Turning to his bride, he said, "Madam," and offered his hand to help her into the waiting car. When she was settled, he began to step in after her, but Sally caught his elbow.

"Wait, Jesse," she said, pulling an envelope from Sam's pocket and handing it to Jesse. "Here's something for you to open once you get under way."

Jesse looked down at the envelope and handed it to Clare. "Okay, Sal, thanks."

Jesse settled in next to Clare and they turned and looked out the back window, waving goodbye as the car moved slowly down the driveway. Many of the children followed as far as the first corner, shouting and waving, until the car picked up speed and pulled away. It quickly cruised through town and had pulled onto the two-lane country road leading toward the airport when they remembered the envelope.

Jesse handed it to Clare and draped his arm across her shoulder as she opened it and pulled out the card. It was made by hand, with a Beatles collage, cut from magazines and newspapers, pasted onto the front. They looked at each other and smiled, then opened the card to read its simple message:

"...and in **The End**, the love
you take is equal to the
love you make."

–John Lennon & Paul McCartney

90

Part II: The Guide

Chapter 10

Getting Started

Okay, guys, this is where we separate the ordinary men from the real Romeos. If you want to become a multi-orgasmic man, and enjoy marathon sex like you've never imagined with an eager, responsive partner, it's time for you to get down to business. You are about to learn the secret of an Everlasting Love(r).

Three Major Principles

In our story, Sam loaned his brother a book[1] which explains the whole concept of the multi-orgasmic male. (The ideas in the book date back *thousands* of years—Eastern cultures are way ahead of Westerners on this one!) From this book Jesse learns three major principles that are the foundation for a fulfilling sexual relationship: 1) the separation of orgasm and ejaculation, or, understanding that—believe it or not—*ejaculation does not need to occur simultaneously with orgasm*, 2) the importance of female satisfaction, and 3) the regulation of ejaculation, that is, gaining conscious control of your ejaculation for increased sexual pleasure, and avoiding frequent ejaculation for improved health (more on the health benefits later). *Becoming multi-orgasmic will give you conscious control of your ejaculation and enable you to*

---

[1] *The Tao of Love and Sex*, by Jolan Chang

keep your erection and make love for longer periods while you experience two, three, or more intense, satisfying orgasms without *ejaculating.* You will easily be able to continue until both you and your partner are satisfied, and at that point, you may choose to end the lovemaking by having an orgasm with a simultaneous ejaculation.

These three principles give a good summary of the basis for multiple male orgasms. But in this "Age of Information," the modern man wants step-by-step guidelines for developing the skills needed to become multi-orgasmic. That's why you picked up this book, right? Well, read on...

Some General Guidelines

Before you begin, here are a few guidelines to keep in mind. As you go through the exercises described here, you will be most successful if you follow these suggestions:

1. When practicing the exercises, it is best to avoid using drugs. Many men have the mistaken notion that drinking will lessen their arousal and help them to "last longer." Although alcohol is an anesthetic that numbs sensation, it also reduces your ability to control your ejaculation. It seems ironic, but to gain control of your ejaculation the answer is to *increase* your sensitivity, not decrease it. Marijuana can also hinder your progress, since daily use results in lower levels of androgens, the hormone that is responsible for your sex drive. Butyl nitrite, amyl nitrite, and similar drugs increase the heartbeat to dangerous levels, and often result in a pounding headache. So stay clean and sober to practice the exercises. When you master the skills of an Everlasting Love(r), the highs you'll

experience with your partner will beat anything that pharmaceuticals have to offer!

2. Focus your awareness totally on the physical sensations you experience. To control your ejaculation and become multi-orgasmic, you must become sensitive to, and learn to recognize, the subtle physical changes in your body at different levels of arousal.

3. Keep your mind in the present. As the saying goes: "Mind and body are one." You can't expect to make steady progress if you physically practice the exercises while you're mentally painting the house or planning your next business trip.

4. Relax, relax, relax. This is not a race or a contest, so don't put pressure on yourself to perform. Every man will progress at his own pace, but if you have unrealistic expectations of yourself or are obsessed with success, you will only sabotage your efforts and delay your ultimate mastery of these techniques.

At this point you may be thinking, *Just how long is it going to take me to learn this?* How long does it take someone to learn to dance? The answer depends a great deal on how they practice, how often they practice, and if they practice with a partner. Becoming a multi-orgasmic man, like learning anything, will depend on a variety of things. These techniques can be mastered in two weeks or several months, but for most men the actual time it takes probably falls somewhere in between. *The most important factor for success is the degree of your motivation. If you are patient and persistent, you will eventually master these techniques.* (Sex therapist Barbara Keesling, Ph.D, author of *How to Make Love All Night Long (And Drive a Woman Wild)*, reported that *every* man she had worked with who was committed to becoming multi-orgasmic had been successful.) At any rate, the effort involved in learning these techniques is far less than other projects you might take on as part of a relationship—for example, building a deck, doing the taxes, or taking a second job—and the process is a lot more enjoyable!

Are you ready to get started?

Chapter 11

Preliminary Conditioning

First things first. Before you can increase your endurance during intercourse, you will need to strengthen a very important muscle: the pubococcygeus muscle (also called the PC muscle.)

The PC muscle is actually a group of muscles that extends like a hammock from your pubic bone back to your tailbone, beneath your bladder and prostate and surrounding the base of your penis and anus. Stopping the flow of urine midstream is an easy way to feel this muscle working, and the pleasurable feelings you experience during orgasm result from the contractions of the PC muscle, the prostate and the anal-sphincter muscle. (For a diagram of male sexual anatomy, see the illustration on page 98.) The penis has *no* muscle, and although it will not get larger or stronger through exercise, the PC muscle will. And as you will soon learn, a strong PC muscle enables you to have better control over your ejaculation as well as stronger erections and orgasms. A strong PC muscle has also been linked to better prostate health, an important fact considering that prostate cancer occurs in almost ten percent of American men.

Before you start, just remember: *A strong PC muscle is an important key to becoming multi-orgasmic. These first two conditioning exercises may seem insignificant, but if you dismiss them as unimportant, you will delay your progress!*

Okay, on to the first exercise.

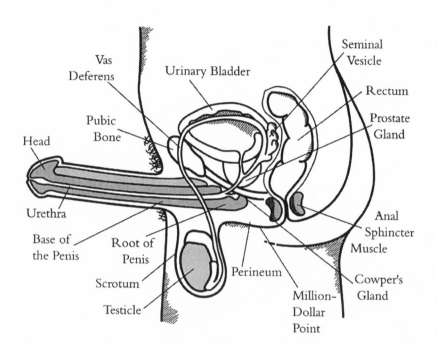

Exercise #1: PC Power

This exercise and the next (*PC Power Plus*) can be done at anytime during the day when you find it most convenient. To maintain a regular schedule with the exercises, it's a good idea to combine them with some part of your usual daily routine, like shaving or driving to work.

Be sure you are comfortable and relaxed (you may be sitting, standing, or lying down), then contract your PC muscle tightly for one or two seconds and release. Do twenty repetitions and repeat this sequence three times a day. That's all! But remember, *consistency is the key*.Think of this like weight lifting. If you started a weight lifting program, you know that to gain strength you would need to gradually increase the weights through regular workouts, so don't expect to make much progress if you skip a few days of the PC squeezes and then do three hundred the next day.

Do these exercises for two or three weeks. If you feel some soreness in the beginning, that's a natural result. After all, those muscles are getting a workout!

Exercise #2: PC Power Plus

This exercise is a simple variation of the first one that further strengthens your PC muscle. Continue with the sequence described above, doing twenty reps of the quick squeeze three times a day, but now add repetitions of a long, slow squeeze. Take five seconds to completely tense the PC muscle, hold the tension for five seconds, then take five seconds to slowly release the tension. You want to do ten reps a day. When you are able to do that, continue this sequence (twenty quick squeezes three times a day and ten reps of the slow squeezes once a day) for two or three weeks.

Depending on your age, health, fitness level, and other factors, these PC exercises may be somewhat difficult at first. You may find that you have to build up to the recommended number of repetitions. If that's the case, don't worry. *The PC muscle will respond to exercise just like any other muscle, and through consistent practice it will get stronger.* Just remember to take it one step at a time and don't pressure yourself.

99

Chapter 12

Sensory Awareness

Regardless of your current age, weight, or overall fitness level, if you've done your PC exercises you are now in great shape for an Everlasting Love(r)! You're ready for the next stage in becoming a multi-orgasmic man.

The next four exercises are designed to increase your sensitivity to the physical sensations you experience during sex and help you to identify the subtle changes in your body at different levels of arousal. Researchers often use the term *ejaculation inevitablity* to describe that there's-no-turning-back-I-can't-stop-it-now point when your ejaculation is involuntarily triggered. An essential skill in controlling your ejaculation and becoming multi-orgasmic is learning to recognize that point, and these graduated exercises will help you to do that.

Although the following exercises can be practiced with a partner, they are intended to be done first as solo exercises. That is, they involve self-stimulation, or what most people would refer to as masturbation. Depending on your background and basic beliefs, you may have reservations about using this approach. If so, an explanation of the advantages of solo practice will help you to see its value.

Self-stimulation has three basic advantages. First, it is simply more convenient. These exercises are for *your* learning, and while practicing with a partner may be pleasurable, sometimes it is difficult to arrange the best time when both people are available and willing to participate. Consistent practice is essential to learning these skills, so purely for the sake of convenience, it is usually far simpler for you to schedule your time to practice regularly without having to juggle your partner's schedule as well.

Second, solo practice in the early stages is also preferable because it relieves you of any pressure to perform. You don't need to be concerned about your partner and whether you are meeting her needs, but rather, you are free to just focus on what is important to *you*.

Minimizing physical and emotional intensity is the third advantage to self-stimulation. Staying relaxed and aware is essential to developing the sensitivity and control of a multi-orgasmic lover, and that is usually a lot easier to do during self-stimulation, when you are able to easily monitor the activity as the intensity starts to build. Because of this, men are generally more successful learning these techniques *first* through solo practice before moving on to practice with a partner.

Okay, it's time to take the next step to dramatically enhancing your love life. Just one reminder—while practicing the exercises, *stay relaxed and forget about any performance expectations.*

Exercise #3: Know Thyself

For this exercise, use any position you find comfortable either lying down or sitting in a chair. Using some massage oil or other lubrication, close your eyes and slowly begin caressing yourself. If you like, start on your chest or thighs, then slowly move toward your genitals. Stroke and massage not only your penis, but your scrotum and perineum as well, and *simply focus on the physical sensations you are experiencing.* When you are touching your penis, do *not* use a strong or quick stroke. Your object is not to achieve an erection, but whether you do or don't is fine. The main point is just to stay in the present and enjoy the physical sensations. Continue caressing yourself, breathing easily and feeling relaxed, for twenty to thirty minutes. The emphasis should be on *sensuality* as opposed to *sexuality*.

This exercise, like the strengthening exercises for the PC muscle, may seem unimportant. Again, remember that no one learns to run before learning how to walk. This exercise allows you to experience pleasurable sensations without being distracted, to focus your awareness in the present, and to relieve yourself of any pressure. In order to become multi-orgasmic, you must learn to do all these things, and this is a way to practice with a low level of intensity before venturing into the "big league" of intercourse. Practice this exercise several times over the course of a week or two until you're confident you have a feel for it.

Exercise #4: Controlled Peaks

Before beginning this exercise, you will establish an "arousal scale" to use for all the remaining exercises. This is a scale from one to ten that reflects the increasing intensity of your feelings as you move through different stages of arousal. Stage 1 is the end of the scale with no sexual thoughts or physical arousal, and Stage 10 is—you guessed it—orgasm. In between, at Stages 2 and 3, are those first little twinges of sexual interest that you feel at the base of your penis. By Stage 4 there is a definite feeling of excitement. It's pleasurable but the intensity level is still low—you're interested but not totally committed at this point. Moving into Stage 5 and 6, your arousal is strong enough that you wouldn't want to stop—it's feeling really good now. At Stage 7 and 8, your heart rate has increased, you probably feel a little out of breath, and your face may flush. Stage 9 is the most intense:

your awareness has narrowed to the sensations in your groin, and you are very close to orgasm. At 9.9, you reach ejaculatory inevitablity, and your body goes over the crest into orgasm.

The signposts of these different stages may vary slightly with the individual, but what is important is that you establish a frame of reference to gauge your intensity with each level of arousal. And although you are using a numbered scale, keep in mind this is not the Olympics! Don't use this scale as a means to judge your performance. A 7 is not better than a 5 and a 9 is not better than an 8—they are just different. Your job is to distinguish their subtle differences.

For this next exercise, begin by lying or sitting in a comfortable position, lubricate your hands, and start to give yourself a genital caress as described in Exercise #3 (*Know Thyself*). Stay relaxed and stroke yourself slowly, moving into your Stage 4 level of arousal. When you reach this point, stop the caress, take a slow, deep breath, stay relaxed, and wait until you feel your arousal drop down to Stage 2. Reaching a certain point of arousal and then letting the intensity drop down one or two levels is called "peaking."

Now, from Stage 2, begin the stimulation again and continue to Stage 6, speeding up your stroking action if necessary. Again, once you reach this higher peak, stop the stimulation, relax and breathe slowly and deeply until your arousal drops to about a 4. Continue this process, striving to stimulate yourself to gradually higher stages, then breathing, relaxing and letting your arousal drop in between peaks. (As you peak at higher and higher levels of intensity, it may become more difficult to relax as you wait for your arousal to drop. Taking longer, deeper breaths in between peaks will help.) Work toward four or five peaks, taking a total of twenty or thirty minutes for the complete exercise.

If you don't reach the higher stages the first time you try this exercise, don't worry. With practice you will get there. By the end of the exercise, you may feel a need to ejaculate; if that's the case, then go ahead. Just remember, don't rush during the exercise and don't try to shoot quickly through several stages, like going from a 4 to a 9. Keep in mind that you are training yourself to distinguish the small changes in your body that signal different degrees of arousal.

Exercise #5: The Squeeze Play

Now that you have a clear idea of the subtle changes in your body at the different stages, you are ready to use that strong PC muscle of yours. Think of your PC muscle like the brakes in a car. Just as you would use brakes to help control a car, you will learn to use your PC muscle to control your ejaculation. By squeezing this muscle, you will eventually be able to enjoy the excitement of multiple orgasms *without* losing control and ejaculating, much like enjoying the thrills of driving a fast car on a long, winding road without skidding into a crash.

Sit or lie down in a comfortable position and with lubrication start a genital caress. Let your arousal level rise gradually by using a slow, gentle stroke. When you peak at Stage 4, don't stop the stimulation. Instead, continue stroking yourself while you step on the brakes by squeezing the PC muscle. (This could be done with one long, hard squeeze, or a few quick squeezes. Each man is different, so you will need to find what works best for you.) Now right away, take a long, deep breath, then stop the stimulation and check to be sure your body is relaxed. As a result of this process, you should feel that even though you continued caressing yourself, when you squeezed the PC muscle it stopped your arousal from climbing higher. If you weren't successful on your first try, don't worry. Just keep at it and eventually you'll get there.

After stopping your arousal at Stage 4, do the same with a Stage 6 peak. Gradually work your way up to higher stages, taking fifteen or twenty minutes for the complete exercise. *Keep in mind that as you reach the higher levels, you will need to squeeze the PC muscle harder and take longer and deeper breaths afterwards.* Practice this exercise as often as you like over a period of time until you feel you are able to prevent your arousal from increasing by using the PC squeeze. When you feel confident with this skill, you are ready to move on and learn the last technique necessary before "payday," when you can actually start experiencing multiple orgasms!

Exercise #6: Surfing a Plateau

A plateau is nothing more than an extended peak. Up until this point, the peaks you have experienced in the previous exercises lasted only one or two seconds. What you will do now is learn to stretch the peaks out to five seconds, ten seconds, or more, before letting them drop off. This skill will give you a more sustained and exhilarating ride, like surfing a big wave! The four basic ways to do this are by 1) making a change in your breathing, 2) tensing the PC muscle, 3) making a change in your movement, or 4) changing your focus.

As before, begin by sitting or lying comfortably, then lubricate your hands and begin the genital caress. Build up to a Stage 5 peak, being especially aware of your arousal level. Continue the stimulation, then just before hitting Stage 6, simply slow your breathing. Without making any other changes, your arousal should begin to drop. After it falls below Stage 5, begin breathing very fast until you feel yourself moving back up to Stage 5 or higher. Continue this process of changing your breathing as you hover at Stage 5 (give or take about a half a level). At the risk of hyperventilating, don't try to stay there too long—ten or fifteen seconds will be fine. Next, take a break until your arousal drops a level or two.

After resting, begin the stimulation again, this time working to continue the caress and hover around Stage 6 by using the PC squeeze. That's it. Don't make any other changes, but try to ride that Stage 6 plateau for ten to fifteen seconds by tensing your PC muscle.

The third method for "surfing" a plateau is to change your motion. This time, stroke yourself until you reach Stage 7, then slow down your movements. Again, without stopping the stimulation, try to stretch the peak into a ten- to fifteen-second plateau simply by changing the speed of your stroke.

All right, now you're ready for the fourth technique: changing your focus. This time, try for Stage 8, and when you reach that, simply change the area that you are stimulating (for example, moving from the head of the penis to the shaft or the testicles). Do not stop the stimulation, just change the focus as you again strive for a ten- to fifteen-second plateau.

Like Exercise #5 *(The Squeeze Play)*, practice this exercise often over a period of time until you feel confident that you can extend peaks into plateaus while keeping your arousal under control. *Remember that learning to stay relaxed as you continue the stimulation is crucial to your success.* Eventually, *if you practice*, you will be able to surf a plateau at the highest, most intense stages. And when you reach that point, you will be very close to the ultimate reward in pleasure—multiple orgasms!

Chapter 13

Putting it All Together

If you've been practicing the graduated exercises described here and stayed with it until you've mastered the skills at each stage, you've really come a long way! At this point you are in the home stretch, and much closer to achieving your goal than you may realize. But just as the last quarter-mile of a long run are the most trying, the final steps to becoming multi-orgasmic will be the most challenging. Throughout the rest of your "training," *focus on how far you have come and don't lose sight of your goal.* Soon you will be an Olympic-caliber lover!

Exercise #7: Eyes Wide Open

In this exercise you will use everything you have learned to make that leap and experience an orgasm without ejaculating or losing your erection. This exercise is like a shortcut. It may not work the first time, and it doesn't work for every man, but some men have good success with it. (If it doesn't work for you, just move on to Exercise # 8, which is actually more foolproof but takes a little more time.) *If you are not successful with this short-cut, there is no reason for you to be discouraged. Just keep trying. Perhaps you will need to go back and make your PC muscle stronger, or fine-tune a skill from an earlier exercise, but if you keep working with these techniques you will succeed in becoming multi-orgasmic.*

Begin this exercise as you did for Exercise # 4 (*Controlled Peaks*). Peak at Stage 4, then 6, 8, and 9. Take your time, going through this cycle in about fifteen or twenty minutes. Once more, stimulate yourself and peak at Stage 9.5. Now keep stroking intensely, heading straight for the dragon's lair of ejaculation! Just at the point of inevitability, (not a second later), slam on the "brakes" by squeezing the PC muscle as tightly as you can while you keep stroking. Breathe deeply and *open your eyes.* (For some mysterious reason, this exercise works *only* if you open your eyes.) Hold the PC muscle as tight as you can for about ten seconds, keeping your eyes open the whole time. If all goes well, you will experience an orgasm but that long, hard squeeze will prevent your ejaculation. Now take a deep breath, slow the stimulation and let your arousal drop to Stage 7 or 8 for a little rest period. Then begin stroking again and let your arousal rise. This time, just continue the stimulation until you have a full orgasm with an ejaculation. Guess what? Your hard work has paid off, because you just had a multiple orgasm! Congratulations!

Exercise #8: The Majority Method

If you didn't quite make it with Exercise #7, don't worry. For the majority of men, this second method is more fail-safe. Through this exercise, you will learn to identify the two stages of ejaculation, the *emission stage* and the *expulsion stage,* in order to pinpoint the exact moment of inevitablity and how much time you have to work with in preventing your ejaculation.

The emission stage is the period when the semen is moved into the urethra by the contractions of the prostate (like filling a water pistol), and the expulsion stage occurs when the PC muscle contracts to discharge the semen out the penis (like pulling the trigger on the water pistol). The PC contractions during the expulsion stage is involuntary for most men, but as a multi-orgasmic man you will voluntarily prevent an ejaculation while still experiencing the pleasurable contractions and feeling of release of an orgasm.

Begin this exercise like Exercise #4 (*Controlled Peaks*). Using some lubrication, peak at Stage 4 then drop down, peak at 6 then drop down, then do the same at 8 and 9. Don't rush the process; take a minimum of three minutes with each peak. After letting your Stage 9 peak drop down, intensify your stroking until your arousal reaches the point of inevitability. Now completely stop the stimulation, and with your eyes open, focus your awareness totally on your genitals. Stay relaxed and breathe deeply as your ejaculation starts. Can you feel the two stages? Can you feel the semen being moved to the base of your penis? Can you feel the contractions of the PC muscle as it moves the semen out through the penis? If you stopped at the right time, this two-second process should actually feel more like several seconds.

Recognizing these two distinct phases will make it easier for you to get your timing right at that critical point of inevitability. You'll see that there is actually plenty of time to "hit the brakes" at that point of inevitability and the expulsion stage, giving you more confidence in your ability to prevent your ejaculation even at the highest levels of arousal.

Now, armed with this new awareness, you can go back to Exercise #7 (*Eyes Wide Open*). Follow the steps, stimulate yourself to the point of inevitability, and work on your timing. It may take several tries over a period of time, but eventually you will find just the right point to squeeze that PC muscle and successfully trigger an orgasm while arresting your ejaculation.

During this learning process, you may have some unusual results before it all clicks. For example, you may experience a "partial orgasm" that leaves you thinking *Is that all?* Or, you may feel like you "missed" an orgasm, or you may have a "partial ejaculation" without an orgasm. You may also experience a *retrograde* ejaculation, in which the semen, instead of being discharged out the penis, backs into the bladder (and is later expelled with urine), with a resulting loss of erection. If you experience any of these things, don't be alarmed. They are normal and not harmful to your body. Actually, you should think of them as a good sign because they indicate progress beyond what you've always done in the past! Just remember—*you're in the home stretch, so don't give up*. With practice and persistence, you will make that jump to the incredible pleasures of multiple orgasms!

Chapter 14

The Main Event

Now that you have gained control of your ejaculation and experienced multiple orgasms through solo practice, it is time for the main event: intercourse. You are about to introduce your partner to the increased pleasures made possible with an Everlasting Love(r). But first, let's consider a few key points that will help you in transferring your skills to actual lovemaking.

Working as a Team

If your partner hasn't read this book yet, or you haven't talked with her about what you have been doing up to this point, now is the time to explain the whole concept of multiple male orgasms. Initially, some women may be a little skeptical or resistant to the idea. They may be concerned that this new approach will turn their lover into some kind of sex robot, and that making love will become too mechanical or unromantic. If your partner expresses any of these concerns, you need to reassure her that *when you learn to consciously control your ejaculation, the pleasure that both of you have during intercourse will increase dramatically.* And, in addition to enjoying more physical satisfaction, *you will also experience greater intimacy.*

As you begin making love with this "new" method, the best way your partner can help is to simply *do nothing.* That is, during intercourse, when your arousal rises to its highest levels of intensity, she can help you prevent ejaculation just by stopping her movement. (You may want to work out with her an easy way to signal this critical stage, perhaps just by stopping your movement, or with a verbal cue.) Although interrupting her movement may be frustrating for her at times, reassure her that the eventual results will be worth it.

Another important way your partner can be of help is to experiment with different positions that may make it easier for you to inhibit your ejaculation. Many men find that when the woman is on top it helps them to maintain their stamina and control. (Conveniently enough, this same position often helps *women* to become multi-orgasmic.) Encourage your partner to try this or other ideas to help you find just the right method that works best for both of you.

A Few Helpful Tips

To control your arousal during intercourse, you will use the same techniques you learned in the solo exercises. By experimenting with variations in your movement, speed, focus, and breathing, you will find a method that works for you, but remember to *emphasize squeezing the PC muscle at the right time while staying relaxed.* Mantak Chia and Douglas Abrams Arava, in their book *The Multi-Orgasmic Man*, point out that many men describe a feeling of "mentally falling *backward* into non-ejaculatory orgasms instead of falling *forward* into ejaculation." The trick is to come close enough to that point of no return, ejaculatory inevitability, to enjoy the pleasurable contractions and sense of release of the emission stage orgasm without crossing the line that triggers ejaculation.

As you continue to apply these methods, here are a few additional "troubleshooting tips" that can aid in your mastery of multi-orgasmic skills:

1. Squeezing the Penis   If your arousal rises too quickly for you to control, you can minimize the intensity, and at the same time strengthen your erection, by squeezing the base of your penis. Simply place your index and middle finger on the underside of your penis, close to your testicles, and with the thumb on the top side, give a firm squeeze.

2. Pressing "The Point"   Ancient Chinese Tao masters refer to the "Million-Gold-Piece-Point," an area in the scrotum just in front of the anus. (According to legend, the name derives from the price paid to the Tao masters to reveal its exact location!) In locating your Million-Gold-Piece-Point, you will find an indentation when you push in at the right spot. During intercourse, it is possible to prevent your ejaculation by squeezing your PC muscle and pressing this point. (You will need to press firmly, pushing in as far as the first joint on your finger.) Many men learn to use this technique successfully during intercourse without needing to withdraw.

3. The Scrotal Tug   Since the testicles must be close to the body in order to trigger ejaculation, pulling them away from your body can be effective prevention. To do this, just circle the top of the scrotal sac with your index finger and thumb, and pull down firmly.

And now a word about condoms. As we move into the next century, the risks of sexual intercourse have changed drastically from only twenty years ago. If you are not currently in a

113

monogamous relationship, *practice safe sex and* _always_ *use a condom.* If you do have an established, monogamous relationship and you typically use condoms for birth control, then continue using them. If you're wondering how they might affect you as a multi-orgasmic man, the advantage—as well as the disadvantage—is that for most men their use does result in decreased sensitivity. This decrease in sensitivity could obviously help in controlling your ejaculation, but at the same time it can make it difficult to keep your erection, or minimize its strength. These disadvantages are certainly not insurmountable, and if you have routinely used condoms in the past, you have likely discovered ways to compensate.

Going From Good to BETTER to **GREAT**

Since ancient times, Chinese Tao masters have practiced ejaculation control because of their belief that ejaculation drains a man's energy—and they would probably have a hard time finding a man who would disagree! (As a matter of fact, the French refer to ejaculation with the term *la petite mort*, which means "the little death.")   According to Eastern philosophy, infrequent ejaculation contributes to better overall health, more energy, and even increased longevity. In *The Multi-Orgasmic Man*, authors Mantak Chia and Douglas Abrams Arava state that a leading physician of ancient China, Sun Ssu-miao, advised that, when combined with exercise and a good diet, "men attain good health and longevity by ejaculating twice a month." Indeed, most multi-orgasmic men will tell you that they need less sleep, have more energy, and maintain better overall health when they ejaculate less often.

As you continue to practice the skills of an Everlasting Love(r), you may frequently choose to finish your lovemaking sessions without ejaculating at all. This may be difficult for your partner to understand or accept, and she may feel hurt or frustrated by this change. She may object because she enjoys feeling you ejaculate, or she may feel that she is less of a woman or less desireable if her man doesn't ejaculate. Or, she may suspect that you can't possibly enjoy yourself fully without ejaculating and are perhaps preventing it just to please her. If any of these possibilities describe your situation when you choose not to ejaculate, assure her that using these skills to prevent your ejaculation provides considerable health benefits without diminishing your pleasure.

Chapter 15

Riding Into the Sunset

For many, if not most men, the primary sources of sex education during their formative years are pornography and their own experiences with masturbation. This method of learning can result in feelings of shame or guilt, and often a fear of getting caught reading or doing something that is forbidden. Under these circumstances, it is not surprising that many men grow to adulthood learning to engage in sex in a way that is both hurried and distracted. For these men, a gradual relearning process may be required to develop the fine awareness necessary to become multi-orgasmic. But the rewards are well worth the effort!

At this point you have gained considerable skill at monitoring your arousal level and controlling your ejaculation. If you have not quite experienced multiple orgasms yet, just keep at it and before long you will. And understand that *one of the best things about becoming multi-orgasmic is that once things "click" for you, they will keep getting better.* At first you may feel that your "dry" orgasms can't compare to those with an ejaculation, but the longer you practice these techniques, the more rewarding it will be. Not only will your orgasms become more intense, you will learn to "surf a plateau" for longer and longer periods, enjoying the ride between orgasms for several minutes instead of several seconds. And, as you gain confidence, *you will feel more and more relaxed, until it becomes almost effortless to make hot, passionate love for much longer periods of time.*

If you practice the exercises described here, and make a consistent, patient effort to master the skills, your reward will be a bounty of pleasure and fulfillment. Not only will you and your partner experience heightened physical passion and increased satisfaction, you will also develop a closer, more loving bond. Remember the saying: "Our world changes when *we* change." All it takes is the desire and commitment to improve your relationship, and if you are willing to stay with it until you achieve success, you will reap the many life-enhancing benefits.

Bibliography

Chang, Jolan. *The Tao of Love and Sex: The Ancient Chinese Way to Ecstacy.* New York, E.P.Dutton, 1977.

Chia, Mantak and Douglas Abrams Arava. *The Multi-Orgasmic Man: Sexual Secrets Every Man Should Know.* San Francisco: HarperSanFranciso, 1996.

Hartman, William, and Marilyn Fithian. *Any Man Can: The Multiple Orgasmic Technique for Every Loving Man.* New York: St. Martin's Press, 1984.

Keesling, Barbara. *How to Make Love All Night (And Drive a Woman Wild).* New York: HarperCollins Publishers, 1994.

Thornton, James S. "Man and the Multiple Orgasm," Self Magazine, May 1992.

About the Author

Before graduating from the University of California, Ms. Joiner wore many hats, including those of a bank courier, a cocktail waitress, an asparagus picker, and a nude figure model (minus the hat). Her interests include martial arts and music; she is a Fourth Degree Black Belt in karate, and "maybe a green belt" in piano. She lives in northern California with her husband and their "too big" cat, Neko.

Order Form

---

*   Fax orders: (707) 575-9815

☎   Toll free telephone orders: 1-800-865-1105. Have your
VISA or Mastercard ready.

✉   Postal orders: Moonstruck Publishers, 5299 Hall Road,
Santa Rosa, CA 95401-5566

Please send _____ copy(ies) of *An Everlasting Love(r)* to:

Name (please print): _____

Address: _____

City: _____ State: _____ Zip: _____

Telephone: (_____) _____

_____ Book(s) @ $11.95 each: _____

7.75% Sales tax (CA residents *only*):   _____

Shipping/handling:

   ($2 first book, $1 each additional book)   _____

TOTAL: _____

*(I understand that if I am not satisfied I may return the book(s) for a full
refund.)*

Payment choice: ❑ Check   ❑ VISA   ❑ Mastercard

Card #:_____ Expires: ___/___

CALL TOLL FREE TO ORDER AT ANY TIME!

007

PRAISE FOR IAN FLEMING AND
THE MAN WITH THE GOLDEN GUN

"Bond is what every   like
to be, and what   would
like to have   sheets."
—Raymo

"A gory, glittering saga…the
James Bond spirit soars on."
—*New York Times*

"Fleming keeps you riveted."
—*Sunday Telegraph*

"For those who like to escape to
Bondsville, the old boom-town
hasn't changed a scrap."
—*Listener*

"Mr. Fleming is in a class by
himself."—*Daily Mail*

"One of the most cunningly
synthesised heroes in crime-fiction."
—*Observer*

"Mr. Fleming is splendid; he stops at
nothing."—*New Statesman*

"Mr. Fleming is a most
compelling story-teller."
—*The Times*

"Our foremost literary magician."
—*New York Herald Tribune*

THE JAMES BOND BOOKS

Casino Royale

Live and Let Die

Moonraker

Diamonds Are Forever

From Russia With Love

Dr No

Goldfinger

For Your Eyes Only

Thunderball

The Spy Who Loved Me

On Her Majesty's Secret Service

You Only Live Twice

The Man with the Golden Gun

Octopussy *and* The Living Daylights

THE MAN WITH THE GOLDEN GUN

Published by Thomas & Mercer
P.O. Box 400818
Las Vegas, NV 89140

ISBN-13: 9781612185576
ISBN-10: 1612185576
Library of Congress Control Number: 2012913451

THE MAN WITH
THE GOLDEN GUN

IAN FLEMING

fTHOMAS & MERCER

CONTENTS

1 | 'CAN I HELP YOU?' 1

2 | ATTENTAT! 11

3 | 'PISTOLS' SCARAMANGA 20

4 | THE STARS FORETELL............32

5 | NO. 3½ LOVE LANE 45

6 | THE EASY GRAND...........55

7 | UN-REAL ESTATE 63

8 | PASS THE CANAPÉS! 74

9 | MINUTES OF THE MEETING 83

10 | BELLY-LICK, ETC. 92

11 | BALLCOCK, AND OTHER, TROUBLE...........101

12 | IN A GLASS, VERY DARKLY...........111

13 | HEAR THE TRAIN BLOW!...........120

14 | THE GREAT MORASS...........128

15 | CRAB-MEAT 137

16 | THE WRAP-UP 145

17 | ENDIT 154

1 .... 'CAN I HELP YOU?'

THE SECRET Service holds much that is kept secret even from very senior officers in the organization. Only M. and his Chief of Staff know absolutely everything there is to know. The latter is responsible for keeping the Top Secret record known as 'The War Book' so that, in the event of the death of both of them, the whole story, apart from what is available to individual Sections and Stations, would be available to their successors.

One thing that James Bond, for instance, didn't know was the machinery at Headquarters for dealing with the public, whether friendly or otherwise – drunks, lunatics, bona fide applications to join the Service, and enemy agents with plans for penetration or even assassination.

On that cold, clear morning in November he was to see the careful cog-wheels in motion.

The girl at the switchboard at the Ministry of Defence flicked the switch to 'Hold' and said to her neighbour, 'It's another nut who says he's James Bond. Even knows his code number. Says he wants to speak to M. personally.'

The senior girl shrugged. The switchboard had had quite a few such calls since, a year before, James Bond's death on a mission to Japan had been announced in the Press. There had even been one pestiferous woman who, at every full moon, passed on messages from Bond from Uranus where it seemed he had got stuck while awaiting entry into heaven. She said, 'Put him through to Liaison, Pat.'

The Liaison Section was the first cog in the machine, the first sieve. The operator got back on the line: 'Just a moment, sir. I'll put you on to an officer who may be able to help you.'

James Bond, sitting on the edge of his bed, said, 'Thank you.'

He had expected some delay before he could establish his identity. He had been warned to expect it by the charming 'Colonel Boris' who had been in charge of him for the past few months after he had finished his treatment in the luxurious Institute on the Nevsky Prospekt in Leningrad. A man's voice came on the line. 'Captain Walker speaking. Can I help you?'

James Bond spoke slowly and clearly. 'This is Commander James Bond speaking. Number 007. Would you put me through to M., or his secretary, Miss Moneypenny. I want to make an appointment.'

Captain Walker pressed two buttons on the side of his telephone. One of them switched on a tape recorder for the use of his department, the other alerted one of the duty officers in the Action Room of the Special Branch at Scotland Yard that he should listen to the conversation, trace the call, and at once put a tail on the caller. It was now up to Captain Walker, who was in fact an extremely bright ex-prisoner-of-war interrogator from Military Intelligence, to keep the subject talking for as near five minutes as possible. He said, 'I'm afraid I don't know either of these two people. Are you sure you've got the right number?'

James Bond patiently repeated the Regent number which was the main outside line for the Secret Service. Together with so much else, he had forgotten it, but Colonel Boris had known it and had made him write it down among the small print on the front page of his forged British passport that said his name was Frank Westmacott, company director.

'Yes,' said Captain Walker sympathetically. 'We seem to have got that part of it right. But I'm afraid I can't place these people you want to talk to. Who exactly are they? This Mr Em, for instance. I don't think we've got anyone of that name at the Ministry.'

'Do you want me to spell it out? You realize this is an open line?'

Captain Walker was rather impressed by the confidence in the speaker's voice. He pressed another button and, so that Bond would hear it, a telephone bell rang. He said, 'Hang on a moment, would you? There's someone on my other line.' Captain Walker got on to the head of his Section. 'Sorry, sir. I've got a chap on who says he's James Bond and wants to talk to M. I know it sounds crazy and I've gone through the usual motions with the Special Branch and so on, but would you mind listening for a minute? Thank you, sir.'

Two rooms away a harassed man, who was the Chief Security Officer for the Secret Service, said 'Blast!' and pressed a switch. A microphone on his desk came to life. The Chief Security Officer sat very still. He badly needed a cigarette, but his room was now 'live' to Captain Walker and to the lunatic who called himself 'James Bond'. Captain Walker's voice came over at full strength. 'I'm so sorry. Now then. This man Mr Em you want to talk to. I'm sure we needn't worry about security. Could you be more specific?'

James Bond frowned. He didn't know that he had frowned and he wouldn't have been able to explain why he had done so.

He said, and lowered his voice, again inexplicably, 'Admiral Sir Miles Messervy. He is head of a department in your Ministry. The number of his room used to be twelve on the eighth floor. He used to have a secretary called Miss Moneypenny. Good-looking girl. Brunette. Shall I give you the Chief of Staff's name? No? Well let's see, it's Wednesday. Shall I tell you what'll be the main dish on the menu in the canteen? It should be steak-and-kidney pudding.'

The Chief Security Officer picked up the direct telephone to Captain Walker. Captain Walker said to James Bond, 'Damn! There's the other telephone again. Shan't be a minute.' He picked up the green telephone. 'Yes, sir?'

'I don't like that bit about the steak-and-kidney pudding. Pass him on to the Hard Man. No. Cancel that. Make it the Soft. There was always something odd about 007's death. No body. No solid evidence. And the people on that Japanese island always seemed to me to be playing it pretty close to the chest. The Stone Face act. It's just possible. Keep me informed, would you?'

Captain Walker got back to James Bond. 'Sorry about that. It's being a busy day. Now then, this inquiry of yours. Afraid I can't help you myself. Not my part of the Ministry. The man you want is Major Townsend. He should be able to locate this man you want to see. Got a pencil? It's No. 44 Kensington Cloisters. Got that? Kensington double five double five. Give me ten minutes and I'll have a word with him and see if he can help. All right?'

James Bond said dully, 'That's very kind of you.' He put down the telephone. He waited exactly ten minutes and picked up the receiver and asked for the number.

James Bond was staying at the Ritz Hotel. Colonel Boris had told him to do so. Bond's file in the K.G.B. Archive described him as a high-liver, so, on arrival in London, he must stick to the K.G.B. image of the high life. Bond went down in the lift to the Arlington Street entrance. A man at the newsstand got a good profile of him with a buttonhole Minox. When Bond went down the shallow steps to the street and asked the commissionaire for a taxi, a canonflex with a telescopic lens clicked away busily from a Red Roses laundry van at the neighbouring goods entrance and, in due course, the same van followed Bond's taxi while a man inside the van reported briefly to the Action Room of the Special Branch.

No. 44 Kensington Cloisters was a dull Victorian mansion in grimy red brick. It had been chosen for its purpose because it had once been the headquarters of the Empire League for Noise Abatement, and its entrance still bore the brass plate of this long-defunct organization, the empty shell of which had been purchased by the Secret Service through the Commonwealth Relations Office. It also had a spacious old-fashioned basement, re-equipped as detention cells, and a rear exit into a quiet mews.

The Red Roses laundry van watched the front door shut behind James Bond and then moved off at a sedate speed to its garage not far from Scotland Yard while the process of developing the canonflex film went on in its interior.

'Appointment with Major Townsend,' said Bond.

'Yes. He's expecting you, sir. Shall I take your raincoat?' The powerful-looking doorman put the coat on a coat-hanger and hung it up on one of a row of hooks beside the door. As soon as Bond was safely closeted with Major Townsend, the coat would go swiftly to the laboratory on the first floor where its provenance would be established from an examination of the fabric. Pocket dust would be removed for more leisurely research. 'Would you follow me, sir?'

It was a narrow corridor of freshly painted clapboard with a tall, single window which concealed the Fluoroscope triggered automatically from beneath the ugly patterned carpet. The findings of its X-ray eye would be fed into the laboratory above the passage. The passage ended in two facing doors marked 'A' and 'B'. The doorman knocked on Room B and stood aside for Bond to enter.

It was a pleasant, very light room, close-carpeted in dove-grey Wilton. The military prints on the cream walls were expensively framed. A small, bright fire burned under an Adam mantelpiece which bore a number of silver trophies and two photographs in leather frames – one of a nice-looking woman and the other of three nice-looking children. There was a central table with a bowl of flowers and two comfortable club chairs on either side of the fire. No desk or filing cabinets, nothing official-looking. A tall man, as pleasant as the room, got up from the far chair, dropped *The Times* on the carpet beside it, and came forward with a welcoming smile. He held out a firm, dry hand.

This was the Soft Man.

'Come in. Come in. Take a pew. Cigarette? Not the ones I seem to remember you favour. Just the good old Senior Service.'

Major Townsend had carefully prepared the loaded remark – a reference to Bond's liking for the Morland Specials with the three gold rings. He noted Bond's apparent lack of comprehension. Bond took a cigarette and accepted a light. They sat down facing one another. Major Townsend crossed his legs comfortably. Bond sat up straight. Major Townsend said, 'Well now. How can I help you?'

Across the corridor, in Room A, a cold Office-of-Works cube with no furniture but a hissing gas fire, an ugly desk with two facing wooden chairs under the naked neon, Bond's reception by the Hard Man, the ex-police superintendent ('ex' because of a brutality case in Glasgow for which he had taken the rap) would have been very different. There, the man who went under the name of Mr Robson would have given him the full intimidation treatment – harsh, bullying interrogation, threats of imprisonment for false representation and God knows what else, and, perhaps, if he had shown signs of hostility or developing a nuisance value, a little judicious roughing-up in the basement.

Such was the ultimate sieve which sorted out the wheat from the chaff from those members of the public who desired access to 'The Secret Service'. There were other people in the building who dealt with the letters. Those written in pencil or in multicoloured inks, and those enclosing a photograph, remained unanswered. Those which threatened or were litigious were referred to the Special Branch. The solid, serious ones were passed, with a comment from the best graphologist in the business, to the Liaison Section at Headquarters for 'further action'. Parcels went automatically, and fast, to the Bomb Disposal Squad at Knightsbridge Barracks. The eye of the needle was narrow. On the whole, it discriminated appropriately. It was an expensive set-up, but it is the first duty of a Secret Service to remain not only secret but secure.

There was no reason why James Bond, who had always been on the operative side of the business, should know anything about the entrails of the service, any more than he should have understood the mysteries of the plumbing or electricity supply of his flat in Chelsea, or the working of his own kidneys. Colonel Boris, however, had known the whole routine. The secret services of all the great powers know the public face of their opponents, and Colonel Boris had very accurately described the treatment that James Bond must expect before he was 'cleared' and was allowed access to the office of his former chief.

So now James Bond paused before he replied to Major Townsend's question about how he could be of help. He looked at the Soft Man and then into the fire. He added up the accuracy of the description he had been given of Major Townsend's appearance and, before he said what he had been told to say, he gave Colonel Boris ninety out of a hundred. The big, friendly

face, the wide-apart, pale-brown eyes, bracketed by the wrin-
kles of a million smiles, the military moustache, the rimless
monocle dangling from a thin black cord, the brushed-back,
thinning sandy hair, the immaculate double-breasted blue
suit, stiff white collar and Brigade tie – it was all there. But
what Colonel Boris hadn't said was that the friendly eyes were
as cold and steady as gun barrels and that the lips were thin
and scholarly.

James Bond said patiently: 'It's really quite simple. I'm who I
say I am. I'm doing what I naturally would do, and that's report
back to M.'

'Quite. But you must realize' (a sympathetic smile) 'that you've
been out of contact for nearly a year. You've been officially posted
as "missing believed killed". Your obituary has even appeared in
The Times. Have you any evidence of identity? I admit that you
look very much like your photographs, but you must see that we
have to be very sure before we pass you on up the ladder.'

'A Miss Mary Goodnight was my secretary. She'd recognize
me all right. So would dozens of other people at H.Q.'

'Miss Goodnight's been posted abroad. Can you give me a
brief description of H.Q., just the main geography?'

Bond did so.

'Right. Now, who was a Miss Maria Freudenstadt?'

'Was?'

'Yes, she's dead.'

'Thought she wouldn't last long. She was a double, working
for K.G.B. Section 100 controlled her. I wouldn't get any thanks
for telling you any more.'

Major Townsend had been primed with this very secret top
question. He had been given the answer, more or less as Bond had
put it. This was the clincher. This *had* to be James Bond. 'Well,
we're getting on fine. Now, it only remains to find out where

you've come from and where you've been all these months and I won't keep you any longer.'

'Sorry. I can only tell that to M. personally.'

'I see.' Major Townsend put on a thoughtful expression. 'Well, just let me make a telephone call or two and I'll see what can be done.' He got to his feet. 'Seen today's *Times*?' He picked it up and handed it to Bond. It had been specially treated to give good prints. Bond took it. 'Shan't be long.'

Major Townsend shut the door behind him and went across the passage and through the door marked 'A' where he knew that 'Mr Robson' would be alone. 'Sorry to bother you, Fred. Can I use your scrambler?' The chunky man behind the desk grunted through the stem of his pipe and remained bent over the midday *Evening Standard* racing news.

Major Townsend picked up the green receiver and was put through to the Laboratory. 'Major Townsend speaking. Any comment?' He listened, carefully, said 'thank you', and got through to the Chief Security Officer at Headquarters. 'Well, sir, I think it must be 007. Bit thinner than his photographs. I'll be giving you his prints as soon as he's gone. Wearing his usual rig – dark-blue single-breasted suit, white shirt, thin black knitted silk tie, black casuals – but they all look brand new. Raincoat bought yesterday from Burberry's. Got the Freudenstadt question right, but says he won't say anything about himself except to M. personally. But whoever he is, I don't like it much. He fluffed on his special cigarettes. He's got an odd sort of glazed, sort of far-away look, and the "Scope" shows that he's carrying a gun in his right-hand coat pocket – curious sort of contraption, doesn't seem to have got a butt to it. I'd say he's a sick man. I wouldn't personally recommend that M. should see him, but I wouldn't know how we're to get him to talk unless he does.' He paused. 'Very good, sir. I'll stay by the telephone. I'm on Mr Robson's extension.'

There was silence in the room. The two men didn't get on well together. Major Townsend gazed into the gas fire, wondering about the man next door. The telephone burred. 'Yes, sir? Very good, sir. Would your secretary send along a car from the pool? Thank you, sir.'

Bond was sitting in the same upright posture, *The Times* still unopened in his hand. Major Townsend said cheerfully, 'Well, that's fixed. Message from M. that he's tremendously relieved you're all right and he'll be free in about half an hour. Car should be here in ten minutes or so. And the Chief of Staff says he hopes you'll be free for lunch afterwards.'

James Bond smiled for the first time. It was a thin smile which didn't light up his eyes. He said, 'That's very kind of him. Would you tell him I'm afraid I shan't be free.'

2 .... ATTENTAT!

THE CHIEF of Staff stood in front of M.'s desk and said firmly, 'I really wouldn't do it, sir. I can see him, or someone else can. I don't like the smell of it at all. I think 007's round the bend. There's no doubt it's him all right. The prints have just been confirmed by Chief of Security. And the pictures are all right – and the recording of his voice. But there are too many things that don't add up. This forged passport we found in his room at the Ritz, for instance. All right. So he wanted to come back into the country quietly. But it's too good a job. Typical K.G.B. sample. And the last entry is West Germany, day before yesterday. Why didn't he report to Station B or W? Both those Heads of Station are friends of his, particularly 016 in Berlin. And why didn't he go and have a look at his flat? He's got some sort of a housekeeper there, Scots woman called May, who's always sworn he was still alive and has kept the place going on her savings. The Ritz is sort of "stage" Bond. And these new clothes. Why did he have to bother? Doesn't matter what he was wearing when he came in through Dover. Normal thing, if he was in rags, would have been to give me a ring – he had my home number – and get me to fix him up. Have a few drinks and run over his story and then report here. Instead of that we've got this typical penetration approach and Security worried as hell.'

The Chief of Staff paused. He knew he wasn't getting through. As soon as he had begun, M. had swivelled his chair sideways and had remained, occasionally sucking at an unlighted pipe, gazing moodily out through the window at the jagged skyline of London. Obstinately, the Chief of Staff concluded, 'Do you think you could leave this one to me, sir? I can get hold of Sir James Molony in no time and have 007 put into The Park for observation and treatment. It'll all be done very gently. V.I.P. handling and so on. I can say you've been called to the Cabinet or something. Security says 007's looking a bit thin. Build him up. Convalescence and all that. That can be the excuse. If he cuts up rough, we can always give him some dope. He's a good friend of mine. He won't hold it against us. He obviously needs to be got back in the groove – if we can do it, that is.'

M. slowly swivelled his chair round. He looked up at the tired, worried face that showed the strain of being the equivalent of Number Two in the Secret Service for ten years and more. M. smiled. 'Thank you, Chief of Staff. But I'm afraid it's not as easy as all that. I sent 007 out on his last job to shake him out of his domestic worries. You remember how it all came about. Well, we had no idea that what seemed a fairly peaceful mission was going to end up in a pitched battle with Blofeld. Or that 007 was going to vanish off the face of the earth for a year. Now we've got to know what happened during that year. And 007's quite right. I sent him out on that mission and he's got every right to report back to me personally. I know 007. He's a stubborn fellow. If he says he won't tell anyone else, he won't. Of course I want to hear what happened to him. You'll listen in. Have a couple of good men at hand. If he turns rough, come and get him. As for his gun' – M. gestured vaguely at the ceiling – 'I can look after that. Have you tested the damned thing?'

'Yes, sir. It works all right. But …'

M. held up a hand. 'Sorry, Chief of Staff. It's an order.' A light winked on the intercom. 'That'll be him. Send him straight in, would you?'

'Very good, sir.' The Chief of Staff went out and closed the door.

James Bond was standing smiling vaguely down at Miss Moneypenny. She looked distraught. When James Bond shifted his gaze and said 'Hullo, Bill' he still wore the same distant smile. He didn't hold out his hand. Bill Tanner said, with a heartiness that rang with a terrible falsity in his ears, 'Hullo, James. Long time no see.' At the same time, out of the corner of his eye, he saw Miss Moneypenny give a quick, emphatic shake of the head. He looked her straight in the eyes. 'M. would like to see 007 straight away.'

Miss Moneypenny lied desperately: 'You know M.'s got a Chiefs of Staff meeting at the Cabinet Office in five minutes?'

'Yes. He says you must somehow get him out of it.' The Chief of Staff turned to James Bond. 'Okay, James. Go ahead. Sorry you can't manage lunch. Come and have a gossip after M.'s finished with you.'

Bond said, 'That'll be fine.' He squared his shoulders and walked through the door over which the red light was already burning.

Miss Moneypenny buried her face in her hands. 'Oh, Bill!' she said desperately. 'There's something wrong with him. I'm frightened.'

Bill Tanner said, 'Take it easy, Penny. I'm going to do what I can.' He walked quickly into his office and shut the door. He went over to his desk and pressed a switch. M.'s voice came into the room: 'Hullo, James. Wonderful to have you back. Take a seat and tell me all about it.'

Bill Tanner picked up the office telephone and asked for Head of Security.

James Bond took his usual place across the desk from M. A storm of memories whirled through his consciousness like badly cut film on a projector that had gone crazy. Bond closed his mind to the storm. He must concentrate on what he had to say, and do, and on nothing else.

'I'm afraid there's a lot I still can't remember, sir. I got a bang on the head' (he touched his right temple) 'somewhere along the line on that job you sent me to do in Japan. Then there's a blank until I got picked up by the police on the waterfront at Vladivostok. No idea how I got there. They roughed me up a bit and in the process I must have got another bang on the head because suddenly I remembered who I was and that I wasn't a Japanese fisherman which was what I thought I was. So then of course the police passed me on to the local branch of the K.G.B. – it's a big grey building on the Morskaya Ulitsa facing the harbour near the railway station, by the way – and when they belinographed my prints to Moscow there was a lot of excitement and they flew me there from the military airfield just north of the town at Vtoraya Rechka and spent weeks interrogating me – or trying to, rather, because I couldn't remember anything except when they prompted me with something they knew themselves and then I could give them a few hazy details to add to their knowledge. Very frustrating for them.'

'Very,' commented M. A small frown had gathered between his eyes. 'And you told them everything you could? Wasn't that rather, er, generous of you?'

'They were very nice to me in every way, sir. It seemed the least I could do. There was this Institute place in Leningrad.

They gave me V.I.P. treatment. Top brain-specialists and every-thing. They didn't seem to hold it against me that I'd been working against them for most of my life. And other people came and talked to me very reasonably about the political situation and so forth. The need for East and West to work together for world peace. They made clear a lot of things that hadn't occurred to me before. They quite convinced me.' Bond looked obstinately across the table into the clear blue sailor's eyes that now held a red spark of anger. 'I don't suppose you understand what I mean, sir. You've been making war against someone or other all your life. You're doing so at this moment. And for most of my adult life you've used me as a tool. Fortunately that's all over now.'

M. said fiercely, 'It certainly is. I suppose among other things you've forgotten is reading reports of our P.O.W.s in the Korean war who were brainwashed by the Chinese. If the Russians are so keen on peace, what do they need the K.G.B. for? At the last estimate, that was about one hundred thousand men and women "making war" as you call it against us and other countries. This is the organization that was so charming to you in Leningrad. Did they happen to mention the murder of Horcher and Stutz in Munich last month?'

'Oh yes, sir.' Bond's voice was patient, equable. 'They have to defend themselves against the secret services of the West. If you would demobilize all this,' Bond waved a hand, 'they would be only too delighted to scrap the K.G.B. They were quite open about it all.'

'And the same thing applies to their two hundred divisions and their U-boat fleet and their I.C.B.M.s, I suppose?' M's voice rasped.

'Of course, sir.'

'Well, if you found these people so reasonable and charming, why didn't you stay there? Others have. Burgess is dead, but you could have chummed up with Maclean.'

'We thought it more important that I should come back and fight for peace here, sir. You and your agents have taught me certain skills for use in the underground war. It was explained to me how these skills could be used in the cause of peace.'

James Bond's hand moved nonchalantly to his right-hand coat pocket. M., with equal casualness, shifted his chair back from his desk. His left hand felt for the button under the arm of the chair.

'For instance?' said M. quietly, knowing that death had walked into the room and was standing beside him and that this was an invitation for death to take his place in the chair.

James Bond had become tense. There was a whiteness round his lips. The blue-grey eyes still stared blankly, almost unseeingly at M. The words rang out harshly, as if forced out of him by some inner compulsion. 'It would be a start if the warmongers could be eliminated, sir. This is for number one on the list.'

The hand, snub-nosed with black metal, flashed out of the pocket, but, even as the poison hissed down the barrel of the bulb-butted pistol, the great sheet of Armourplate glass hurtled down from the baffled slit in the ceiling and, with a last sigh of hydraulics, braked to the floor. The jet of viscous brown fluid splashed harmlessly into its centre and trickled slowly down, distorting M.'s face and the arm he had automatically thrown up for additional protection.

The Chief of Staff had burst into the room, followed by the Head of Security. They threw themselves on James Bond. Even as they seized his arms his head fell forward on his chest and he would have slid from his chair to the ground if they hadn't supported him. They hauled him to his feet. He was in a dead faint. The Head of Security sniffed. 'Cyanide,' he said curtly. 'We must all get out of here. And bloody quick!' (The emergency had snuffed out Headquarters 'manners'.) The pistol lay on the carpet where it had fallen. He kicked it away. He said to M., who had walked out from behind his glass shield, 'Would you mind leaving the room, sir? Quickly. I'll have this cleaned up during the lunch hour.' It was an order. M. went to the open door. Miss Moneypenny stood with her clenched hand up to her mouth. She watched with horror as James Bond's supine body was hauled out and, the heels of its shoes leaving tracks on the carpet, taken into the Chief of Staff's room.

M. said sharply, 'Close that door, Miss Moneypenny. Get the duty M.O. up right away. Come along, girl! Don't just stand there gawking! And not a word of this to anyone. Understood?'

Miss Moneypenny pulled herself back from the edge of hysterics. She said an automatic 'Yes, sir', pulled the door shut and reached for the inter-office telephone.

M. walked across and into the Chief of Staff's office and closed the door. Head of Security was on his knees beside Bond. He had loosened his tie and collar button and was feeling his pulse. Bond's face was white and bathed in sweat. His breathing was a desperate rattle, as if he had just run a race. M. looked briefly down at him and then, his face hidden from the others, at the wall beyond the body. He turned to the Chief of Staff. He said briskly, 'Well, that's that. My predecessor died in that chair. Then it was a simple bullet, but from much the same sort of a crazed officer. One can't legislate against the lunatic. But the Office of Works certainly did a good job with that gadget. Now then, Chief of Staff. This is of course to go no further. Get Sir James Molony as soon as you can and have 007 taken down to The Park. Ambulance, surreptitious guard. I'll explain things to Sir James this afternoon. Briefly, as you heard, the K.G.B. got hold of him. Brainwashed him. He was already a sick man. Amnesia of some kind. I'll tell you all I know later. Have his things collected from the Ritz and his bill paid. And put something out to the Press Association. Something on these lines: "The Ministry of Defence is pleased," no, say delighted, "to announce that Commander James Bond etc., who was posted as missing, believed killed while on a mission to Japan last November, has returned to this country after a hazardous journey across the Soviet Union which is expected to yield much valuable information. Commander Bond's health has inevitably suffered from his experiences and he is convalescing under medical supervision."' M. smiled frostily. 'That bit about information'll give no joy to Comrade Semichastny and his troops. And add a "D" Notice to editors: "It is particularly requested, for security reasons, that the minimum of speculation or comment be added to the above communiqué and that no attempts be made to trace Commander Bond's whereabouts." All right?'

Bill Tanner had been writing furiously to keep up with M. He looked up from his scratch pad, bewildered. 'But aren't you going to make any charges, sir? After all, treason and attempted murder ... I mean, not even a court martial?'

'Certainly not.' M.'s voice was gruff. '007 was a sick man. Not responsible for his actions. If one can brainwash a man, presumably one can un-brainwash him. If anyone can, Sir James can. Put him back on half pay for the time being, in his old Section. And see he gets full back pay and allowances for the past year. If the K.G.B. has the nerve to throw one of my best men at me, I have the nerve to throw him back at them. 007 was a good agent once. There's no reason why he shouldn't be a good agent again. Within limits, that is. After lunch, give me the file on Scaramanga. If we can get him fit again, that's the right-sized target for 007.'

The Chief of Staff protested, 'But that's suicide, sir! Even 007 could never take him.'

M. said coldly, 'What would 007 get for this morning's bit of work? Twenty years? As a minimum, I'd say. Better for him to fall on the battlefield. If he brings it off, he'll have won his spurs back again and we can all forget the past. Anyway, that's my decision.'

There was a knock on the door and the duty Medical Officer came into the room. M. bade him good afternoon and turned stiffly on his heel and walked out through the open door.

The Chief of Staff looked at the retreating back. He said, under his breath, 'You cold-hearted bastard!' Then, with his usual minute thoroughness and sense of duty, he set about the tasks he had been given. His not to reason why!

3 .... 'PISTOLS' SCARAMANGA

At Blades, M. ate his usual meagre luncheon – a grilled Dover sole followed by the ripest spoonful he could gouge from the club Stilton. And as usual he sat by himself in one of the window seats and barricaded himself behind *The Times*, occasionally turning a page to demonstrate that he was reading it, which, in fact, he wasn't. But Porterfield commented to the head waitress, Lily, a handsome, much-loved ornament of the club, that 'there's something wrong with the old man today. Or maybe not exactly wrong, but there's something up with him.' Porterfield prided himself on being something of an amateur psychologist. As head waiter, and father confessor to many of the members, he knew a lot about all of them and liked to think he knew everything, so that, in the tradition of incomparable servants, he could anticipate their wishes and their moods. Now, standing with Lily in a quiet moment behind the finest cold buffet on display at that date anywhere in the world, he explained himself. 'You know that terrible stuff Sir Miles always drinks? That Algerian red wine that the wine committee won't even allow on the wine list. They only have it in the club to please Sir Miles. Well, he explained to me once that in the navy they used to call it "The Infuriator" because if you drank too much of it, it seems that it used to put you into a rage. Well now, in the ten years that I've had the pleasure of looking after Sir Miles, he's never ordered more than half a carafe of the stuff.' Porterfield's benign, almost priestly countenance assumed an expression of theatrical solemnity as if he had read something really terrible in the tea leaves. 'Then what happens today?' Lily clasped her hands tensely and bent her head fractionally closer to get the full impact of the news. 'The old man says, "Porterfield. A bottle of Infuriator. You understand? A full bottle!" So of course I didn't say anything but went off and brought it to him. But mark my words, Lily,' he noticed a lifted hand down the long room and moved off, 'there's something hit Sir Miles hard this morning and no mistake.'

M. sent for his bill. As usual he paid, whatever the amount of the bill, with a five-pound note for the pleasure of receiving in change crisp new pound notes, new silver and gleaming copper pennies, for it is the custom at Blades to give its members only freshly minted money. Porterfield pulled back his table and M. walked quickly to the door, acknowledging the occasional greeting with a preoccupied nod and a brief lifting of the hand. It was two o'clock. The old black Phantom Rolls took him quietly and quickly northwards through Berkeley Square, across Oxford Street and via Wigmore Street into Regent's Park. M. didn't look out at the passing scene. He sat stiffly in the back, his bowler hat squarely set on the middle of his head, and gazed unseeing at the back of the chauffeur's head with hooded, brooding eyes.

For the hundredth time, since he had left his office that morning, he assured himself that his decision was right. If James Bond could be straightened out, and M. was certain that that supreme neurologist, Sir James Molony, could bring it off, it would be ridiculous to re-assign him to normal staff duties in the Double-O Section. The past could be forgiven, but not forgotten – except with the passage of time. It would be most irksome for those in the know to have Bond moving about Headquarters as if nothing had happened. It would be doubly embarrassing for M. to have to face Bond across that desk. And James Bond, if aimed straight at a known target – M. put it in the language of battleships – was a supremely effective firing-piece. Well, the target was there and it desperately demanded destruction. Bond had accused M. of using him as a tool. Naturally. Every officer in the Service was a tool for one secret purpose or another. The problem on hand could only be solved by a killing. James Bond would not possess the Double-O prefix if he had not high talents, frequently proved, as a gunman. So be it! In exchange for the happenings of that morning, in expiation of them, Bond must prove himself at his old skills. If he succeeded, he would have regained his previous status. If he failed, well, it would be a death for which he would be honoured. Win or lose, the plan would solve a vast array of problems. M. closed his mind once and for all on his decision. He got out of the car and went up in the lift to the eighth floor and along the corridor, smelling the smell of some unknown disinfectant more and more powerfully as he approached his office.

Instead of using his key to the private entrance at the end of the corridor M. turned right through Miss Moneypenny's door. She was sitting in her usual place, typing away at the usual routine correspondence. She got to her feet.

'What's this dreadful stink, Miss Moneypenny?'

'I don't know what it's called, sir. Head of Security brought along a squad from Chemical Warfare at the War Office. He says your office is all right to use again but to keep the windows open for a while. So I've turned on the heating. Chief of Staff isn't back from lunch yet, but he told me to tell you that everything you wanted done is under way. Sir James is operating until four but will expect your call after that. Here's the file you wanted, sir.'

M. took the brown folder with the red Top Secret star in its top right-hand corner. 'How's 007? Did he come round all right?' Miss Moneypenny's face was expressionless. 'I gather so, sir. The M.O. gave him a sedative of some kind and he was taken off on a stretcher during the lunch hour. He was covered up. They took him down in the service lift to the garage. I haven't had any inquiries.'

'Good. Well, bring me in the signals, would you. There's been a lot of time wasted today on all these domestic excitements.' Bearing the file M. went through the door into his office. Miss Moneypenny brought in the signals and stood dutifully beside him while he went through them, occasionally dictating a comment or a query. She looked down at the bowed, iron-grey head with the bald patch polished for years by a succession of naval caps and wondered, as she had wondered so often over the past ten years, whether she loved or hated this man. One thing was certain. She respected him more than any man she had known or had read of.

M. handed her the file. 'Thank you. Now just give me a quarter of an hour, and then I'll see whoever wants me. The call to Sir James has priority of course.'

M. opened the brown folder, reached for his pipe and began absent-mindedly filling it as he glanced through the list of subsidiary files to see if there was any other docket he immediately needed. Then he set a match to his pipe and settled back in his chair and read:

'FRANCISCO (PACO) "PISTOLS" SCARAMANGA.' And underneath, in lower-case type, 'Freelance assassin mainly under K.G.B. control through D.S.S., Havana, Cuba, but often as an independent operator for other organizations, in the

Caribbean and Central American states. Has caused widespread damage, particularly to the S.S., but also to C.I.A. and other friendly services, by murder and scientific maiming, since 1959, the year when Castro came to power and which seems also to have been the trigger for Scaramanga's operations. Is widely feared and admired in said territory throughout which he appears, despite police precautions, to have complete freedom of access. Has thus become something of a local myth and is known in his "territory" as "The Man with the Golden Gun" – a reference to his main weapon which is a gold-plated, long-barrelled, single-action Colt .45. He uses special bullets with a heavy, soft (24 ct) gold core jacketed with silver and cross-cut at the tip, on the dum-dum principle, for maximum wounding effect. Himself loads and artifices this ammunition. Is responsible for the death of 267 (British Guiana), 398 (Trinidad), 943 (Jamaica) and 768 and 742 (Havana) and for the maiming and subsequent retirement from the S.S., of 098, Area Inspection Officer, by bullet wounds in both knees. (See above references in Central Records for Scaramanga's victims in Martinique, Haiti and Panama.)

'DESCRIPTION: Age about 35. Height 6 ft. 3 in. Slim and fit. Eyes, light brown. Hair reddish in a crew cut. Long sideburns. Gaunt, sombre face with thin "pencil" moustache, brownish. Ears very flat to the head. Ambidextrous. Hands very large and powerful and immaculately manicured. Distinguishing marks: a third nipple about two inches below his left breast. (N.B. in Voodoo and allied local cults this is considered a sign of invulnerability and great sexual prowess.) Is an insatiable but indiscriminate womanizer who invariably has sexual intercourse shortly before a killing in the belief that it improves his "eye". (N.B. a belief shared by many professional lawn tennis players, golfers, gun and rifle marksmen and others.)

'ORIGINS: A relative of the Catalan family of circus managers of the same name with whom he spent his youth. Self-educated. At the age of 16, after the incident described below, emigrated illegally to the United States where he lived a life of petty crime on the fringes of the gangs until he graduated as a full-time gunman for the "Spangled Mob" in Nevada with the cover of pitboy in the casino of the Tiara Hotel in Las Vegas where in fact he acted as executioner of cheats and other transgressors within and outside "The Mob". In 1958 was forced to flee the States as the result of a famous duel against his opposite number for the Detroit Purple Gang, a certain Ramon "The Rod" Rodriguez, which took place by moonlight on the third green of the Thunderbird golf course at Las Vegas. (Scaramanga got two bullets into the heart of his opponent before the latter had fired a shot. Distance 20 paces.) Believed to have been compensated by "The Mob" with 100,000 dollars. Travelled the whole Caribbean area investing fugitive funds for various Las Vegas interests and later, as his reputation for keen and successful dealing in real estate and plantations became consolidated, for Trujillo of Dominica and Batista of Cuba. In 1959 settled in Havana and, seeing the way the wind blew, while remaining ostensibly a Batista man, began working undercover for the Castro party and, after the revolution, obtained an influential post as foreign "enforcer" for the D.S.S. In this capacity, on behalf, that is, of the Cuban Secret Police, he undertook the assassinations mentioned above.

'PASSPORTS: Various, including Cuban diplomatic.

'DISGUISES: None. They are not necessary. The myth surrounding this man, the equivalent, let us say, of that surrounding the most famous film star, and the fact that he has no police record, have hitherto given him complete freedom of movement and indemnity from interference in "his" territory. In most of the islands and mainland republics which constitute this territory, he has groups of admirers (e.g. the Rastafari in Jamaica) and commands powerful pressure groups who give him protection and succour when called upon to do so. Moreover, as the ostensible purchaser, and usually the legal front, for the "hot money" properties mentioned above, he has legitimate access, frequently supported by his diplomatic status, to any part of his territory.

'RESOURCES: Considerable but of unknown extent. Travels on various credit cards of the Diners' Club variety. Has a numbered account with the Union des Banques de Crédit, Zurich, and appears to have no difficulty in obtaining foreign currency from the slim resources of Cuba when he needs it.

'MOTIVATION: (Comment by C. C.) –' M. refilled and relit his pipe, which had died. What had gone before was routine information which added nothing to his basic knowledge of the man. What followed would be of more interest. 'C. C.' covered the identity of a former Regius Professor of History at Oxford who lived a – to M. – pampered existence at Headquarters in a small and, in M.'s opinion, over-comfortable office. In between, again in M.'s opinion, over-luxurious and over-long meals at the Garrick Club, he wandered, at his ease, into Headquarters, examined such files as the present one, asked questions and had signals of inquiry sent, and then delivered his judgement. But M., for all his prejudices against the man, his haircut, the casualness of his clothes, what he knew of his way of life, and the apparently haphazard processes of his ratiocination, appreciated the sharpness of the mind, the knowledge of the world, that C. C. brought to his task and, so often, the accuracy of his judgements. In short, M. always enjoyed what C. C. had to say and he now picked up the file again with relish.

'I am interested in this man,' wrote C. C., 'and I have caused inquiries to be made on a somewhat wider front than usual, since it is not common to be confronted with a secret agent who is at once so much of a public figure and yet appears to be infinitely successful in the difficult and dangerous field of his choice – that of being, in common parlance, "a gun for hire". I think I may have found the origin of this partiality for killing his fellow men in cold blood, men against whom he has no personal animosity but merely the reflected animosity of his employers, in the following bizarre anecdote from his youth. In the travelling circus of his father, Enrico Scaramanga, the boy had several roles. He was a most spectacular trick shot, he was a stand-in strong man in the acrobatic troop, often taking the place of the usual artiste as bottom man in the "human pyramid" act, and he was the mahout, in gorgeous turban, Indian robes, etc., who rode the leading elephant in a troupe of three. This elephant, by the name of Max, was a male and it is a peculiarity of the male elephant, which I have learned with much interest and verified with eminent zoologists, that, at intervals during the year, they go "on heat" sexually. During these periods, a mucous deposit forms behind the animals' ears and this needs to be scraped off since otherwise it causes the elephant intense irritation. Max developed this symptom during a visit of the circus to Trieste, but, through an oversight, the condition was not noticed and given the necessary treatment. The "Big Top" of the circus had been erected on the outskirts of the town adjacent to the coastal railway line and, on the night which was, in my opinion, to determine the future way of life of the young Scaramanga, Max went berserk, threw the youth and, screaming horrifically, trampled his way through the auditorium, causing many casualties, and charged off across the fairground and on to the railway line down which (a frightening spectacle under the full moon which, as newspaper cuttings record, was shining on that night) he galloped at full speed. The local carabiniere were alerted and set off in pursuit by car along the main road that flanks the railway line. In due course they caught up with the unfortunate monster, which, its frenzy expired, stood peacefully facing back the way it had come. Not realizing that the elephant, if approached by its handler, could now be led peacefully back to its stall, the police opened rapid fire and bullets from their carbines and revolvers wounded the animal superficially in many places. Infuriated afresh, the miserable beast, now pursued by the police car from which the hail of fire continued, charged off again along the railway line. On arrival at the fairground, the elephant seemed to recognize its "home", the "Big Top", and, turning off the railway line, lumbered back through the fleeing spectators to the centre of the deserted arena and there, weakened by loss of blood, pathetically continued with its interrupted act. Trumpeting dreadfully in its agony, the mortally wounded Max endeavoured again and again to raise itself and stand upon one leg. Meanwhile the young Scaramanga, now armed with his pistols, tried to throw a lariat over the animal's head while calling out the "elephant talk" with which he usually controlled him. Max seems to have recognized the youth and – it must have been a truly pitiful sight – lowered its trunk to allow the youth to be hoisted to his usual seat behind the elephant's head. But at this moment the police burst into the sawdust ring and their captain, approaching very close, emptied his revolver into the elephant's right eye at a range of a few feet, upon which Max fell dying to the ground. Upon this, the young Scaramanga who, according to the Press, had a deep devotion for his charger, drew one of his pistols and shot the policeman through the heart and fled off into the crowd of bystanders pursued by the other policemen who could not fire because of the throng of people. He made good his escape, found his way south to Naples and thence, as noted above, stowed away to America.

'Now, I see in this dreadful experience a possible reason for the transformation of Scaramanga into the most vicious gunman of recent years. In him was, I believe, born on that day a cold-blooded desire to avenge himself on all humanity. That the elephant had run amok and trampled many innocent people, that the man truly responsible was his handler and that the police were only doing their duty, would be, psychopathologically, either forgotten or deliberately suppressed by a youth of hot-blooded stock whose subconscious had been so deeply lacerated. At all events, Scaramanga's subsequent career requires some explanation, and I trust I am not being fanciful in putting forward my own prognosis from the known facts.'

M. rubbed the bowl of his pipe thoughtfully down the side of his nose. Well, fair enough! He turned back to the file.

'I have comment', wrote C. C., 'to make on this man's alleged sexual potency when seen in relation to his profession. It is a Freudian thesis, with which I am inclined to agree, that the pistol, whether in the hands of an amateur or of a professional gunman, has significance for the owner as a symbol of virility – an extension of the male organ – and that excessive interest in guns (e.g. gun collections and gun clubs) is a form of fetishism. The partiality of Scaramanga for a particularly showy variation of weapon, and his use of silver and gold bullets, clearly point, I think, to his being a slave to this fetish and, if I am right, I have doubts about his alleged sexual prowess, for the lack of which his gun fetish would be either a substitute or a compensation. I have also noted, from a "profile" of this man in *Time* magazine, one fact which supports my thesis that Scaramanga may be sexually abnormal. In listing his accomplishments, *Time* notes, but does not comment upon, the fact that this man cannot whistle. Now it may only be myth, and it is certainly not medical science, but there is a popular theory that a man who cannot whistle has homosexual tendencies. (At this point, the reader may care to experiment and, from his self-knowledge, help to prove or disprove this item of folklore! C. C.)' (M. hadn't whistled since he was a boy. Unconsciously his mouth pursed and a clear note was emitted. He uttered an impatient 'tchah!' and continued with his reading.) 'So I would not be surprised to learn that Scaramanga is not the Casanova of popular fancy. Passing to the wider implications of gunmanship, we enter the realms of the Adlerian power urge as compensation for the inferiority complex, and here I will quote some well-turned phrases of a certain Mr Harold L. Peterson in his preface to his finely illustrated *The Book of the Gun*, published by Paul Hamlyn. Mr Peterson writes: "In the vast array of things man has invented to better his condition, few have fascinated him more than the gun. Its function is simple; as Oliver Winchester said, with Nineteenth Century complacency, 'A gun is a machine for throwing balls.' But its ever-increasing efficiency in performing this task, and its awesome ability to strike home from long range, have given it tremendous psychological appeal.

' "For possession of a gun and the skill to use it enormously augments the gunner's personal power, and extends the radius of his influence and effect a thousand times beyond his arm's length. And since strength resides in the gun, the man who wields it may be less than strong without being disadvantaged. The flashing sword, the couched lance, the bent longbow performed to the limit of the man who held it. The gun's power is inherent and needs only to be released. A steady eye and an accurate aim are enough. Wherever the muzzle points the bullet goes, bearing the gunner's wish or intention swiftly to the target ... Perhaps more than any other implement, the gun has shaped the course of nations and the destiny of men." '

C. C. commented: 'In the Freudian thesis, "his arm's length" would become the length of the masculine organ. But we need not linger over these esoterica. The support for my premise is well expressed in Mr Peterson's sinewy prose and, though I would substitute the printing press for the gun in his concluding paragraph, his points are well taken. The subject, Scaramanga, is, in my opinion, a paranoiac in subconscious revolt against the father figure (i.e. the figure of authority) and a sexual fetishist with possible homosexual tendencies. He has other qualities which are self-evident from the earlier testimony. In conclusion, and having regard to the damage he has already wrought upon the personnel of the S.S., I conclude that his career should be terminated with the utmost dispatch – if necessary by the inhuman means he himself employs, in the unlikely event an agent of equal courage and dexterity can be made available.' Signed 'C. C.'

Beneath, at the end of the docket, the Head of the Caribbean and Central American Section had minuted 'I concur', signed 'C.A.', and the Chief of Staff had added, in red ink, 'Noted. C.O.S.'

M. gazed into space for perhaps five minutes. Then he reached for his pen and, in green ink, scrawled the word 'Action?' followed by the italic, authoritative '*M*'.

Then he sat very still for another five minutes and wondered if he had signed James Bond's death warrant.

4 .... THE STARS FORETELL

THERE ARE few less prepossessing places to spend a hot after-noon than Kingston International Airport in Jamaica. All the money has been spent on lengthening the runway out into the harbour to take the big jets and little was left over for the comfort of transit passengers. James Bond had come in an hour before on a B.W.I.A. flight from Trinidad and there were two hours to go before his connection with a Cuban Airways flight for Havana. He had taken off his coat and tie and now sat on a hard bench gloomily surveying the contents of the In-Bond shop with its expensive scents, liquor and piles of over-decorated native ware. He had had luncheon on the plane, it was the wrong time for a drink and it was too hot and too far to take a taxi into Kingston even had he wanted to. He wiped his already soaking handker-chief over his face and neck and cursed softly and fluently.

A cleaner ambled in and, with the exquisite languor of such people throughout the Caribbean, proceeded to sweep very small bits of rubbish hither and thither, occasionally dipping a bone-less hand into a bucket to sprinkle water over the dusty cement floor. Through the slatted jalousies a small breeze, reeking of the mangrove swamps, briefly stirred the dead air and then was gone. There were only two other passengers in the 'lounge', Cubans perhaps, with jippa-jappa luggage. A man and a woman. They sat close together against the opposite wall and stared fixedly at James Bond, adding minutely to the oppression of the atmosphere. Bond got up and went over to the shop. He bought a *Daily Gleaner* and returned to his place. Because of its inconsequence and occasionally bizarre choice of news the *Gleaner* was a favourite paper of Bond's. Almost the whole of that day's front page was taken up with new ganja laws to prevent the consumption, sale and cultivation of this local version of marijuana. The fact that de Gaulle had just sensationally announced his recognition of Red China was boxed well down the page. Bond read the whole paper – 'country newsbits' and all – with the minute care bred of desperation. His horoscope said: 'CHEER UP! Today will bring a pleasant surprise and the fulfilment of a dear wish. But you must earn your good fortune by watching closely for the golden opportunity when it presents itself and then seizing it with both hands.' Bond smiled grimly. He would be unlikely to get on the scent of Scaramanga on his first evening in Havana. It was not even certain that Scaramanga was there. This was a last resort. For six weeks, Bond had been chasing his man round the Caribbean and Central America. He had missed him by a day in Trinidad and by only a matter of hours in Caracas. Now he had rather reluctantly taken the decision to try and ferret him out on his home ground, a particularly inimical home ground, with which Bond was barely familiar. At least he had fortified himself in British Guiana with a diplomatic passport and he was now 'Courier' Bond with splendidly engraved instructions from Her Majesty to pick up the Jamaican diplomatic bag in Havana and return with it. He had even borrowed an example of the famous Silver Greyhound, the

British Courier's emblem for three hundred years. If he could do his job and then get a few hundred yards' start, this would at least give him sanctuary in the British Embassy. Then it would be up to the F.O. to bargain him out. If he could find his man. If he could carry out his instructions. If he could get away from the scene of the shooting. If, if, if ... Bond turned to the advertisements on the back page. At once an item caught his eye. It was so typically 'old' Jamaica. This is what he read:

[FOR SALE BY AUCTION]
[AT 77 HARBOUR STREET, KINGSTON]
[At 10.30 a.m. on WEDNESDAY,]
[28th MAY]
[under Powers of Sale contained in a mortgage]
[from Cornelius Brown *et ux]*
[No. 3½ LOVE LANE, SAVANNAH LA MAR.]

Containing the substantial residence and all that parcel of land by measurement on the Northern Boundary three chains and five perches, on the Southern Boundary five chains and one perch, on the Eastern Boundary two chains exactly and on the Western Boundary four chains and two perches be the same in each case and more or less and butting Northerly on No. 4 Love Lane.

[THE C. D. ALEXANDER CO. LTD.]
[77 HARBOUR STREET, KINGSTON]
[PHONE 4897.]

James Bond was delighted. He had had many assignments in Jamaica and many adventures on the island. The splendid address and all the stuff about chains and perches and the old-fashioned abracadabra at the end of the advertisement brought back all the authentic smell of one of the oldest and most romantic of former British possessions. For all her newfound 'Independence' he would bet his bottom dollar that the statue of Queen Victoria in the centre of Kingston had not been destroyed or removed to a museum as similar relics of an historic infancy had been in the resurgent African states. He looked at his watch. The *Gleaner* had consumed a whole hour for him. He picked up his coat and brief-case. Not much longer to go! In the last analysis, life wasn't all that dismal. One must forget the bad and remember the good. What were a couple of hours of heat and boredom in this island compared with memories of Beau Desert and Honeychile Rider and his survival against the mad Dr No? James Bond smiled to himself as the dusty pictures clicked across his brain. How long ago it all was! What had happened to her? She never wrote. The last he had heard, she had had two children by the Philadelphia doctor she had married. He wandered off into the grandly named 'Concourse' where the booths of many airlines stood empty, and promotion folders and little company flags on their counters gathered the dust blown in with the mangrove breeze.

There was the customary central display-stand holding messages for incoming and outgoing passengers. As usual, Bond wondered whether there would be something for him. In all his life there never had been. Automatically he ran his eye over the scattered envelopes, held, under tape, beneath each parent letter. Nothing under 'B' and nothing under his alias 'H' for 'Hazard, Mark' of the 'Transworld Consortium', successor to the old 'Universal Export', that had recently been discarded as cover for the Secret Service. Nothing. He ran a bored eye over the other envelopes. He suddenly froze. He looked around him, languidly, casually. The Cuban couple were out of sight. Nobody else was looking. He reached out a quick hand, wrapped in his handkerchief, and pocketed the buff envelope that said, 'Scaramanga. B.O.A.C. passenger from Lima'. He stayed where he was for a few minutes and then wandered slowly off to the door marked 'Men'.

He locked the door and sat down. The envelope was not sealed. It contained a B.W.I.A. message form. The neat B.W.I.A. writing said: 'Message received from Kingston at 12.15: the samples will be available at No. 3½ S.L.M. as from midday tomorrow.' There was no signature. Bond uttered a short bark of laughter and triumph. S.L.M. – Savannah La Mar. Could it be? It must be! At last the three red stars of a jackpot had clicked into line. What was it his *Gleaner* horoscope had said? Well, he would go nap on this clue from outer space – seize it with both hands as the *Gleaner* had instructed. He read the message again and carefully put it back in the envelope. His damp handkerchief had left marks on the buff envelope. In this heat they would dry out in a matter of minutes. He went out and sauntered over to the stand. There was no one in sight. He slipped the message back into its place under 'S' and walked over to the Cuban Airlines booth and cancelled his reservation. He then went to the B.O.A.C. counter and looked through the timetable. Yes, the Lima flight for Kingston, New York and London was due in at 13.15 the next day. He was going to need help. He remembered the name of Head of Station J. He went over to the telephone booth and got through to the High Commissioner's Office. He asked for Commander Ross. After a moment a girl's voice came on the line. 'Commander Ross's assistant. Can I help you?'

There was something vaguely familiar in the lilt of the voice. Bond said, 'Could I speak to Commander Ross? This is a friend from London.'

The girl's voice became suddenly alert. 'I'm afraid Commander Ross is away from Jamaica. Is there anything I can do?' There was a pause. 'What name did you say?'

'I didn't say any name. But in fact it's ...'

The voice broke in excitedly, 'Don't tell me. It's James!'

Bond laughed. 'Well I'm damned! It's Goodnight! What the hell are you doing here?'

'More or less what I used to do for you. I heard you were back, but I thought you were ill or something. How absolutely marvellous! But where are you talking from?'

'Kingston Airport. Now listen, darling. I need help. We can talk later. Can you get cracking?'

'Of course. Wait till I get a pencil. Right.'

'First I need a car. Anything that'll go. Then I want the name of the top man at Frome, you know, the WISCO estate beyond Savannah La Mar. Large-scale survey map of that area, a hundred pounds in Jamaican money. Then be an angel and ring up Alexander's the auctioneers and find out anything you can about a property that's advertised in today's *Gleaner*. Say you're a prospective buyer. Three and a half Love Lane. You'll see the details. Then I want you to come out to Morgan's Harbour where I'm going in a minute, be staying the night there, and we'll have dinner and swop secrets until the dawn steals over the Blue Mountains. Can do?'

'Of course. But that's the hell of a lot of secrets. What shall I wear?'

'Something that's tight in the right places. Not too many buttons.'

She laughed. 'You've established your identity. Now I'll get on with all this. See you about seven. 'Bye.'

Gasping for air, James Bond pushed his way out of the little sweat box. He ran his handkerchief over his face and neck. He'd be damned! Mary Goodnight, his darling secretary from the old days in the OO Section! At Headquarters they had said she was abroad. He hadn't asked any questions. Perhaps she had opted for a change when he had gone missing. Anyway, what a break! Now he'd got an ally, someone he knew. Good old *Gleaner*! He got his bag from the Cuban Airlines booth and went out and hailed a taxi and said 'Morgan's Harbour' and sat back and let the air from the open windows begin to dry him.

The romantic little hotel is on the site of Port Royal at the tip of the Palisadoes. The proprietor, an Englishman who had once been in Intelligence himself and who guessed what Bond's job was, was glad to see him. He showed Bond to a comfortable air-conditioned room with a view of the pool and the wide mirror of Kingston harbour. He said, 'What is it this time? Cubans or smuggling? They're the popular targets these days.'

'Just on my way through. Got any lobsters?'

'Of course.'

'Be a good chap and save two for dinner. Broiled with melted butter. And a pot of that ridiculously expensive foie gras of yours. All right?'

'Wilco. Celebration? Champagne on the ice?'

'Good idea. Now I must get a shower and some sleep. That Kingston Airport's murder.'

James Bond awoke at six. At first he didn't know where he was. He lay and remembered. Sir James Molony had said that his memory would be sluggish for a while. The E.C.T. treatment at The Park, a discreet so-called 'convalescent home' in a vast mansion in Kent, had been fierce. Twenty-four bashes at his brain from the black box in thirty days. After it was over, Sir James had confessed that, if he had been practising in America, he wouldn't have been allowed to administer more than eighteen. At first, Bond had been terrified at the sight of the box and of the two cathodes that would be cupped to each temple. He had heard that people undergoing shock treatment had to be strapped down, that their jerking, twitching bodies, impelled by the volts, often hurtled off the operating-table. But that, it seemed, was old hat. Now there was the longed-for needle with the pentathol, and Sir James said there was no movement of the body when the current flashed through except a slight twitching of the eyelids. And the results had been miraculous. After the pleasant, quiet-spoken analyst had explained to him what had been done to him in Russia, and after he had passed through the mental agony of knowing what he had nearly done to M., the old fierce hatred of the K.G.B. and all its works had been reborn in him and, six weeks after he had entered The Park, all he wanted was to get back at the people who had invaded his brain for their own murderous purposes. And then had come his physical rehabilitation and the inexplicable amount of gun practice he had had to do at the Maidstone police range. And then the day arrived when the Chief of Staff had come down and explained about the gun practice and had spent the day with him and given him his orders, the scribble of green ink, signed 'M.', that wished him luck, and then the excitement of the ride to London Airport on his way across the world.

Bond took another shower and dressed in shirt, slacks and sandals and wandered over to the little bar on the waterfront and ordered a double Walker's de Luxe Bourbon on the rocks and watched the pelicans diving for their dinner. Then he had another drink with a water chaser to break it down and wondered about 3½ Love Lane and what the 'samples' would consist of and how he would take Scaramanga. This had been worrying him since he had been given his orders. It was all very fine to be told to 'eliminate' the man, but James Bond had never liked killing in cold blood and to provoke a draw against a man who was possibly the fastest gun in the world was suicide. Well, he would just have to see which way the cards fell. The first thing to do was to clean up his cover. The diplomatic passport he would leave with Goodnight. He would now be 'Mark Hazard' of the 'Transworld Consortium', the splendidly vague title which could cover almost any kind of human activity. His business would have to be with the West Indies Sugar Company because that was the only business, apart from Kaiser Bauxite, that existed in the comparatively deserted western districts of Jamaica. There was also the Negril project for developing one of the most spectacular beaches in the world, beginning with the building of the Thunderbird Hotel. He could be a rich man looking around for a building site. If his hunch was right, and the childish predictions of his horoscope, and if he came up with Scaramanga at the romantic Love Lane address, it would be a question of playing it by ear.

The prairie fire of the sunset raged briefly in the west and the molten sea cooled off into moonlit gunmetal.

A naked arm smelling of Chanel No. 5 snaked round his neck and warm lips kissed the corner of his mouth. As he reached up to hold the arm where it was, a breathless voice said, 'Oh, James! I'm sorry. I just had to! It's so wonderful to have you back.'

Bond put his hand under the soft chin and lifted up her mouth and kissed her full on the half-open lips. He said, 'Why didn't we ever think of doing that before, Goodnight? Three years with only that door between us! What must we have been thinking of?'

She stood away from him. The golden bell of hair fell back to embrace her neck. She hadn't changed. Still only the faintest trace of make-up, but now the face was golden with sunburn from which the wide-apart blue eyes, now ablaze with the moon, shone out with that challenging directness that had disconcerted him when they had argued over some office problem. Still the same glint of health over the good bones and the broad uninhibited smile from the full lips that, in repose, were so exciting.

But now the clothes were different. Instead of the severe shirt and skirt of the days at Headquarters, she was wearing a single string of pearls and a one-piece short-skirted frock in the colour of a pink gin with a lot of bitters in it – the orangey-pink of the inside of a conch shell. It was all tight against the bosom and the hips. She smiled at his scrutiny. 'The buttons are down the back. This is standard uniform for a tropical Station.'

'I can just see Q Branch dreaming it up. I suppose one of the pearls has a death pill in it.'

'Of course. But I can't remember which. I'll just have to swallow the whole string. Can I have a daiquiri, please, instead?'

Bond gave the order. 'Sorry, Goodnight. My manners are slipping. I was dazzled. It's so tremendous finding you here. And I've never seen you in your working clothes before. Now then, tell me the news. Where's Ross? How long have you been here? Have you managed to cope with all that junk I gave you?'

Her drink came. She sipped it carefully. Bond remembered that she rarely drank and didn't smoke. He ordered another for himself and felt vaguely guilty that this was his third double and that she wouldn't know it and when it came wouldn't recognize it as a double. He lit a cigarette. Nowadays he was trying to keep to twenty and failing by about five. He stabbed the cigarette out. He was getting near to his target and the rigid training rules that had been drilled into him at The Park must from now on be observed meticulously. The champagne wouldn't count. He was amused by the conscience this girl had awakened in him. He was also surprised and impressed.

Mary Goodnight knew that the last question was the one he would want answered first. She reached into a plain straw handbag on a gold metal chain and handed him a thick envelope. She said, 'Mostly in used singles. A few fivers. Shall I debit you direct or put it in as expenses?'

'Direct, please.'

'The car's outside. You remember Strangways? Well it's his old Sunbeam Alpine. The Station bought it and now I use it. The tank's full and it goes like a bird. The top man at Frome is a man called Tony Hugill. Ex-navy. Nice man. Nice wife. Nice children. Does a good job. Has a lot of trouble with cane burning and other small sabotage – mostly with thermite bombs brought in from Cuba. Cuba's sugar crop is Jamaica's chief rival and with Hurricane Flora and all the rains they've been having over there, the Cuban crop is going to be only about three million tons this year, compared with a Batista level of about seven, and very late, because the rains have played havoc with the sucrose content.' She smiled her wide smile. 'No secrets. Just reading the *Gleaner*. So it's worth Castro's trouble to try and keep the world price up by doing as much damage as he can to rival crops so that he's in a better position to bargain with Russia. He's only got his sugar to sell and he wants food badly. This wheat the Americans are selling to Russia. A lot of that will find its way back to Cuba, in exchange for sugar, to feed the Cuban sugar croppers.' She smiled again. 'Pretty daft business, isn't it? I don't think Castro can hold out much longer. The missile business in Cuba must have cost Russia about a billion pounds. And now they're having to pour money into Cuba, money and goods, to keep the place on its feet. I can't help thinking they'll pull out soon and leave Castro to go the way Batista went. It's a fiercely Catholic country and Hurricane Flora was considered as the final judgment from heaven. It sat over the island and simply whipped it, day after day, for five days. No hurricane in history has ever behaved like that. The churchgoers don't miss an omen like that. It was a straight indictment of the regime.'

Bond said with admiration, 'Goodnight, you're a treasure. You've certainly been doing your homework.'

The direct blue eyes looked straight into his, dodging the compliment. 'This is the stuff I live with here. It's built into the Station. But I thought you might like some background to Frome and what I've said explains why WISCO are getting these cane fires. At least we think it is. Apparently there's a tremendous chess game going on all over the world in sugar – in what they call sugar futures, that's sort of buying the stuff forward for delivery dates later in the year. Washington's trying to keep the price down, to upset Cuba's economy, but there's increased world consumption and a shortage largely due to Flora and the tremendous rains we've been having here after Flora which have delayed the Jamaican crop. I don't understand it all, but it's in Cuba's interest to do as much damage as possible to the Jamaican crop and this place Frome you're interested in produces about a quarter of Jamaica's total output.' She took a sip at her drink. 'Well, that's all about sugar. The top man there is this man Hugill. We've had a lot to do with him, so he'll be friendly. He was in Naval Intelligence during the war, sort of commando job, so he knows the score. The car's a bit aged but it's still pretty fast and it won't let you down. It's rather bashed about so it won't be conspicuous. I've put the survey map in the glove compartment.'

'That's fine. Now, last question and then we'll go and have dinner and tell each other our life stories. But, by the way, what's happened to your chief, Ross?'

Mary Goodnight looked worried. 'To tell you the truth, I don't exactly know. He went off last week on some job to Trinidad. It was to try and locate a man called Scaramanga. He's a local gunman of some sort. I don't know much about him. Apparently Headquarters want him traced for some reason.' She smiled ruefully. 'Nobody ever tells me anything that's interesting. I just do the donkey work. Well, Commander Ross was due back two days ago and he hasn't turned up. I've had to send off a Red Warning, but I've been told to give him another week.'

'Well, I'm glad he's out of the way. I'd rather have his Number Two. Last question. What about this 3½ Love Lane? Did you get anywhere?'

Mary Goodnight blushed. 'Did I not! That was a fine question to get me mixed up with. Alexander's were non-committal and I finally had to go to the Special Branch. I shan't be able to show my face there for weeks. Heaven knows what they must think of you. That place is a, is a, er –' She wrinkled her nose. 'It's a famous disorderly house in Sav' La Mar.'

Bond laughed out loud at her discomfiture. He teased her with malicious but gentle sadism. 'You mean it's a whorehouse?'

'James! For heaven's sake! Must you be so crude?'

5 . . . . NO. 3½ LOVE LANE

THE SOUTH coast of Jamaica is not as beautiful as the north, and it is a long 120-mile hack over very mixed road surfaces from Kingston to Savannah La Mar. Mary Goodnight had insisted on coming along, 'to navigate and help with the punctures'. Bond had not demurred.

Spanish Town, May Pen, Alligator Pond, Black River, Whitehouse Inn, where they had luncheon – the miles unrolled under the fierce sun until, around four in the afternoon, a stretch of good straight road brought them among the spruce little villas, each with its patch of brownish lawn, bougainvillaea, and single bed of canna lilies and crotons, which make up the 'smart' suburbs of the modest little coastal township that is, in the vernacular, Sav' La Mar.

Except for the old quarter on the waterfront, it is not a typically Jamaican town, nor a very attractive one. The villas, built for the senior staff of the Frome sugar estates, are drably respectable, and the small straight streets smack of a most un-Jamaican bout of town planning around the 1920s. Bond stopped at the first garage, took in petrol and put Mary Goodnight into a hired car for the return trip. He had told her nothing of his assignment and she had asked no questions when Bond told her vaguely that it was 'something to do with Cuba'. Bond said he would keep in touch when he could, and get back to her when his job was done and then, businesslike, she was off back down the dusty road and Bond drove slowly down to the waterfront. He identified Love Lane, a narrow street of broken-down shops and houses that meandered back into the town from the jetty. He circled the area to get the neighbouring geography clear in his mind and parked the car in a deserted area near the spit of sand on which fishing canoes were drawn up on raised stilts. He locked the car and sauntered back and into Love Lane. There were a few people about, poor people of the fisherman class. Bond bought a packet of Royal Blend at a small general store that smelled of spices. He asked where No. 3½ was and got a look of polite curiosity. 'Further up de street. Mebbe a chain. Big house on de right.' Bond moved over to the shady side and strolled on. He slit open the packet with his thumbnail and lit a cigarette to help the picture of an idle tourist examining a corner of old Jamaica. There was only one big house on the right. He took some time lighting the cigarette while he examined it.

It must once have had importance, perhaps as the private house of a merchant. It was of two storeys with balconies running all the way round and it was wooden built with silvering shingles, but the gingerbread tracery beneath the eaves was broken in many places and there was hardly a scrap of paint left on the jalousies that closed off all the upstairs windows and most of those below. The patch of 'yard' bordering the street was inhabited by a clutch of vulturine-necked chickens that pecked at nothing and three skeletal Jamaican black-and-tan mongrels. They gazed lazily across the street at Bond and scratched and bit at invisible flies. But, in the background, there was one very beautiful *lignum vitae* tree in full blue blossom. Bond guessed that it was as old as the house – perhaps fifty years. It certainly owned the property by right of strength and adornment. In its delicious black shade a girl in a rocking chair sat reading a magazine. At the range of about thirty yards she looked tidy and pretty. Bond strolled up the opposite side of the street until a corner of the house hid the girl. Then he stopped and examined the house more closely.

Wooden steps ran up to an open front door, over whose lintel, whereas few of the other buildings in the street bore numbers, a big enamelled metal sign announced '3½' in white on dark blue. Of the two broad windows that bracketed the door, the left-hand one was shuttered, but the right-hand one was a single broad sheet of rather dusty glass through which tables and chairs and a serving-counter could be seen. Over the door a swinging sign said 'Dreamland Cafe' in sun-bleached letters, and round this window were advertisements for Red Stripe beer, Royal Blend, Four Aces cigarettes and Coca-Cola. A hand-painted sign said 'SNAX' and, underneath, 'Hot Cock Soup Fresh Daily'.

Bond walked across the street and up the steps and parted the bead curtain that hung over the entrance. He walked over to the counter and was inspecting its contents, a plate of dry-looking ginger cakes, a pile of packeted banana crisps, and some sweet jars, when he heard quick steps outside. The girl from the garden came in. The beads clashed softly behind her. She was an octoroon, pretty as, in Bond's imagination, the word octoroon suggested. She had bold, brown eyes, slightly uptilted at the corners, beneath a fringe of silken black hair. (Bond reflected that there would be Chinese blood somewhere in her past.) She was dressed in a short frock of shocking pink which went well with the coffee and cream of her skin. Her wrists and ankles were tiny. She smiled politely. The eyes flirted. 'Evenin'.'

'Good evening. Could I have a Red Stripe?'

'Sure.' She went behind the counter. She gave him a quick glimpse of fine bosoms as she bent to the door of the icebox – a glimpse not dictated by the geography of the place. She nudged the door shut with a knee, deftly uncapped the bottle and put it on the counter beside an almost clean glass. 'That'll be one and six.'

Bond paid. She rang the money into the cash register. Bond drew up a stool to the counter and sat down. She rested her arms on the wooden top and looked across at him. 'Passing through?'

'More or less. I saw this place was for sale in yesterday's *Gleaner*. I thought I'd take a look at it. Nice big house. Does it belong to you?'

She laughed. It was a pity, because she was a pretty girl, but the teeth had been sharpened by munching raw sugar cane. 'What a hope! I'm sort of, well sort of manager. There's the café' (she pronounced it caif) 'and mebbe you heard we got other attractions.'

Bond looked puzzled. 'What sort?'

'Girls. Six bedrooms upstairs. Very clean. It only cost a pound. There's Sarah up there now. Care to meet up with her?'

'Not today, thanks. It's too hot. But do you only have one at a time?'

'There's Lindy, but she's engaged. She's a big girl. If you like them big, she'll be free in half an hour.' She glanced at the kitchen clock on the wall behind her. 'Around six o'clock. It'll be cooler then.'

'I prefer girls like you. What's your name?'

She giggled. 'I only do it for love. I told you I just manage the place. They call me Tiffy.'

'That's an unusual name. How did you come by it?'

'My momma had six girls. Called them all after flowers. Violet, Rose, Cherry, Pansy and Lily. Then when I came, she couldn't think of any more flower names so she called me "Artificial".'

48

Tiffy waited for him to laugh. When he didn't, she went on. 'When I went to school they all said it was a wrong name and laughed at me and shortened it to Tiffy and that's how I've stayed.'

'Well, I think it's a very pretty name. My name's Mark.'

She flirted. 'You a saint too?'

'No one's ever accused me of it. I've been up at Frome doing a job. I like this part of the island and it crossed my mind to find some place to rent. But I want to be closer to the sea than this. I'll have to look around a bit more. Do you rent rooms by the night?'

She reflected. 'Sure. Why not. But you may find it a bit noisy. There's sometimes a customer who's taken some drinks too many. And there's not too much plumbing.' She leaned closer and lowered her voice. 'But I wouldn't have advised you to rent the place. The shingles are in bad shape. Cost you mebbe five hunnerd, mebbe a thousand to get the roof done.'

'It's nice of you to tell me that. But why's the place being sold? Trouble with the police?'

'Not so much. We operate a respectable place. But in the *Gleaner*, after Mr Brown, that's my boss, you read that "*et ux*"?'

'Yes.'

'Well, seems that means "and his wife". And Mistress Brown, Mistress Agatha Brown, she was Church of England, but she just done gone to the Catholics. And it seems they don't hold with places like 3½, not even when they're decently run. And their church here, just up the street, seems that needs a new roof like here. So Mistress Brown figures to kill two birds with the same stone and she goes on at Mr Brown to close the place down and sell it and with her portion she goin' fix the roof for the Catholics.'

'That's a shame. It seems a nice quiet place. What's going to happen to you?'

'Guess I'll move to Kingston. Live with one of my sisters and mebbe work in one of the big stores – Issa's mebbe, or Nathan's.

Sav' La Mar is sort of quiet.' The brown eyes became introspective. 'But I'll sure miss the place. Folks have fun here and Love Lane's a pretty street. We're all friends up and down the Lane. It's got sort of, sort of ...'

'Atmosphere.'

'Right. That's what it's got. Like sort of old Jamaica. Like it must have been in the old days. Everyone's friends with each other. Help each other when they have trouble.

You'd be surprised how often the girls do it for free if the man's a good feller, regular customer sort of, and he's short.' The brown eyes gazed inquiringly at Bond to see if he understood the strength of the evidence.

'That's nice of them. But it can't be good for business.'

She laughed. 'This ain't no business, Mister Mark. Not while I'm running it. This is a public service, like water and electricity and health and education and ...' She broke off and glanced over her shoulder at the clock which said 5.45. 'Hell! You got me talking so much I've forgot Joe and May. It's their supper.' She went to the café window and wound it down. At once, from the direction of the *lignum vitae* tree, two large black birds, slightly smaller than a raven, whirled in, circled the interior of the café amidst a metallic clangour of song unlike the song of any other bird in the world, and untidily landed on the counter within reach of Bond's hand. They strutted up and down imperiously, eyeing Bond without fear from bold, golden eyes and went through a piercing repertoire of tinny whistles and trills, some of which required them to ruffle themselves up to almost twice their normal size.

Tiffy went back behind the bar, took two pennies out of her purse, rang them up on the register and took two ginger cakes out of the flyblown display case. She broke off bits and fed the two birds, always the smaller of the two, the female, first, and they greedily seized the pieces from her fingers, and, holding the scraps to the wooden counter with a claw, tore them into smaller fragments and devoured them. When it was all over, and Tiffy had chided them both for pecking her fingers, they made small, neat white messes on the counter and looked pleased with themselves. Tiffy took a cloth and cleaned up the messes. She said, 'We call them kling-klings but learned folk call them Jamaican grackles. They're very friendly folk. The Doctor Bird, the humming bird with the streamer tail, is the Jamaican national bird, but I like these best. They're not so beautiful, but they're the friendliest birds and they're funny besides. They seem to know it. They're like naughty black thieves.' The kling-klings eyed the cake stand and complained stridently that their supper was over. James Bond produced twopence and handed it over. 'They're wonderful. Like mechanical toys. Give them a second course from me.'

Tiffy rang up the money and took out two more cakes. 'Now listen, Joe and May. This nice gemmun's been nice to Tiffy and he's now being nice to you. So don't you peck my fingers and make messes or mebbe he won't visit us again.' She was half-way through feeding the birds when she cocked an ear. There was the noise of creaking boards somewhere overhead and then the sound of quiet footsteps treading stairs. All of a sudden Tiffy's animated face became quiet and tense. She whispered to Bond: 'That's Lindy's man. Important man. He's a good customer here. But he don't like me because I won't go with him. So he can talk rough sometimes. And he don't like Joe and May because he reckons they make too much noise.' She shooed the birds in the direction of the open window, but they saw there was half their cake to come and they just fluttered into the air and then down to the counter again. Tiffy appealed to Bond. 'Be a good friend and just sit quiet whatever he says. He likes to get people mad. And then ...' She stopped. 'Will you have another Red Stripe, mister?'

Bead curtains swished in the shadowy back of the room.

Bond had been sitting with his chin propped on his right hand. He now dropped the hand to the counter and sat back. The Walther PPK inside the waistband of his trousers to the left of his flat stomach signalled its presence to his skin. The fingers of his right hand curled slightly, ready to receive its butt. He moved his left foot off the rail of the stool on to the floor. He said, 'That'd be fine.' He unbuttoned his coat with his left hand and then, with the same hand, took out his handkerchief and wiped his face with it. 'It always gets extra hot around six before the Undertaker's Wind has started to blow.'

'Mister, the undertaker's right here. You care to feel his wind?'

James Bond turned his head slowly. Dusk had crept into the big room and all he could see was a pale, tall outline. The man was carrying a suitcase. He put it down on the floor and came forward. He must have been wearing rubber-soled shoes for his feet made no sound. Tiffy moved nervously behind the counter and a switch clicked. Half a dozen low-voltage bulbs came to life in rusty brackets around the walls.

Bond said easily, 'You made me jump.'

Scaramanga came up and leant against the counter. The description in Records was exact, but it had not caught the cat-like menace of the big man, the extreme breadth of the shoulders and the narrow waist, or the cold immobility of the eyes that now examined Bond with an expression of aloof disinterest. He was wearing a well-cut, single-breasted tan suit and 'co-respondent' shoes in brown and white. Instead of a tie, he wore a high stock in white silk secured by a gold pin the shape of a miniature pistol. There should have been something theatrical about the get-up but, perhaps because of the man's fine figure, there wasn't.

He said, 'I sometimes make 'em dance. Then I shoot their feet off.' There was no trace of a foreign accent underneath the American.

Bond said, 'That sounds rather drastic. What do you do it for?'

'The last time it was five thousand dollars. Seems like you don't know who I am. Didn't the cool cat tell you?'

Bond glanced at Tiffy. She was standing very still, her hands by her sides. The knuckles were white.

Bond said, 'Why should she? Why would I want to know?'

There was a quick flash of gold. The small black hole looked directly at Bond's navel. 'Because of this. What are you doing here, stranger? Kind of a coincidence finding a city slicker at 3½. Or at Sav' La Mar for the matter of that. Not by any chance from the police? Or any of their friends?'

'Kamerad!' Bond raised his hands in mock surrender. He lowered them and turned to Tiffy. 'Who is this man? A one-man takeover bid for Jamaica? Or a refugee from a circus? Ask him what he'd like to drink. Whoever he is, it was a good act.' James Bond knew that he had very nearly pulled the trigger of the gun. Hit a gunman in his vanity … He had a quick vision of himself writhing on the floor, his right hand without the power to reach for his own weapon. Tiffy's pretty face was no longer pretty. It was a taut skull. She stared at James Bond. Her mouth opened but no sound came from the gaping lips. She liked him and she knew he was dead. The kling-klings, Joe and May, smelled the same electricity. With a tremendous din of metallic squawks, they fled for the open window like black thieves escaping into the night.

The explosions from the Colt .45 were deafening. The two birds disintegrated against the violet back-drop of the dusk, the scraps of feathers and pink flesh blasting out of the yellow light of the café into the limbo of the deserted street like shrapnel.

There was a moment of deafening silence. James Bond didn't move. He sat where he was, waiting for the tension of the deed to relax. It didn't. With an inarticulate scream, that was half a filthy word, Tiffy took James Bond's bottle of Red Stripe off the counter and clumsily flung it. There came a distant crash of glass from the back of the room. Then, having made her puny gesture, Tiffy fell to her knees behind the counter and went into sobbing hysterics.

James Bond drank down the rest of his beer and got slowly to his feet. He walked towards Scaramanga and was about to pass him when the man reached out a languid left arm and caught him at the biceps. He held the snout of his gun to his nose, sniffing delicately. The expression in the dead brown eyes was far-away. He said, 'Mister, there's something quite extra about the smell of death. Care to try it?' He held out the glittering gun as if he was offering James Bond a rose.

Bond stood quite still. He said, 'Mind your manners. Take your hand off me.'

Scaramanga raised his eyebrows. The flat, leaden gaze seemed to take in Bond for the first time.

He released his grip.

James Bond went on round the edge of the counter. When he came opposite the other man, he found the eyes were now looking at him with faint, scornful curiosity. Bond stopped. The sobbing of the girl was the crying of a small dog. Somewhere down the street a 'Sound System' – a loudspeaker record player – began braying calypso.

Bond looked the man in the eye. He said, 'Thanks. I've tried it. I recommend the Berlin vintage. 1945.' He smiled a friendly, only slightly ironical smile. 'But I expect you were too young to be at that tasting.'

6 . . . . THE EASY GRAND

BOND KNELT down beside Tiffy and gave her a couple of sharp slaps on the right cheek. Then on the left. The wet eyes came back into focus. She put her hand up to her face and looked at Bond with surprise. Bond got to his feet. He took a cloth and wetted it at the tap, then leant down and put his arm round her and wiped the cloth gently over her face. Then he lifted her up and handed her her bag that was on a shelf behind the counter. He said, 'Come on, Tiffy. Make up that pretty face again. Business'll be warming up soon. The leading lady's got to look her best.'

Tiffy took the bag and opened it. She looked past Bond and saw Scaramanga for the first time since the shooting. The pretty lips drew back in a snarl. She whispered fiercely so that only Bond could hear, 'I'm goin' fix that man, but good. There's Mother Edna up Orange Hill way. She's an obeah top woman. I'll go up there tomorrow. Come a few days, he won't know what hit him.' She took out a mirror and began doing up her face. Bond reached into his hip pocket and counted out five one-pound notes. He stuffed them into her open bag.

'You forget all about it. This'll buy you a nice canary in a cage to keep you company. Anyway, another pair of klings'll come along if you put some food out.' He patted her shoulder and moved away. When he came up with Scaramanga he stopped and said, 'That may have been a good circus act' (he used the word again on purpose) 'but it was rough on the girl. Give her some money.'

Scaramanga said, 'Shove it,' out of the corner of his mouth. He said suspiciously, 'And what's all this yack about circuses?' He turned to face Bond. 'Just stop where you are, Mister, and answer a few questions. Like I said, are you from the police? You've sure got the smell of cops around you. If not, what are you doing hereabouts?'

Bond said, 'People don't tell me what to do. I tell them.' He walked on into the middle of the room and sat down at a table. He said, 'Come and sit down and stop trying to lean on me. I'm unleanable-on.'

Scaramanga shrugged. He took two long strides, picked up one of the metal chairs, twirled it round and thrust it between his legs and sat bassackwards, his left arm lying along the back of the chair. His right arm rested on his thigh, inches from the ivory pistol butt that showed above the waistband of his trousers. Bond recognized that it was a good working position for a gunman, the metal back of the chair acting as a shield for most of the body. This was certainly a most careful and professional man.

Bond, both hands in full view on the table top, said cheerfully, 'No. I'm not from the police. My name's Mark Hazard. I'm from a company called "Transworld Consortium". I've been doing a job at Frome, the WISCO sugar place. Know it?'

'Sure I know it. What you been doing there?'

'Not so fast, my friend. First of all, who are you and what's your business?'

'Scaramanga. Francisco Scaramanga. Labour relations. Ever heard of me?'

Bond frowned. 'Can't say I have? Should I have?'

'Some people who hadn't are dead.'

'A lot of people who haven't heard of me are dead.' Bond leaned back. He crossed one leg over the other, above the knee, and grasped the ankle in a clubman pose. 'I do wish you'd stop talking in heroics. For instance, seven hundred million Chinese have certainly heard of neither of us. You must be a frog in a very small pool.'

Scaramanga did not rise to the jibe. He said reflectively, 'Yeah. I guess you could call the Caribbean a pretty small pool. But there's good pickin's to be had from it. "The man with the golden gun." That's what they call me in these parts.'

'It's a handy tool for solving labour problems. We could do with you up at Frome.'

'Been having trouble up there?' Scaramanga looked bored.

'Too many cane fires.'

'Was that your business?'

'Sort of. One of the jobs of my company is insurance investigation.'

'Security work. I've come across guys like you before. Thought I could smell the cop-smell.' Scaramanga looked satisfied that his guess had been right. 'Did you get anywhere?'

'Picked up a few Rastafari. I'd have liked to get rid of the lot of them. But they went crying to their union that they were being discriminated against because of their religion so we had to call a halt. So the fires'll begin again soon. That's why I say we could do with a good enforcer up there.' Bond added blandly, 'I take it that's another name for your profession?'

Again Scaramanga dodged the sneer. He said, 'You carry a gun?'

'Of course. You don't go after the Rastas without one.'

'What kind of a gun?'

'Walther PPK. 7.65 millimetre.'

'Yes, that's a stopper all right.' Scaramanga turned towards the counter. 'Hey, cool cat. Couple of Red Stripes, if you're in business again.' He turned back and the blank eyes looked hard at Bond. 'What's your next job?'

'Don't know. I'll have to contact London and find out if they've got any other problems in the area. But I'm in no hurry. I work for them more or less on a freelance basis. Why? Any suggestions?'

The other man sat quiet while Tiffy came out from behind the counter. She came over to the table and placed the tin tray with the bottles and glasses in front of Bond. She didn't look at Scaramanga. Scaramanga uttered a harsh bark of laughter. He reached inside his coat and took out an alligator-skin billfold. He extracted a hundred-dollar bill and threw it on the table. 'No hard feelings, cool cat. You'd be okay if you didn't always keep your legs together. Go buy yourself some more birds with that. I like to have smiling people around me.'

Tiffy picked up the note. She said, 'Thanks, Mister. You'd be surprised what I'm going to spend your money on.' She gave him a long, hard look and turned on her heel.

Scaramanga shrugged. He reached for a bottle of beer and a glass and both men poured and drank. Scaramanga took out an expensive cigar case, selected a pencil-thin cheroot and lit it with a match. He let the smoke dribble out between his lips and inhaled the thin stream up his nostrils. He did this several times with the same mouthful of smoke until the smoke was dissipated. All the while he stared across the table at Bond, seeming to weigh up something in his mind. He said, 'Care to earn yourself a grand – a thousand bucks?'

Bond said, 'Possibly.' He paused and added, 'Probably.' What he meant was, 'Of course! If it means staying close to you, my friend.'

Scaramanga smoked a while in silence. A car stopped outside and two laughing men came quickly up the steps. When they came through the bead curtains, working-class Jamaicans, they stopped laughing and went quietly over to the counter and began whispering to Tiffy. Then they both slapped a pound note on the counter and, making a wide detour away from the white men, disappeared through the curtains at the back of the room. Their laughter began again as Bond heard their footsteps on the stairs.

Scaramanga hadn't taken his eyes from Bond's face. Now he said, keeping his voice low, 'I got myself a problem. Some partners of mine, they've taken an interest in this Negril development. Far end of the property. Place called Bloody Bay. Know it?'

'I've seen it on the map. Just short of Green Island Harbour.'

'Right. So I've got some shares in the business. So we start building a hotel and get the first storey finished and the main living-rooms and restaurant and so on. So then the tourist boom slackens off – Americans get frightened of being so close to Cuba or some such crap. And the banks get difficult and money begins to run short. Follow me?'

'So you're a stale bull of the place?'

'Right. So I came over a few days ago and I'm staying at the Thunderbird and I've got a half-dozen of the main stockholders to fly in for a meeting on the spot. Sort of look the place over and get our heads together and figure what to do next. Now, I want to give these guys a good time so I've got a smart combo over from Kingston, calypso singers, limbo, plenty of girls – all that jazz. And there's swimming and one of the features of the place is a small-scale railway that used to handle the sugar cane. Runs to Green Island Harbour where I gotta forty-foot Chris-Craft Roamer. Deep-sea fishing. That'll be another outing. Get me? Give the fellers a real good time.'

'So that they'll get all enthusiastic and buy out your share of the stock?'

Scaramanga frowned angrily. 'I'm not paying you a grand to get the wrong ideas. Or any ideas for the matter of that.'

'What for then?'

For a moment or two Scaramanga went through his smoking routine, the little pillars of smoke vanishing again and again into the black nostrils. It seemed to calm him. His forehead cleared. He said, 'Some of these men are kind of rough. We're all stock-holders, of course, but that don't necessarily mean we're friends. Understand? I'll be wanting to hold some meetings, private meetings, with mebbe only two or three guys at a time, sort of sounding out the different interests. Could be that some of the other guys, the ones not invited to a particular meeting, might get it into their heads to bug a meeting or try and get wise to what goes on in one way or another. So it jes' occurs to me that you being live to security and such, that you could act as a kind of guard at these meetings, clean the room for mikes, stay outside the door and see that no one comes nosing around, see that when I want to be private I git private. D'you get the photo?'

Bond had to laugh. He said, 'So you want to hire me as a kind of personal bodyguard. Is that it?'

The frown was back. 'And what's so funny about that, Mister? It's good money, ain't it? Three, mebbe four days in a luxury joint like the Thunderbird. A thousand bucks at the end of it? What's so screwy about that proposition, eh?' Scaramanga mashed out the butt of his cigar against the underside of the table. A shower of sparks fell. He let them lie.

Bond scratched the back of his head as if reflecting. Which he was – furiously. He knew that he hadn't heard the full story. He also knew that it was odd, to say the least of it, for this man to hire a complete stranger to do this job for him. The job itself stood up, but only just. It made sense that Scaramanga would not want to hire a local man, an ex-policeman for instance, even if one could be found. Such a man might have friends in the hotel business who would be interested in the speculative side of the Negril development. And, of course, on the plus side, Bond would be achieving what he had never thought possible – he would have got right inside Scaramanga's guard. Or would he? There was the strong smell of a trap. But, assuming that Bond had not, by some obscure bit of ill luck, been blown, he couldn't for the life of him see what the trap could be. Well, clearly, he must make the gamble. In so many respects it was a chance in a million.

Bond lit a cigarette. He said, 'I was only laughing at the idea of a man of your particular skills wanting protection. But it all sounds great fun. Of course I'll come along. When do we start? I've got a car at the bottom of the road.'

Scaramanga thrust out an inside wrist and looked at a thin gold watch on a two-coloured gold bracelet. He said, '6.32. My car'll be outside.' He got up. 'Let's go. But don't forget one thing, Mister Whoosis. I rile mighty easy. Get me?'

Bond said easily, 'I saw how annoyed you got with those inoffensive birds.' He stood up. 'I don't see any reason why either of us should get riled.'

Scaramanga said indifferently, 'Okay, then.' He walked to the back of the room and picked up his suitcase, new-looking but cheap, strode to the exit and clashed through the bead curtain and down the steps.

Bond went quickly over to the counter. 'Goodbye, Tiffy. Hope I'll be coming by again one day. If anyone should ask after me, say I'm at the Thunderbird Hotel at Bloody Bay.'

Tiffy reached out a hand and timidly touched his sleeve. 'Go careful over there, Mister Mark. There's gangster money in that place. And watch out for yourself.' She jerked her head towards the exit: 'That's the worstest man I ever heard tell of.' She leaned forward and whispered, 'That's a thousand pound worth of ganja he's got in that bag. Rasta left it for him this morning. So I smelled the bag.' She drew quickly back.

Bond said, 'Thanks, Tiffy. See Mother Edna puts a good hex on him. I'll tell you why some day. I hope. 'Bye!' He went quickly out and down into the street where a red Thunderbird convertible was waiting, its exhaust making a noise like an expensive motor-boat. The chauffeur was a Jamaican, smartly dressed, with a peaked cap. A red pennant on the wireless aerial said 'The Thunderbird Hotel' in gold. Scaramanga was sitting beside the chauffeur. He said impatiently, 'Get in the back. Lift you down to your car. Then follow along. It gets a good road after a while.'

James Bond got into the car behind Scaramanga and wondered whether to shoot the man now, in the back of the head – the old Gestapo-K.G.B. point of puncture. A mixture of reasons prevented him – the itch of curiosity, an inbuilt dislike of cold murder, the feeling that this was not the predestined moment, the likelihood that he would have to murder the chauffeur also – these, combined with the softness of the night and the fact that the 'Sound System' was now playing a good recording of one of his favourites, 'After You've Gone', and that cicadas were singing from the *lignum vitae* tree, said 'No'. But at that moment, as the car coasted down Love Lane towards the bright mercury of the sea, James Bond knew that he was not only disobeying orders, or at best dodging them, he was also being a bloody fool.

7 .... UN-REAL ESTATE

WHEN HE arrives at a place on a dark night, particularly in an alien land which he has never seen before – a strange house, perhaps, or an hotel – even the most alert man is assailed by the confused sensations of the meanest tourist.

James Bond more or less knew the map of Jamaica. He knew that the sea had always been close to him on his left and, as he followed the twin red glares of the leading car through an impressive entrance gate of wrought iron and up an avenue of young Royal palms, he heard the waves scrolling into a beach very close to his car. The fields of sugar cane would, he guessed from the approach, come close up against the new high wall that surrounded the Thunderbird property, and there was a slight smell of mangrove swamp coming down from below the high hills whose silhouette he had occasionally glimpsed under a scudding three-quarter moon on his right. But otherwise he had no clue to exactly where he was or what sort of place he was now approaching and, particularly for him, the sensation was an uncomfortable one.

The first law for a secret agent is to get his geography right, his means of access and exit, and assure his communications with the outside world. James Bond was uncomfortably aware that, for the past hour, he had been driving into limbo and that his nearest contact was a girl in a brothel thirty miles away. The situation was not reassuring.

Half a mile ahead, someone must have seen the approaching lights of the leading car and pressed switches, for there was a sudden blaze of brilliant yellow illumination through the trees and a final sweep of the drive revealed the hotel. With the theatrical lighting and the surrounding blackness to conceal any evidence of halted construction work, the place made a brave show. A vast pale-pink-and-white pillared portico gave the hotel an aristocratic frontage and, when Bond drew up behind the other car at the entrance, he could see through the tall Regency windows a vista of black-and-white marble flooring beneath blazing chandeliers. A bell captain and his Jamaican staff in red jackets and black trousers hurried down the steps and, after showing great deference to Scaramanga, took his suitcase and Bond's, then the small cavalcade moved into the entrance hall where Bond wrote 'Mark Hazard' and the Kensington address of Transworld Consortium in the register.

Scaramanga had been talking to a man who appeared to be the manager, a young American with a neat face and a neat suit. He turned to Bond. 'You're in Number 24 in the West Wing. I'm close by in Number 20. Order what you want from Room Service. See you about ten in the morning. The guys'll be coming in from Kingston around midday. Okay?' The cold eyes in the gaunt face didn't mind whether it was or not. Bond said it was. He followed one of the bell boys with his suitcase across the slippery marble floor and through an archway on the left of the hall and down a long white corridor with a close-fitted carpet in royal blue Wilton.

There was a smell of new paint and Jamaican cedar. The numbered doors and the light fittings were in good taste. Bond's room was almost at the end on the left. No. 20 was opposite. The bell hop unlocked No. 24 and held the door for Bond. Air-conditioned air gushed out. It was a pleasant modern double bedroom and bath in grey and white. When he was alone, Bond went to the air-conditioning control and turned it to zero. Then he threw back the curtains and wound down the two broad windows to let in real air. Outside, the sea whispered softly on an invisible beach and the moonlight splashed the black shadows of palms across trim lawns. To his left, where the yellow light of the entrance showed a corner of the gravel sweep, Bond heard his car being started up and driven away, presumably to a parking lot which would, he guessed, be at the rear so as not to spoil the impact of the façade. He turned back into his room and inspected it minutely. The only objects of suspicion were a large picture on the wall above the two beds and the telephone. The picture was a Jamaican market scene painted locally. Bond lifted it off its nail, but the wall behind was innocent. He then took out a pocket knife, laid the telephone carefully, so as not to shift the receiver, upside down on a bed, and very quietly and carefully unscrewed the bottom plate. He smiled his satisfaction. Behind the plate was a small microphone joined by leads to the main cable inside the cradle. He screwed back the plate with the same care and put the telephone quietly back on the night table. He knew the gadget. It would be transistorized and of sufficient power to pick up a conversation in normal tones anywhere in the room. It crossed his mind to say very devout prayers out loud before he went to bed. That would be a fitting prologue for the central recording device!

James Bond unpacked his few belongings and called Room Service. A Jamaican voice answered. Bond ordered a bottle of Walker's de Luxe Bourbon, three glasses, ice and, for nine o'clock,

Eggs Benedict. The voice said, 'Sure, sir.' Bond then took off his clothes, put his gun and holster under a pillow, rang for the valet and had his suit taken away to be pressed. By the time he had taken a hot shower followed by an ice-cold one and pulled on a fresh pair of Sea Island cotton underpants the bourbon had arrived.

The best drink in the day is just before the first one (the Red Stripe didn't count). James Bond put ice in the glass and three fingers of the bourbon and swilled it round the glass to cool it and break it down with the ice. He pulled a chair up to the window, put a low table beside it, took *Profiles in Courage* by Jack Kennedy out of his suitcase, happened to open it at Edmund G. Ross ('I looked down into my open grave'), then went and sat down, letting the scented air, a compound of sea and trees, breathe over his body, naked save for the underpants. He drank the bourbon down in two long draughts and felt its friendly bite at the back of his throat and in his stomach. He filled up his glass again, this time with more ice to make it a weaker drink, and sat back and thought about Scaramanga.

What was the man doing now? Talking long distance with Havana or the States? Organizing things for tomorrow? It would be interesting to see these fat, frightened stockholders! If Bond knew anything, they would be a choice bunch of hoods, the type that had owned the Havana hotels and casinos in the old Batista days, the men that held the stock in Las Vegas, that looked after the action in Miami. And whose money was Scaramanga representing? There was so much hot money drifting around the Caribbean that it might be any of the syndicates, any of the banana dictators from the islands or the mainland. And the man himself? It had been damned fine shooting that had killed the two birds swerving through the window of 3½. How in hell was Bond going to take him? On an impulse, Bond went over to his bed and took the Walther from under the pillow. He slipped out the magazine and pumped the single round on to the counterpane. He tested the spring of the magazine and of the breech and drew a quick bead on various objects round the room. He found he was aiming an inch or so high. But that would be because the gun was lighter without its loaded magazine. He snapped the magazine back and tried again. Yes, that was better. He pumped a round into the breech, put up the safety and replaced the gun under the pillow. Then he went back to his drink and picked up the book and forgot his worries in the high endeavours of great men.

The eggs came and were good. The mousseline sauce might have been mixed at Maxim's. Bond had the tray removed, poured himself a last drink and prepared for bed. Scaramanga would certainly have a master key. Tomorrow, Bond would whittle himself a wedge to jam the door. For tonight, he up-ended his suitcase just inside the door and balanced the three glasses on top of it. It was a simple booby trap but it would give him all the warning he needed. Then he took off his shorts and got into bed and slept.

A nightmare woke him, sweating, around two in the morning. He had been defending a fort. There were other defenders with him, but they seemed to be wandering around aimlessly, ineffectively, and when Bond shouted to rally them they seemed not to hear him. Out on the plain, Scaramanga sat bassackwards on the café chair beside a huge golden cannon. Every now and then, he put his long cigar to the touch-hole and there came a tremendous flash of soundless flame. A black cannon ball, as big as a football, lobbed up high in the air and crashed down into the fort with a shattering noise of breaking timber. Bond was armed with nothing but a longbow, but even this he could not fire because, every time he tried to fit the notch of the arrow into the gut, the arrow slipped out of his fingers to the ground. He cursed his clumsiness. Any moment now and a huge cannon ball would land on the small open space where he was standing! Out on the plain, Scaramanga reached his cigar to the touch-hole. The black ball soared up. It was coming straight for Bond! It landed just in front of him and came rolling very slowly towards him, getting bigger and bigger, smoke and sparks coming from its shortening fuse. Bond threw up an arm to protect himself. Painfully, the arm crashed into the side of the night table and Bond woke up.

Bond got out of bed, gave himself a cold shower and drank a glass of water. By the time he was back in bed, he had forgotten the nightmare and he went quickly to sleep and slept dreamlessly until 7.30 in the morning. He put on swimming trunks, removed the barricade from in front of the door and went out into the passage. To his left, a door into the garden was open and sun streamed in. He went out and was walking over the dewy grass towards the beach when he heard a curious thumping noise from among the palms on his right. He walked over. It was Scaramanga, in trunks, attended by a good-looking young Negro holding a flame-coloured Terry cloth robe, doing exercises on a trampoline. Scaramanga's body gleamed with sweat in the sunshine as he hurled himself high in the air from the stretched canvas and bounded back, sometimes from his knees or his buttocks and sometimes even from his head. It was an impressive exercise in gymnastics. The prominent third nipple over the heart made an obvious target! Bond walked thoughtfully down to the beautiful crescent of white sand fringed with gently clashing palm trees. He dived in and, because of the other man's example, swam twice as far as he had intended.

James Bond had a quick and small breakfast in his room, dressed, reluctantly because of the heat, in his dark suit, armed himself and went for a walk round the property. He quickly got the picture. The night, and the lighted façade, had covered up a half-project. The East Wing on the other side of the lobby was still lath and plaster. The body of the hotel – the restaurant, night club and living-rooms that were the tail of the T-shaped structure, were mock-ups – stages for a dress rehearsal hastily assembled with the essential props, carpets, light fixtures and a scattering of furniture, but stinking of fresh paint and wood shavings. Perhaps fifty men and women were at work, tacking up curtains, Hoovering carpets, fixing the electricity, but no one was employed on the essentials, the big cement mixers, the drills, the ironwork, that lay about behind the hotel like the abandoned toys of a giant. At a guess, the place would need another year and another five million dollars to become what the plans had said it was to be. Bond saw Scaramanga's problem. Someone was going to complain about this. Others would want to get out. But then again, others would want to buy in, but cheaply, and use it as a tax-loss to set against more profitable enterprises elsewhere. Better to have a capital asset, with the big tax concessions that Jamaica gave, than pay the money to Uncle Sam, Uncle Fidel, Uncle Trujillo, Uncle Leoni of Venezuela. So Scaramanga's job would be to blind his guests with pleasure, send them back half drunk to their syndicates. Would it work? Bond knew such people and he doubted it. They might go to bed drunk with a pretty coloured girl, but they would awake sober or they wouldn't have their jobs, they wouldn't be coming here with their discreet brief-cases.

He walked farther back on the property. He wanted to locate his car. He found it in a deserted lot behind the West Wing. The sun would get at it where it was so he drove it forward and into the shade of a giant ficus tree. He checked the petrol and pocketed the ignition key. There were not too many small precautions he could take.

On the parking lot, the smell of the swamps was very strong. While it was still comparatively cool, he decided to walk farther. He soon came to the end of the young shrubs and guinea grass the landscaper had laid on. Behind these was desolation – a great area of sluggish streams and swampland from which the hotel land had been recovered. Egrets, shrikes and Louisiana herons rose and settled lazily, and there were strange insect noises and the call of frogs and gekkos. On what would probably be the border of the property a biggish stream meandered towards the sea, its muddy banks pitted with the holes of land crabs and water rats. As Bond approached there was a heavy splash and a man-sized alligator left the bank and showed its snout before submerging. Bond smiled to himself. No doubt, if the hotel got off the ground, all this area would be turned into an asset. There would be native boatmen, suitably attired as Arawak Indians, a landing-stage and comfortable boats, with fringed shades, from which the guests could view the 'tropical jungle' for an extra ten dollars on the bill.

Bond glanced at his watch. He strolled back. To the left, not yet screened by the young oleanders and crotons that had been planted for this eventual purpose, were the kitchens and laundry and staff quarters, the usual back quarters of a luxury hotel, and music, the heartbeat thump of Jamaican calypso, came from their direction – presumably the Kingston combo rehearsing. Bond walked round and under the portico into the main lobby. Scaramanga was at the desk talking to the manager. When he heard Bond's footsteps on the marble, he turned and looked and gave Bond a curt nod. He was dressed as on the previous day, and the high white cravat suited the elegance of the hall. He said 'Okay, then' to the manager and, to Bond, 'Let's go take a look at the conference room.'

Bond followed him through the restaurant door and then through another door to the right that opened into a lobby, one of whose walls was taken up with the glasses and plates of a buffet. Beyond this was another door. Scaramanga led the way through into what would one day perhaps be a card room or writing-room.

Now there was nothing but a round table in the centre of a wine-red carpet and seven white leatherette arm-chairs with scratch pads and pencils in front of them. The chair facing the door, presumably Scaramanga's, had a white telephone in front of it.

Bond went round the room and examined the windows and the curtains and glanced at the wall brackets of the lighting. He said, 'The brackets could be bugged. And of course there's the telephone. Like me to go over it?'

Scaramanga looked at Bond stonily. He said, 'No need to. It's bugged all right. By me. Got to have a record of what's said.'

Bond said, 'All right, then. Where do you want me to be?'

'Outside the door. Sitting reading a magazine or something. There'll be the general meeting this afternoon around four. Tomorrow there'll mebbe be one or two smaller meetings, mebbe just me and one of the guys. I want all these meetings not to be disturbed. Got it?'

'Seems simple enough. Now, isn't it about time you told me the names of these men and more or less who they represent and which ones, if any, you're expecting trouble from?'

Scaramanga said, 'Take a chair and a paper and pencil.' He strolled up and down the room. 'First there's Mr Hendriks. Dutchman. Represents the European money, mostly Swiss. You needn't bother with him. He's not the arguing type. Then there's Sam Binion from Detroit.'

'The Purple Gang?'

Scaramanga stopped in his stride and looked hard at Bond. 'These are all respectable guys, Mister Whoosis.'

'Hazard is the name.'

'All right. Hazard, then. But respectable, you understand. Don't go getting the notion that this is another Appalachian. These are all solid business men. Get me? This Sam Binion, for instance. He's in real estate. He and his friends are worth mebbe twenty million bucks. See what I mean? Then there's Leroy Gengerella. Miami. Owns Gengerella Enterprises. Big shot in the entertainment world. He may cut up rough. Guys in that line of business like quick profits and a quick turnover. And Ruby Rotkopf, the hotel man from Vegas. He'll ask the difficult questions because he'll already know most of the answers from experience. Hal Garfinkel from Chicago. He's in Labour Relations, like me. Represents a lot of Teamster Union funds. He shouldn't be any trouble. Those unions have got so much money they don't know where to put it. That makes five. Last comes Louie Paradise from Phoenix, Arizona. Owns Paradise Slots, the biggest people in the one-armed bandit business. Got casino interests too. I can't figure which way he'll bet. That's the lot.'

'And who do you represent, Mr Scaramanga?'

'Caribbean money.'

'Cuban?'

'I said Caribbean. Cuba's in the Caribbean, isn't it?'

'Castro or Batista?'

The frown was back. Scaramanga's right hand balled into a fist. 'I told you not to rile me, Mister. So don't go prying into my affairs or you'll get hurt. And that's for sure.' As if he could hardly control himself longer, the big man turned on his heel and strode brusquely out of the room.

James Bond smiled. He turned back to the list in front of him. A strong reek of high gangsterdom rose from the paper. But the name he was most interested in was Mr Hendriks who represented 'European money'. If that was his real name, and he was a Dutchman, so, James Bond reflected, was he.

He tore off three sheets of paper to efface the impression of his pencil and walked out and along into the lobby. A bulky man was approaching the desk from the entrance. He was sweating mightily in his unseasonable woollen-looking suit. He might have been anybody – an Antwerp diamond merchant, a German dentist, a Swiss bank manager. The pale, square-jowled face was totally anonymous. He put a heavy brief-case on the desk and said in a thick Central European accent, 'I am Mr Hendriks. I think it is that you have a room for me, isn't it?'

8 . . . . PASS THE CANAPÉS!

THE CARS began rolling up. Scaramanga was in evidence. He switched a careful smile of welcome on and off. No hands were shaken. The host was greeted either as 'Pistol' or 'Mr S' except by Mr Hendriks, who called him nothing.

Bond stood within earshot of the desk and fitted the names to the men. In general appearance they were all much of a muchness. Dark-faced, clean-shaven, around five feet six, hard-eyed above thinly smiling mouths, curt of speech to the manager. They all held firmly on to their brief-cases when the bell boys tried to add them to the luggage on the rubber-tyred barrows. They dispersed to their rooms along the East Wing. Bond took out his list and added hat-check notations to each one except Hendriks who was clearly etched in Bond's memory. Gengerella became 'Italian origin, mean, pursed mouth'; Rotkopf, 'Thick neck, totally bald, Jew'; Binion, 'bat ears, scar down left cheek, limp'; Garfinkel, 'the toughest. Bad teeth, gun under right armpit'; and, finally, Paradise, 'Showman type, cocky, false smile, diamond ring'.

Scaramanga came up. 'What you writing?'

'Just notes to remember them by.'

'Gimme.' Scaramanga held out a demanding hand.

Bond gave him the list.

Scaramanga ran his eyes down it. He handed it back. 'Fair enough. But you needn't have mentioned the only gun you noticed. They'll all be protected. Except Hendriks, I guess. These kinda guys are nervous when they move abroad.'

'What of?'

Scaramanga shrugged. 'Mebbe the natives.'

'The last people who worried about the natives were the redcoats, perhaps a hundred and fifty years ago.'

'Who cares? See you in the bar around twelve. I'll be introducing you as my Personal Assistant.'

'That'll be fine.'

Scaramanga's brows came together. Bond strolled off in the direction of his bedroom. He proposed to needle this man, and go on needling until it came to a fight. For the time being the other man would probably take it because it seemed he needed Bond. But there would come a moment, probably on an occasion when there were witnesses, when his vanity would be so sharply pricked that he would draw. Then Bond would have a small edge, for it would be he who had thrown down the glove. The tactic was a crude one, but Bond could think of no other.

Bond verified that his room had been searched at some time during the morning – and by an expert. He always used a Hoffritz safety razor patterned on the old-fashioned heavy-toothed Gillette type. His American friend Felix Leiter had once bought him one in New York to prove that they were the best, and Bond had stayed with them. The handle of a safety razor is a reasonably sophisticated hideout for the minor tools of espionage – codes, microdot developers, cyanide and other pills. That morning Bond had set a minute nick on the screw base of the handle in line with the 'Z' of the maker's name engraved on the shaft. The nick was now a millimetre to the right of the 'Z'. None of his other little traps, handkerchiefs with indelible dots in particular places arranged in a certain order, the angle of his suitcase with the wall of the wardrobe, the semi-extracted lining of the breast pocket of his spare suit, the particular symmetry of certain dents in his tube of Maclean's toothpaste, had been bungled or disturbed. They all might have been by a meticulous servant, a trained valet. But Jamaican servants, for all their charm and willingness, are not of this calibre. No. Between nine and ten, when Bond was doing his rounds and was well away from the hotel, his room had received a thorough going-over by someone who knew his business.

Bond was pleased. It was good to know that the fight was well and truly joined. If he found a chance of making a foray into No. 20, he hoped that he would do better. He took a shower. Afterwards, as he brushed his hair, he looked at himself in the mirror with inquiry. He was feeling a hundred per cent fit, but he remembered the dull, lacklustre eyes that had looked back at him when he shaved after first entering The Park – the tense, preoccupied expression on his face. Now the grey-blue eyes looked back at him from the tanned face with the brilliant glint of suppressed excitement and accurate focus of the old days. He smiled ironically back at the introspective scrutiny that so many people make of themselves before a race, a contest of wits, a trial of some sort. He had no excuses. He was ready to go.

The bar was through a brass-studded leather door opposite the lobby to the conference room. It was – in the fashion – a mock-English public-house saloon bar with luxury accessories. The scrubbed wooden chairs and benches had foam-rubber squabs in red leather. Behind the bar, the tankards were of silver, or simulated silver, instead of pewter. The hunting prints, copper and brass hunting horns, muskets and powder horns, on the walls could have come from the Parker Galleries in London. Instead of tankards of beer, bottles of champagne in antique coolers stood on the tables and, instead of yokels, the hoods stood around in what looked like Brooks Brothers 'tropical' attire and carefully sipped their drinks while 'Mine Host' leant against the polished mahogany bar and twirled his golden gun round and round on the first finger of his right hand like the snide poker cheat out of an old Western.

As the door closed behind Bond with a pressurised sigh, the golden gun halted in mid-whirl and sighted on Bond's stomach. 'Fellers,' said Scaramanga, mock boisterous, 'meet my Personal Assistant, Mr Mark Hazard, from London, England. He's come along to make things run smoothly over this week-end. Mark, come over and meet the gang and pass round the canapés.' He lowered the gun and shoved it into his waistband.

James Bond stitched a Personal Assistant smile on his face and walked up to the bar. Perhaps because he was an Englishman, there was a round of handshaking. The red-coated barman asked him what he would have and he said, 'Some pink gin. Plenty of bitters. Beefeater's.' There was desultory talk about the relative merits of gins. Everyone else seemed to be drinking champagne except Mr Hendriks who stood away from the group and nursed a Schweppes Bitter Lemon. Bond moved among the men. He made small talk about their flight, the weather in the States, the beauties of Jamaica. He wanted to fit the voices to the names. He gravitated towards Mr Hendriks. 'Seems we're the only two Europeans here. Gather you're from Holland. Often passed through. Never stayed there long. Beautiful country.'

The very pale blue eyes regarded Bond unenthusiastically. 'Sank you.'

'What part do you come from?'

'Den Haag.'

'Have you lived there long?'

'Many, many years.'

'Beautiful town.'

'Sank you.'

'Is this your first visit to Jamaica?'

'No.'

'How do you like it?'

'It is a beautiful place.'

Bond nearly said, 'Sank you.' He smiled encouragingly at Mr Hendriks as much as to say, 'I've made all the running so far. Now you say something.'

Mr Hendriks looked past Bond's right ear at nothing. The pressure of the silence built up. Mr Hendriks shifted his weight from one foot to the other and finally broke down. His eyes shifted and looked thoughtfully at Bond. 'And you. You are from London, isn't it?'

'Yes. Do you know it?'

'I have been there, yes.'

'Where do you usually stay?'

There was hesitation. 'With friends.'

'That must be convenient.'

'Pliss?'

'I mean it's pleasant to have friends in a foreign town. Hotels are so much alike.'

'I have not found this. Excuse pliss.' With a Germanic bob of the head Mr Hendriks moved decisively away from Bond and went up to Scaramanga, who was still lounging in solitary splendour at the bar. Mr Hendriks said something. His words acted like a command on the other man. Mr Scaramanga straightened himself and followed Mr Hendriks into a far corner of the room. He stood and listened with deference as Mr Hendriks talked rapidly in a low tone.

Bond, joining the other men, was interested. It was his guess that no other man in the room could have buttonholed Scaramanga with so much authority. He noticed that many fleeting glances were cast in the direction of the couple apart. For Bond's money, this was either the Mafia or K.G.B. Probably even the other five wouldn't know which, but they would certainly recognize the secret smell of 'The Machine' which Mr Hendriks exuded so strongly.

Luncheon was announced. The Jamaican head waiter hovered between two richly prepared tables. There were place cards. Bond found that, while Scaramanga was host at one of them, he himself was at the head of the other table between Mr Paradise and Mr Rotkopf. As he expected, Mr Paradise was the better value of the two and, as they went through the conventional shrimp cocktail, steak, fruit salad of the Americanized hotel abroad, Bond cheerfully got himself involved in an argument about the odds at roulette when there are one zero or two. Mr Rotkopf's only contribution was to say, through a mouthful of steak and French fries, that he had once tried three zeros at the Black Cat Casino in Miami but that the experiment had failed. Mr Paradise said that so it should have. 'You got to let the suckers win sometimes, Ruby, or they won't come back. Sure, you can squeeze the juice out of them, but you oughta leave them the pips. Like with my slots. I tell the customers, don't be too greedy. Don't set 'em at thirty per cent for the house. Set 'em at twenty. You ever heard of Mr J. B. Morgan turning down a net profit of twenty per cent? Hell, no! So why try and be smarter than guys like that?'

Mr Rotkopf said sourly, 'You got to make big profits to put against a bum steer like this.' He waved a hand. 'If you ask me,' he held up a bit of steak on his fork, 'you're eating the only money you're going to see out of this dump at this minute.'

Mr Paradise leaned across the table and said softly, 'You know something?'

Mr Rotkopf said, 'I always told my money that the bindweed would get this place. The dam' fools wouldn't listen. And look where we are in three years! Second mortgage nearly run out and we've only got one storey up. What I say is ...'

The argument went off into the realms of high finance. At the next-door table there was not even this amount of animation. Scaramanga was a man of few words. There were clearly none available for social occasions. Opposite him, Mr Hendriks exuded a silence as thick as Gouda cheese. The three hoods addressed an occasional glum sentence to anyone who would listen. James Bond wondered how Scaramanga was going to electrify this unpromising company into 'having a good time'.

Luncheon broke up and the company dispersed to their rooms. James Bond wandered round to the back of the hotel and found a discarded shingle on a rubbish dump. It was blazing hot under the afternoon sun, but the Doctor's wind was blowing in from the sea. For all its air-conditioning, there was something grim about the impersonal grey and white of Bond's bedroom. Bond walked along the shore, took off his coat and tie and sat in the shade of a bush of sea grapes and watched the fiddler crabs about their minuscule business in the sand while he whittled two chunky wedges out of the Jamaican cedar. Then he closed his eyes and thought about Mary Goodnight. She would now be having her siesta in some villa on the outskirts of Kingston. It would probably be high up in the Blue Mountains for the coolness. In Bond's imagination, she would be lying on her bed under a mosquito net. Because of the heat, she would have nothing on, and one could see only an ivory and gold shape through the fabric of the net. But one would know that there were small beads of sweat on her upper lip and between her breasts and the fringes of the golden hair would be damp. Bond took off his clothes and lifted up the corner of the mosquito net, not wanting to wake her until he had fitted himself against her thighs. But she turned, in half sleep, towards him and held out her arms. 'James …'

Under the sea-grape bush, a hundred and twenty miles away from the scene of the dream, James Bond's head came up with a jerk. He looked quickly, guiltily, at his watch. 3.30. He went off to his room and had a cold shower, verified that his cedar wedges would do what they were meant to do, and strolled down the corridor to the lobby.

The manager with the neat suit and neat face came out from behind his desk. 'Er, Mr Hazard.'

'Yes.'

'I don't think you've met my assistant, Mr Travis.'

'No, I don't think I have.'

'Would you care to step into the office for a moment and shake him by the hand?'

'Later perhaps. We've got this conference on in a few minutes.'

The neat man came a step closer. He said quietly, 'He particularly wants to meet you, Mr – er – Bond.'

Bond cursed himself. This was always happening in his particular trade. You were looking in the dark for a beetle with red wings. Your eyes were focused for that particular pattern on the bark of the tree. You didn't notice the moth with cryptic colouring that crouched quietly near by, itself like a piece of the bark, itself just as important to the collector. The focus of your eyes was too narrow. Your mind was too concentrated. You were using 1 x 100 magnification and your 1 x 10 was not in focus. Bond looked at the man with the recognition that exists between crooks, between homosexuals, between secret agents. It is the look common to men bound by secrecy – by common trouble. 'Better make it quick.'

The neat man stepped behind his desk and opened a door. Bond went in and the neat man closed the door behind them. A tall, slim man was standing at a filing cabinet. He turned. He had a lean, bronzed Texan face under an unruly mop of straight, fair hair, and, instead of a right hand, a bright steel hook. Bond stopped in his tracks. His face split into a smile broader than he had smiled for what? Was it three years or four? He said, 'You goddamned, lousy crook. What in hell are you doing here?' He went up to the man and hit him hard on the biceps of the left arm.

The grin was slightly more creased than Bond remembered, but it was just as friendly and ironical. Mr Travis said, 'The name is Leiter, Mr Felix Leiter. Temporary accountant on loan from Morgan Guarantee Trust to the Thunderbird Hotel. We're just checking up on your credit rating, Mr Hazard. Would you kindly, in your royal parlance, extract your finger, and give me some evidence that you are who you claim to be?'

9 . . . . MINUTES OF THE MEETING

JAMES BOND, almost light-headed with pleasure, picked up
a handful of travel literature from the front desk, said 'Hi!' to Mr
Gengerella, who didn't reply, and followed him into the conference room lobby. They were the last to show. Scaramanga, beside
the open door to the conference room, looked pointedly at his
watch and said to Bond, 'Okay, feller. Lock the door when we're
all settled and don't let anyone in even if the hotel catches fire.' He
turned to the barman behind the loaded buffet. 'Get lost, Joe. I'll
call for you later.' He said to the room, 'Right. We're all set. Let's
go.' He led the way into the conference room and the six men
followed. Bond stood by the door and noted the seating order
round the table. He closed the door and locked it and quickly also
locked the exit from the lobby. Then he picked up a champagne
glass from the buffet, pulled over a chair and sited the chair very
close to the door of the conference room. He placed the bowl of
the champagne glass as near as possible to a hinge of the door
and, holding the glass by the stem, put his left ear up against its
base. Through the crude amplifier, what had been the rumble of

a voice became Mr Hendriks speaking, '... and so it is that I will now report from my superiors in Europe ...' The voice paused and Bond heard another noise, the creak of a chair. Like lightning he pulled the chair back a few feet, opened one of the travel folders on his lap and raised the glass to his lips. The door jerked open and Scaramanga stood in the opening, twirling his pass key on a chain. He examined the innocent figure on the chair. He said, 'Okay, feller. Just checking,' and kicked the door shut. Bond noisily locked it and took up his place again. Mr Hendriks said, 'I have one most important message for our Chairman. It is from a sure source. There is a man that is called James Bond that is looking for him in this territory. This is a man who is from the British Secret Service. I have no informations or descriptions of this man but it seems that he is highly rated by my superiors. Mr Scaramanga, have you heard of this man?'

Scaramanga snorted. 'Hell, no! And should I care? I eat one of their famous secret agents for breakfast from time to time. Only ten days ago, I disposed of one of them who came nosing after me. Man called Ross. His body is now very slowly sinking to the bottom of a pitch lake in Eastern Trinidad – place called La Brea. The oil company, the Trinidad Lake Asphalt people, will obtain an interesting barrel of crude one of these days. Next question, please, Mr Hendriks.'

'Next I am wishing to know what is the policy of The Group in the matter of cane sabotage. At our meeting six months ago in Havana, against my minority vote, it was decided, in exchange for certain favours, to come to the aid of Fidel Castro and assist in maintaining and indeed increasing the world price of sugar to offset the damage caused by Hurricane Flora. Since this time there have been very numerous fires in the cane fields of Jamaica and Trinidad. In this connection, it has come to the ears of my superiors that individual members of The Group, notably,' there was the rustle of paper, 'Messrs Gengerella, Rotkopf and Binion, in addition to our Chairman, have engaged in extensive purchasing of July sugar futures for the benefit of private gain ...'

There came an angry murmur from round the table. 'Why shouldn't we ...? Why shouldn't they ...?' The voice of Gengerella dominated the others. He shouted, 'Who in hell said we weren't to make money? Isn't that one of the objects of The Group? I ask you again, Mr Hendriks, as I asked you six months ago, who in hell is it among your so-called "superiors" who wants to keep the price of raw sugar down? For my money, the most interested party in such a gambit would be Soviet Russia. They're selling goods to Cuba, including, let me say, the recently abortive shipment of missiles to fire against my homeland, in exchange for raw sugar. They're sharp traders, the Reds. In their double-dealing way, even from a friend and ally, they would want more sugar for fewer goods. Yes? I suppose', the voice sneered, 'one of your superiors, Mr Hendriks, would not by any chance be in the Kremlin?'

The voice of Scaramanga cut through the ensuing hubbub. 'Fellers! Fellers!' A reluctant silence fell. 'When we formed the Co-operative, it was agreed that the first object was to co-operate with one another. Okay, then. Mr Hendriks. Let me put you more fully in the picture. So far as the total finances of The Group are concerned, we have a fine situation coming up. As an investment group, we have good bets and bad bets. Sugar is a good bet and we should ride that bet even though certain members of The Group have chosen not to be on the horse. Get me? Now hear me through. There are six ships controlled by The Group at this moment riding at anchor outside New York and other U.S. harbours. These ships are loaded with raw sugar. These ships, Mr Hendriks, will not dock and unload until sugar futures, July futures, have risen another ten cents. In Washington, the Department of Agriculture and the Sugar Lobby know this. They know that we have them by the balls. Meantimes the liquor lobby is leaning on them – let alone Russia. The price of molasses is going up with sugar and the rum barons are kicking up hell and want our ships let in before there's a real shortage and the price goes through the roof. But there's another side to it. We're having to pay our crews and our charter bills and so on, and squatting ships are dead ships, dead losses. So something's going to give. In the business, the situation we've developed is called the Floating Crop Game – our ships lying offshore, lined up against the Government of the United States. All right. So now four of us stand to win or lose ten million bucks or so – us and our backers. And we've got this little business of the Thunderbird on the red side of the sheet. So what do you think, Mr Hendriks? Of course we burn the crops where we can get away with it. I got a good man in with the Rastafaris – that's a beat sect here that grows beards and smokes ganja and mostly lives on a bit of land outside Kingston called the Dungle – the Dunghill – and believes it owes allegiance to the King of Ethiopia, this King Zog or what-have-you, and that that's their rightful home. So I've got a man in there, a man who wants the ganja for them, and I keep him supplied in exchange for plenty fires and troubles on the cane lands. So all right, Mr Hendriks. You just tell your superiors that what goes up must come down and that applies to the price of sugar like anything else. Okay?'

Mr Hendriks said, 'I will pass on your saying, Mr Scaramanga. It will not cause pleasure. Now there is this business of the hotel. How is she standing, if you pliss? I think we are all wishing to know the true situation, isn't it?'

There was a growl of assent.

Mr Scaramanga went off into a long dissertation which was only of passing interest to Bond. Felix Leiter would in any case be getting it all on the tape in a drawer of his filing cabinet. He had reassured Bond on this score. The neat American, Leiter had explained, filling him in with the essentials, was in fact a certain Mr Nick Nicholson of the C.I.A. His particular concern was Mr Hendriks who, as Bond had suspected, was a top man of the K.G.B. The K.G.B. favours oblique control – a man in Geneva being the Resident Director for Italy, for instance – and Mr Hendriks at The Hague was in fact Resident Director for the Caribbean and in charge of the Havana centre. Leiter was still working for Pinkertons, but was also on the reserve of the C.I.A. who had drafted him for this particular assignment because of his knowledge, gained in the past mostly with James Bond, of Jamaica. His job was to get a breakdown of The Group and find out what they were up to. They were all well-known hoods who would normally have been the concern of the F.B.I., but Gengerella was a Capo Mafiosi and this was the first time the Mafia had been found consorting with the K.G.B. – a most disturbing partnership which must at all costs be quickly broken up, by physical elimination if need be. Nick Nicholson, whose 'front' name was Mr Stanley Jones, was an electronics expert. He had traced the main lead to Scaramanga's recording device under the floor of the central switch room and had bled off the microphone cable to his own tape recorder in the filing cabinet. So Bond had not much to worry about. He was listening to satisfy his own curiosity and to fill in on anything that might transpire in the lobby or out of range of the bug in the telephone on the conference room table. Bond had explained his own presence. Leiter had given a long low whistle of respectful apprehension. Bond had agreed to keep well clear of the other two men and to paddle his own canoe, but they had arranged an emergency meeting place and a postal 'drop' in the uncompleted and 'Out of Order' men's room off the lobby. Nicholson had given him a pass key for this place and all other rooms and then Bond had had to hurry off to his meeting. James Bond was immensely reassured by finding these unexpected reinforcements. He had worked with Leiter on some of his most hazardous assignments. There was no man like him when the chips were down. Although Leiter had only a steel hook instead of a right arm – a memento of one of those assignments – he was one of the finest left-handed one-armed shots in the States and the hook itself could be a devastating weapon at close quarters.

Scaramanga was finishing his exposition. 'So the net of it is, gentlemen, that we need to find ten million bucks. The interests I represent, which are the majority interests, suggest that this sum should be provided by a Note issue, bearing interest at ten per cent and repayable in ten years, such an issue to have priority over all other loans.'

The voice of Mr Rotkopf broke in angrily. 'The hell it will! Not on your life, Mister. What about the seven per cent second mortgage put up by me and my friends only a year back? What do you think I'd get if I went back to Vegas with that kind of parley? The old heave-ho! And at that I'm being optimistic.'

'Beggars can't be choosers, Ruby. It's that or close. What do you other fellers have to say?'

Hendriks said, 'Ten per cent on a first charge is good pizzness. My friends and I will take one million dollars. On the understanding, it is natural, that the conditions of the issue are, how shall I say, more substantial, less open to misunderstandings, than the second mortgage of Mr Rotkopf and his friends.'

'Of course. And I and my friends will also take a million. Sam?'

Mr Binion said reluctantly, 'Okay, okay. Count us in for the same. But by golly this has got to be the last touch.'

'Mr Gengerella?'

'It sounds a good bet. I'll take the rest.'

The voices of Mr Garfinkel and Mr Paradise broke in excitedly, Garfinkel in the lead. 'Like hell you will! I'm taking a million.'

'And so am I,' shouted Mr Paradise. 'Cut the cake equally. But dammit. Let's be fair to Ruby. Ruby, you oughta have first pick. How much do you want? You can have it off the top.'

'I don't want a damned cent of your phoney Notes. As soon as I get back, I'm going to reach for the best damned lawyers in the States – all of them. You think you can scrub a mortgage just by saying so, you've all got another think coming.'

There was silence. The voice of Scaramanga was soft and deadly. 'You're making a big mistake, Ruby. You've just got yourself a nice fat tax-loss to put against your Vegas interests. And don't forget that when we formed this Group we all took an oath. None of us was to operate against the interests of the others. Is that your last word?'

'It dam' is.'

'Would this help you change your mind? They've got a slogan for it in Cuba – *Rapido! Seguro! Economico!* This is how the system operates.'

The scream of terror and the explosion were simultaneous. A chair crashed to the floor and there was a moment's silence. Then someone coughed nervously. Mr Gengerella said calmly, 'I think that was the correct solution of an embarrassing conflict of interests. Ruby's friends in Vegas like a quiet life. I doubt if they will even complain. It is better to be a live owner of some finely engraved paper than to be a dead holder of a second mortgage. Put them in for a million, Pistol. I think you behaved with speed and correctness. Now then, can you clean this up?'

'Sure, sure.' Mr Scaramanga's voice was relaxed, happy. 'Ruby's left here to go back to Vegas. Never heard of again. We don't know nuthen'. I've got some hungry crocs out back there in the river.

They'll give him free transportation to where he's going – and his baggage if it's good leather. I shall need some help tonight. What about you, Sam? And you, Louie?'

The voice of Mr Paradise pleaded. 'Count me out, Pistol. I'm a good Catholic.'

Mr Hendriks said, 'I will take his place. I am not a Catholic person.'

'So be it then. Well, fellers, any other business? If not, we'll break up the meeting and have a drink.'

Hal Garfinkel said nervously, 'Just a minute, Pistol. What about that guy outside the door? That limey feller? What's he going to say about the fireworks and all?'

Mr Scaramanga's chuckle was like the dry chuckle of a gekko. 'Just don't you worry your tiny head about the limey, Hal. He'll be looked after when the week-end's over. Picked him up in a bordello in a village nearby. Place where I go get my weed and a bit of black tail. Got only temporary staff here to see you fellers have a good time over the week-end. He's the temporariest of the lot. Those crocs have a big appetite. Ruby'll be the main dish, but they'll need a dessert. Jes' you leave him to me. For all I know he may be this James Bond man Mr Hendriks has told us about. I should worry. I don't like limeys. Like some good yankee once said, "For every Britisher that dies, there's a song in my heart." Remember the guy? Around the time of the Israeli war against them. I dig that viewpoint. Stuck-up bastards. Stuffed shirts. When the time comes, I'm going to let the stuffing out of this one. Jes' you leave him to me. Or let's jes' say leave him to this.'

Bond smiled a thin smile. He could imagine the golden gun being produced and twirled round the finger and stuck back in the waistband. He got up and moved his chair away from the door and poured champagne into the useful glass and leant against the buffet and studied the latest hand-out from the Jamaica Tourist Board.

The click of Scaramanga's pass key sounded in the lock. Scaramanga looked at Bond from the doorway. He ran a finger along the small moustache. 'Okay, feller. I guess that's enough of the house champagne. Cut along to the manager and tell him Mr Ruby Rotkopf'll be checking out tonight. I'll fix the details. And say a major fuse blew during the meeting and I'm going to seal off this room and find out why we're having so much bad workmanship around the place. 'Kay? Then drinks and dinner and bring on the dancing girls. Got the photo?'

James Bond said that he had. He weaved slightly as he went to the lobby door and unlocked it. 'E. & O.E. – Errors and omissions excepted' as the financial prospectuses say, he thought that he had indeed now 'got the photo'. And it was an exceptionally clear print in black and white without 'fuzz'.

10 ....BELLY-LICK, ETC.

IN THE back office, James Bond went quickly over the high-lights of the meeting. Nick Nicholson and Felix Leiter agreed they had enough on the tape, supported by Bond, to send Scaramanga to the chair. That night, one of them would do some snooping while the body of Rotkopf was being disposed of and try and get enough evidence to have Garfinkel and, better still, Hendriks indicted as accessories. But they didn't at all like the outlook for James Bond. Felix commanded him, 'Now don't you move an inch without that old equalizer of yours. We don't want to have to read that obituary of yours in *The Times* all over again. All that crap about what a splendid feller you are nearly made me throw up when I saw it reprinted in the American blatts. I dam' nearly fired off a piece to the *Trib* putting the record straight.'

Bond laughed. He said, 'You're a fine friend, Felix. When I think of all the trouble I've been to to set you a good example all these years.' He went off to his room, swallowed two heavy slugs of bourbon, had a cold shower and lay on his bed and looked at the ceiling until it was 8.30 and time for dinner. The meal was less stuffy than luncheon. Everyone seemed satisfied with the way the business of the day had gone and all except Scaramanga and Mr Hendriks had obviously had plenty to drink. Bond found himself excluded from the happy talk. Eyes avoided his and replies to his attempts at conversation were monosyllabic. He was bad news. He had been dealt the death card by the boss. He was certainly not a man to be pally with. While the meal moved sluggishly on – the conventional 'expensive' dinner of a cruise ship, desiccated smoked salmon with a thimbleful of small-grained black caviar, fillets of some unnamed native fish, possibly silk fish, in a cream sauce, 'poulet suprême', a badly roasted broiler with a thick gravy, and *bombe surprise*, was as predictable as such things are – the dining-room was being turned into a 'tropical jungle' with the help of potted plants, piles of oranges and coconuts and an occasional stem of bananas, as a backdrop for the calypso band which, in wine-red and gold frilled shirts, in due course assembled and began playing 'Linstead Market' too loud. The tune closed. An acceptable but heavily clad girl appeared and began singing 'Belly-Lick' with the printable words. She wore a false pineapple as a head-dress. Bond saw a 'cruise ship' evening stretching ahead. He decided that he was either too old or too young for the worst torture of all, boredom, and got up and went to the head of the table. He said to Mr Scaramanga, 'I've got a headache. I'm going to bed.'

Mr Scaramanga looked up at him under lizard eyelids. 'No. If you figure the evening's not going so good, make it go better. That's what you're being paid for. You act as if you know Jamaica. Okay. Get these people off the pad.'

It was many years since James Bond had accepted a 'dare'. He felt the eyes of The Group on him. What he had drunk had made him careless – perhaps wanting to show off, like the man at the party who insists on playing the drums. Stupidly, he wanted to assert his personality over this bunch of tough guys who rated him insignificant. He didn't stop to think that it was bad tactics, that he would be better off being the ineffectual limey. He said, 'All right, Mr Scaramanga. Give me a hundred-dollar bill and your gun.'

Scaramanga didn't move. He looked up at Bond with surprise and controlled uncertainty. Louie Paradise shouted thickly, 'C'mon, Pistol! Let's see some action! Mebbe the guy can produce.'

Scaramanga reached for his hip pocket, took out his billfold and thumbed out a note. Next he slowly reached to his waistband and took out his gun. The subdued light from the spot on the girl glowed on its gold. He laid the two objects on the table side by side. James Bond, his back to the cabaret, picked up the gun and hefted it. He thumbed back the hammer and twirled the cylinder with a flash of his hands to verify that it was loaded. Then he suddenly whirled, dropped on his knee so that his aim would be above the shadowy musicians in the background and, his arm at full length, let fly. The explosion was deafening in the confined space. The music died. There was a tense silence. The remains of the false pineapple hit something in the dark background with a soft thud. The girl stood under the spot and put her hands to her face and slowly folded to the dance floor like something graceful out of *Swan Lake*. The maître d'hôtel came running from among the shadows.

As chatter broke out among The Group, James Bond picked up the hundred-dollar note and walked out into the spotlight. He bent down and lifted the girl up by her arm. He pushed the dollar bill down into her cleavage. He said, 'That was a fine act we did together, sweetheart. Don't worry. You were in no danger. I aimed for the top half of the pineapple. Now run off and get ready for your next turn.' He turned her round and gave her a sharp pat on the behind. She gave him a horrified glance and scurried off into the shadows.

Bond strolled on and came up with the band. 'Who's in charge here? Who's in command of the show?'

The guitarist, a tall, gaunt Negro, got slowly to his feet. The whites of his eyes showed. He squinted at the golden gun in Bond's hand. He said uncertainly, as if signing his own death warrant, 'Me, sah.'

'What's your name?'

'King Tiger, sah.'

'All right then, King. Now listen to me. This isn't a Salvation Army fork-supper. Mr Scaramanga's friends want some action. And they want it hot. I'll be sending plenty of rum over to loosen things up. Smoke weed if you like. We're private here. No one's going to tell on you. And get that pretty girl back, but with only half the clothes on, and tell her to come up close and sing "Belly-Lick" very clearly with the blue words. And, by the end of the show, she and the other girls have got to end up stripped. Understand? Now get cracking or the evening'll fold and there'll be no tips at the end. Okay? Then let's go.'

There was nervous laughter and whispered exhortation to King Tiger from the six-piece combo. King Tiger grinned broadly. 'Okay, Captain, sah.' He turned to his men. 'Give 'em "Iron Bar", but hot. An' I'll go get some steam up with Daisy and her friends.' He strode to the service exit and the band crashed into its stride.

Bond walked back and laid the pistol down in front of Scaramanga, who gave Bond a long, inquisitive look and slid it back into his waistband. He said flatly, 'We must have a shooting match one of these days, Mister. How about it? Twenty paces and no wounding?'

'Thanks,' said Bond, 'but my mother wouldn't approve. Would you have some rum sent over to the band? These people can't play dry.' He went back to his seat. He was hardly noticed. The five men, or rather four of them because Hendriks sat impassively through the whole evening, were straining their ears to catch the lewd words of the Fanny Hill version of 'Iron Bar' that were coming across clearly from the soloist. Four girls, plump, busty little animals wearing nothing but white sequined G-strings, ran out on to the floor, and, advancing towards the audience, did an enthusiastic belly dance that brought sweat to the temples of Louie Paradise and Hal Garfinkel. The number ended amidst applause, the girls ran off and the lights were dowsed, leaving only the circular spot in the middle of the floor. The drummer, on his calypso box, began a hasty beat like a quickened pulse. The service door opened and shut and a curious object was wheeled into the circle of light. It was a huge hand, perhaps six feet tall at its highest point, upholstered in black leather. It stood, half open on its broad base, with the thumb and fingers outstretched as if ready to catch something. The drummer hastened his beat. The service door sighed. A glistening figure slipped through and, after pausing in the darkness, moved into the pool of light round the hand with a strutting jerk of belly and limbs. There was Chinese blood in her and her body, totally naked and shining with palm oil, was almost white against the black hand. As she jerked round the hand she caressed its outstretched fingers with her hands and arms and then, with well-acted swooning motions, climbed into the palm of the hand and proceeded to perform langorous, but explicit and ingenious acts of passion with each of the fingers in turn. The scene, the black hand, now shining with her oil and seeming to clutch at the squirming white body, was of an incredible lewdness, and Bond, himself aroused, noticed that even Scaramanga was watching with rapt attention, his eyes narrow slits. The drummer had now worked up to his crescendo. The girl, in well-simulated ecstasy, mounted the thumb, slowly expired upon it and then, with a last grind of her rump, slid down it and vanished through the exit. The act was over. The lights came on and everyone, including the band, applauded loudly. The men came out of their separate animal trances. Scaramanga clapped his hand for the band leader, took a note out of his case and said something to him under his breath. The chieftain, Bond suspected, had chosen his bride for the night!

After this inspired piece of sexual dumb crambo, the rest of the cabaret was an anti-climax. One of the girls, only after her G-string had been slashed off with a cutlass by the band leader, was able to squirm under a bamboo balanced just eighteen inches off the floor on the top of two beer bottles. The first girl, the one who had acted as an unwitting pineapple-tee to Bond's William Tell act, came on and combined an acceptable strip-tease with a rendering of 'Belly-Lick' that got the audience straining its ears again, and then the whole team of six girls, less the Chinese beauty, came up to the audience and invited them to dance. Scaramanga and Hendriks refused with adequate politeness and Bond stood the two left-out girls glasses of champagne and learned that their names were Mabel and Pearl while he watched the four others being almost bent in half by the bear-like embraces of the four sweating hoods as they clumsily cha-cha'd round the room to the now riotous music of the half-drunk band. The climax to what could certainly class as an orgy was clearly in sight. Bond told his two girls that he must go to the men's room and slipped away when Scaramanga was looking elsewhere, but, as he went, he noted that Hendriks's gaze, as cool as if he had been watching an indifferent film, was firmly on him as he made his escape.

When Bond got to his room, it was midnight. His windows had been closed and the air-conditioning turned on. He switched it off and opened the windows half-way and then, with heartfelt relief, took a shower and went to bed. He worried for a while about having shown off with the gun, but it was an act of folly which he couldn't undo and he soon went to sleep to dream of three black-cloaked men dragging a shapeless bundle through dappled moonlight towards dark waters that were dotted with glinting red eyes. The gnashing white teeth and the crackling bones resolved themselves into a persistent scrabbling noise that brought him suddenly awake. He looked at the luminous dial of his watch. It said 3.30. The scrabbling became a quiet tapping from behind the curtains. James Bond slid quietly out of bed, took his gun from under his pillow and crept softly along the wall to the edge of the curtains. He pulled them aside with one swift motion. The golden hair shone almost silver in the moonlight. Mary Goodnight whispered urgently, 'Quick, James! Help me in!'

Bond cursed softly to himself. What the hell? He laid his gun down on the carpet and reached for her outstretched hands and half dragged, half pulled her over the sill. At the last moment, her heel caught in the frame and the window banged shut with a noise like a pistol shot. Bond cursed again, softly and fluently, under his breath. Mary Goodnight whispered penitently, 'I'm terribly sorry, James.'

Bond shushed her. He picked up his gun and put it back under his pillow and led her across the room and into the bathroom. He turned on the light and, as a precaution, the shower, and, simultaneously with her gasp, remembered he was naked. He said, 'Sorry, Goodnight,' and reached for a towel and wound it round his waist and sat down on the edge of the bath. He gestured to the girl to sit down on the lavatory seat and said, with icy control, 'What in hell are you doing here, Mary?'

Her voice was desperate. 'I had to come. I had to find you somehow. I got on to you through the girl at that, er, dreadful place. I left the car in the trees down the drive and just sniffed about. There were lights on in some of the rooms and I listened and, er,' she blushed crimson, 'I gathered you couldn't be in any of them and then I saw the open window and I just somehow knew you would be the only one to sleep with his window open. So I just had to take the chance.'

'Well, we've got to get you out of here as quick as we can. Anyway, what's the trouble?'

'A "Most Immediate" in Triple-X came over this evening. I mean yesterday evening. It was to be passed to you at all costs. H.Q. thinks you're in Havana. It said that one of the K.G.B. top men who goes under the name of Hendriks is in the area and that he's known to be visiting this hotel. You're to keep away from him. They know from "a delicate but sure source"' (Bond smiled at the old euphemism for cypher-breaking) 'that among his other jobs is to find you and, er, well, kill you. So I put two and two together, and, what with you being in this corner of the island and the questions you asked me, I guessed that you might be already on his track but that you might be walking into an ambush, sort of. Not knowing, I mean, that while you were after him, he was after you.'

She put out a tentative hand, as if for reassurance that she had done the right thing. Bond took it and patted it absent-mindedly while his mind chewed on this new complication. He said, 'The man's here all right. So's a gunman called Scaramanga. You might as well know, Mary, that Scaramanga killed Ross. In Trinidad.' She put her hand up to her mouth. 'You can report it as a fact, from me. If I can get you out of here, that is. As for Hendriks, he's here all right, but he doesn't seem to have identified me for certain. Did H.Q. say whether he was given a description of me?'

'You were simply described as "the notorious secret agent, James Bond". But this doesn't seem to have meant much to Hendriks because he asked for particulars. That was two days ago.

He may get them cabled or telephoned here at any minute. You do see why I had to come, James?'

'Yes, of course. And thanks, Mary. Now, I've got to get you out of that window and then you must just make your own way. Don't worry about me. I think I can handle the situation all right. Besides, I've got help.' He told her about Felix Leiter and Nicholson. 'You just tell H.Q. you've delivered the message and that I'm here and about the two C.I.A. men. H.Q. can get the C.I.A. angles from Washington direct. Okay?' He got to his feet.

She stood up beside him and looked up at him. 'But you will take care?'

'Sure, sure.' He patted her shoulder. He turned off the shower and opened the bathroom door. 'Now, come on. We must pray for a stroke of luck.'

A silken voice from the darkness at the end of the bed said, 'Well, the Holy Man jes' ain't running for you today, Mister. Step forward both of you. Hands clasped behind the neck.'

11 ....BALLCOCK, AND OTHER, TROUBLE

SCARAMANGA WALKED to the door and turned the lights on. He was naked save for his shorts and the holster below his left arm. The golden gun remained trained on Bond as he moved.

Bond looked at him incredulously, then to the carpet inside the door. The wedges were still there, undisturbed. He could not possibly have got through the window unaided. Then he saw that his clothes cupboard stood open and that light showed through into the next room. It was the simplest of secret doors – just the whole of the back of the cupboard, impossible to detect from Bond's side of the wall and, on the other, probably, in appearance, a locked communicating door.

Scaramanga came back into the centre of the room and stood looking at them both. His mouth and eyes sneered. He said, 'I didn't see this piece of tail in the line-up. Where you been keeping it, buster? And why d'you have to hide it away in the bathroom? Like doing it under the shower?'

Bond said, 'We're engaged to be married. She works in the British High Commissioner's Office in Kingston. Cypher clerk. She found out where I was staying from that place you and I met. She came out to tell me that my mother's in hospital in London. Had a bad fall. Her name's Mary Goodnight. What's wrong with that and what do you mean coming busting into my room in the middle of the night waving a gun about? And kindly keep your foul tongue to yourself.' Bond was pleased with his bluster and decided to take the next step towards Mary Goodnight's freedom. He dropped his hands to his sides and turned to the girl. 'Put your hands down, Mary. Mr Scaramanga must have thought there were burglars about when he heard that window bang. Now, I'll get some clothes on and take you out to your car. You've got a long drive back to Kingston. Are you sure you wouldn't rather stay here for the rest of the night? I'm sure Mr Scaramanga could find us a spare room.' He turned back to Mr Scaramanga. 'It's all right, Mr Scaramanga, I'll pay for it.'

Mary Goodnight chipped in. She had dropped her hands. She picked up her small bag from the bed where she had thrown it, opened it and began busying herself with her hair in a fussy, feminine way. She chattered, falling in well with Bond's bland piece of very British 'Now-look-here-my man-manship'. 'No, honestly, darling, I really think I'd better go. I'd be in terrible trouble if I was late at the office and the Prime Minister, Sir Alexander Bustamante, you know he's just had his eightieth birthday, well he's coming to lunch and you know His Excellency always likes me to do the flowers and arrange the place cards and as a matter of fact,' she turned charmingly towards Mr Scaramanga, 'it's quite a day for me. The party was going to make up thirteen so His Excellency has asked me to be the fourteenth. Isn't that marvellous? But heaven knows what I'm going to look like after tonight. The roads really are terrible in parts aren't they, Mr – er – Scramble. But there it is. And I do apologize for causing all this disturbance and keeping you from your beauty sleep.' She went towards him like the Queen Mother opening a bazaar, her hand outstretched. 'Now you run along off back to bed again and my fiancé' (Thank God she hadn't said James! The girl was inspired!) ''ll see me safely off the premises. Goodbye, Mr, er ...'

James Bond was proud of her. It was almost pure Joyce Grenfell. But Scaramanga wasn't going to be taken by any double talk, limey or otherwise. She almost had Bond covered from Scaramanga. He moved swiftly aside. He said, 'Hold it, lady. And you, mister, stand where you are.' Mary Goodnight let her hand drop to her side. She looked inquiringly at Scaramanga as if he had just rejected the cucumber sandwiches. Really! These Americans! The Golden Gun didn't go for polite conversation. It held dead steady between the two of them. Scaramanga said to Bond, 'Okay, I'll buy it. Put her through the window again. Then I've got something to say to you.' He waved his gun at the girl. 'Okay, bimbo. Get going. And don't come trespassing on other people's lands again. Right? And you can tell His friggin' Excellency where to shove his place cards. His writ don't run over the Thunderbird. Mine does. Got the photo? Okay. Don't bust your stays getting through the window.'

Mary Goodnight said icily, 'Very good, Mr, er ... I will deliver your message. I'm sure the High Commissioner will take more careful note than he has done of your presence on the island. And the Jamaican Government also.'

Bond reached out and took her arm. She was on the edge of overplaying her role. He said, 'Come on, Mary. And please tell mother that I'll be through here in a day or two and I'll be telephoning her from Kingston.' He led her to the window and helped, or rather bundled her out. She gave a brief wave and ran off across the lawn. Bond came away from the window with considerable relief. He hadn't expected the ghastly mess to sort itself out so painlessly.

He went and sat down on his bed. He sat on the pillow. He was reassured to feel the hard shape of his gun against his thighs. He looked across at Scaramanga. The man had put his gun back in the shoulder holster. He leant up against the clothes cupboard and ran his finger reflectively along the black line of his moustache. He said, 'High Commissioner's Office. That also houses the local representative of your famous Secret Service. I suppose, Mister Hazard, that your real name wouldn't be James Bond? You showed quite a turn of speed with the gun tonight. I seem to have read somewhere that this man Bond fancies himself with the hardware. I also have information to the effect that he's somewhere in the Caribbean and that he's looking for me. Funny coincidence department, eh?'

Bond laughed easily. 'I thought the Secret Service packed up at the end of the war. Anyway, 'fraid I can't change my identity to suit your book. All you've got to do in the morning is ring up Frome and ask for Mr Tony Hugill, the boss up there, and check on my story. And can you explain how this Bond chap could possibly have tracked you down to a brothel in Sav' La Mar? And what does he want from you anyway?'

Scaramanga contemplated him silently for a while. Then he said, 'Guess he may be lookin' for a shootin' lesson. Be glad to oblige him. But you've got something about Number 3½. That's what I figgered when I hired you. But coincidence doesn't come in that size. Mebbe I should have thought again. I said from the first I smelled cops. That girl may be your fiancée or she may not, but that ploy with the shower bath. That's an old hood's trick. Probably a Secret Service one too. Unless, that is, you were screwin' her.' He raised one eyebrow.

'I was. Anything wrong with that? What have you been doing with the Chinese girl? Playing mah-jongg?' Bond got to his feet.

He stitched impatience and outrage on his face in equal quantities. 'Now look here, Mr Scaramanga. I've had just about enough
of this. Just stop leaning on me. You go around waving that
damned gun of yours and acting like God Almighty and insinu-
ating a lot of tommy-rot about the Secret Service and you expect
me to kneel down and lick your boots. Well, my friend, you've
come to the wrong address. If you're dissatisfied with the job I'm
doing, just hand over the thousand dollars and I'll be on my way.
Who in hell d'you think you are anyway?'

Scaramanga smiled his thin, cruel smile. 'You may be getting wise to that sooner than you think, shamus.' He shrugged.
'Okay, okay. But just you remember this, mister. If it turns out
you're not who you say you are, I'll blow you to bits. Get me? And
I'll start with the little bits and go on to the bigger ones. Just so
it lasts a heck of a long time. Right? Now you'd better get some
shut-eye. I've got a meeting with Mr Hendriks at ten in the conference room. And I don't want to be disturbed. After that the
whole party goes on an excursion on the railroad I was tellin' you
about. It'll be your job to see that that gets properly organized.
Talk to the manager first thing. Right? Okay, then. Be seeing ya.'
Scaramanga walked into the clothes cupboard, brushed Bond's
suit aside and disappeared. There came a decisive click from the
next room. Bond got to his feet. He said 'Phew!' at the top of his
voice and walked off into the bathroom to wash the last two hours
away in the shower.

He awoke at 6.30, by arrangement with that curious extra-
sensory alarm clock that some people keep in their heads and that
always seems to know the exact time. He put on his bathing trunks
and went out to the beach and did his long swim again. When at
7.15 he saw Scaramanga come out of the East Wing followed by
the boy carrying his towel, he made for the shore. He listened for
the twanging thump of the trampoline and then, keeping well out

of sight of it, entered the hotel by the main entrance and moved quickly down the corridor to his room. He listened at his window to make sure the man was still exercising, then he took the master key Nick Nicholson had given him and slipped across the corridor to No. 20 and was quickly inside. He left the door on the latch. Yes, there was his target, lying on the dressing-table. He strode across the room, picked up the gun and slipped out the round in the cylinder that would next come up for firing. He put the gun down exactly as he had found it, got back to the door, listened, and then was out and across the corridor and into his own room. He went back to the window and listened. Yes, Scaramanga was still at it. It was an amateurish ploy that Bond had executed, but it might gain him just that fraction of a second that, he felt it in his bones, was going to be life or death for him in the next twenty-four hours. In his mind, he smelled that slight whiff of smoke that indicated that his cover was smouldering at the edges. At any moment 'Mark Hazard of the Transworld Consortium' might go up in flames like some clumsy effigy on Guy Fawkes Night and James Bond would stand there, revealed, with nothing between him and a possible force of six other gunmen but his own quick hand and the Walther PPK. So every shade of odds that he could shift to his side of the board would be worthwhile. Undismayed by the prospect, in fact rather excited by it, he ordered a large breakfast, consumed it with relish and after pulling the connecting pin out of the ballcock in his lavatory he went along to the manager's office.

Felix Leiter was on duty. He gave a thin managerial smile and said, 'Good morning, Mr Hazard. Can I help you?' Leiter's eyes were looking beyond Bond, over his right shoulder. Mr Hendriks materialized at the desk before Bond could answer.

Bond said, 'Good morning.'

Mr Hendriks replied with his little Germanic bow. He said to Leiter, 'The telephone operator is saying that there is a long-distance call from my office in Havana. Where is the most private place to take it, pliss?'

'Not in your bedroom, sir?'

'Is not sufficiently private.'

Bond guessed that he too had bowled out the microphone. Leiter looked helpful. He came out from behind his desk. 'Just over here, sir. The lobby telephone. This box is soundproof.'

Mr Hendriks looked stonily at him. 'And the machine. That also is soundproof?'

Leiter looked politely puzzled. 'I'm afraid I don't understand, sir. It is connected directly with the operator.'

'Is no matter. Show me, pliss.' Mr Hendriks followed Leiter to the far corner of the lobby and was shown into the booth. He carefully closed the leather-padded door and picked up the receiver and talked into it. Then he stood waiting, watching Leiter come back across the marble floor and speak deferentially to Bond. 'You were saying, sir?'

'It's my lavatory. Something wrong with the ballcock. Is there anywhere else?'

'I'm so sorry, sir. I'll have the house engineer look at it at once. Yes, certainly. There's the lobby toilet. The decoration isn't completed and it's not officially in use, but it's in perfectly good working order.' He lowered his voice. 'And there's a connecting door with my office. Leave it for ten minutes while I run back the tape of what this bastard's saying. I heard the call was coming through. Don't like the sound of it. May be your worry.' He gave a little bow and waved Bond towards the central table with magazines on it. 'If you'll just take a seat for a few moments, sir, and then I'll take care of you.'

Bond nodded his thanks and turned away. In the booth, Hendriks was talking. His eyes were fixed on Bond with a terrible intensity. Bond felt the skin crawl at the base of his stomach. This was it all right! He sat down and picked up an old *Wall Street Journal*. Surreptitiously he tore a small piece out of the centre of page one. It could have been a tear at the cross-fold. He held the paper up at page two and watched Hendriks through the little hole.

Hendriks watched the back of the paper and talked and listened. He suddenly put down the receiver and came out of the booth. His face gleamed with sweat. He took out a clean white handkerchief and ran it over his face and neck and walked rapidly off down the corridor.

Nick Nicholson, as neat as a pin, came across the lobby and, with a courtly smile and a bow for Bond, took up his place behind the desk. It was 8.30. Five minutes later, Felix Leiter came out from the inner office. He said something to Nicholson and came over to Bond. There was a pale, pinched look round his mouth. He said, 'And now, if you'll follow me, sir.' He led the way across the lobby, unlocked the men's room door, followed Bond in and locked the door behind him. They stood among the carpentry work by the wash-basins. Leiter said tensely, 'I guess you've had it, James. They were talking Russian, but your name and number kept on cropping up. Guess you'd better get out of here just as quickly as that old jalopy of yours'll carry you.'

Bond smiled thinly. 'Forewarned is forearmed, Felix. I knew it already. Hendriks has been told to rub me. Our old friend at K.G.B. headquarters, Semichastny, has got it in for me. I'll tell you why one of these days.' He told Leiter of the Mary Goodnight episode of the early hours. Leiter listened gloomily. Bond concluded, 'So there's no object in getting out now. We shall hear all the dope and probably their plans for me at this meeting at ten.

Then they've got this excursion business afterwards. Personally I guess the shooting match'll take place somewhere out in the country where there are no witnesses. Now, if you and Nick could work out something that'd upset the Away Engagement, I'll make myself responsible for the home pitch.'

Leiter looked thoughtful. Some of the cloud lifted from his face. He said, 'I know the plans for this afternoon. Off on this miniature train through the cane fields, picnic, then the boat out of Green Island Harbour, deep-sea fishing and all that. I've reconnoitred the route for it all.' He raised the thumb of his left hand and pinged the end of his steel hook thoughtfully. 'Ye-e-e-s. It's going to mean some quick action and a heap of luck and I'll have to get the hell up to Frome for some supplies from your friend Hugill. Will he hand over some gear on your say-so? Okay, then. Come into my office and write him a note. It's only a half-hour's drive and Nick can hold the front desk for that time. Come on.' He opened a side door and went through into his office. He beckoned Bond to follow and shut the door behind him. At Leiter's dictation, Bond took down the note to the manager of the WISCO sugar estates and then went out and along to his room. He took a strong nip of straight bourbon and sat on the edge of his bed and looked unseeingly out of the window and across the lawn to the sea's horizon. Like a dozing hound chasing a rabbit in its dreams, or like the audience at an athletics meeting that lifts a leg to help the high-jumper over the bar, every now and then, his right hand twitched involuntarily. In his mind's eye, in a variety of imagined circumstances, it was leaping for his gun.

Time passed and James Bond still sat there, occasionally smoking half-way through a Royal Blend and then absent-mindedly stubbing it out in the bed-table ash-tray. An observer would have made nothing of his thoughts. The pulse in his left temple was beating a little fast. There was some tension, but perhaps only the concentration applied to his thinking, in the slightly pursed lips, but the brooding, blue-grey eyes that saw nothing were relaxed, almost sleepy. It would have been impossible to guess that James Bond was contemplating the possibility of his own death later that day, feeling the soft-nosed bullets tearing into him, seeing his body jerking on the ground, his mouth perhaps screaming. Those were certainly part of his thoughts, but the twitching right hand was evidence that, in much of the whirring film of his thoughts, the enemy's fire was not going unanswered – perhaps had even been anticipated.

James Bond gave a deep relaxed sigh. His eyes came back into focus. He looked at his watch. It said 9.50. He got up, ran both hands down his lean face with a scrubbing motion, and went out and along the corridor to the conference room.

12 .... IN A GLASS, VERY DARKLY

THE SET-UP was the same. Bond's travel literature was on the buffet table where he had left it. He went through into the conference room. It had only been cursorily tidied. Scaramanga had probably said it was not to be entered by the staff. The chairs were roughly in position, but the ash-trays had not been emptied. There were no stains on the carpet and no signs of the carpet having been washed. It had probably been a single shot through the heart. With Scaramanga's soft-nosed bullets, the internal damage would be devastating, but the fragments of the bullet would stay in the body and there would be no bleeding. Bond went round the table, ostentatiously positioning the chairs more accurately. He identified the one where Ruby Rotkopf must have sat, across the table from Scaramanga, because it had a cracked leg. He dutifully examined the windows and looked behind the curtains, doing his job. Scaramanga came into the room followed by Mr Hendriks. He said roughly, 'Okay, Mr Hazard. Lock both doors like yesterday. No one to come in. Right?'

'Yes.' As Bond passed Mr Hendriks he said cheerfully, 'Good morning, Mr Hendriks. Enjoy the party last night?'

Mr Hendriks gave his usual curt bow. He said nothing. His eyes were granite marbles.

Bond went out and locked the doors and took up his position with the brochures and the champagne glass. Immediately, Hendriks began talking, quickly and urgently, fumbling for the English words. 'Mister S. I have bad troubles to report. My Zentrale in Havana spoke with me this morning. They have heard direct from Moscow. This man' – he must have made a gesture towards the door – 'this man is the British secret agent, the man Bond. There is no doubt. I am given the exact descriptions. When he goes swimming this morning, I am examining his body through glasses. The wounds on his body are clearly to be seen. The scar down the right side of the face leaves no doubt. And his shooting last night! The ploddy fool is proud of his shooting. I would like to see a member of my organization behave in zees stupid fashions! I would have him shot immediately.' There was a pause. The man's tone altered, became slightly menacing. His target was now Scaramanga. 'But, Mister S. How can this have come about? How can you possibly have let it arrive? My Zentrale is dumbfounded at the mistake. The man might have done much damage but for the watchfulness of my superiors. Please explain, Mister S. I must be making the very full report. How is it that you are meeting this man? How is it that you are then carrying him efen into the centre of The Group? The details, pliss, Mister. The full accounting. My superiors will be expressing sharp criticism of the lack of vigilance against the enemy.'

Bond heard the rasp of a match against a box. He could imagine Scaramanga sitting back and going through the smoking routine. The voice, when it came, was decisive, uncowed. 'Mr Hendriks, I appreciate your outfit's concern about this and

I congratulate them on their sources of information. But you tell your Central this: I met this man completely by accident, at least I thought so at the time, and there's no use worrying about how it happened. It hasn't been easy to set up this conference and I needed help. I had to get two managers in a hurry from New York to handle the hotel people. They're doing a good job, right? The floor staff and all the rest I had to get from Kingston. But what I really needed was a kind of personal assistant who could be around to make sure that everything went smoothly. Personally, I just couldn't be bothered with all the details. When this guy dropped out of the blue he looked all right to me. So I picked him up. But I'm not stupid. I knew that when this show was over I'd have to get rid of him, just in case he'd learned anything he shouldn't have. Now you say he's a member of the Secret Service. I told you at the beginning of this conference that I eat these people for breakfast when I have a mind to. What you've told me changes just one thing: he'll die today instead of tomorrow. And here's how it's going to happen.' Scaramanga lowered his voice. Now Bond could only hear disjointed words. The sweat ran down from his ear as he pressed it to the base of the champagne glass. 'Our train trip ... rats in the cane ... unfortunate accident ... before I do it ... one hell of a shock ... details to myself ... promise you a big laugh'. Scaramanga must have sat back again. Now his voice was normal. 'So you can rest easy. There'll be nothing left of the guy by this evening. Okay? I could get it over with now by just opening the door. But two blown fuses in two days might stir up gossip around here. And this way there'll be a heap of fun for everyone on the picnic.'

Mr Hendriks's voice was flat and uninterested. He had carried out his orders and action was about to follow, definite action. There could be no complaint of delay in carrying out orders. He said, 'Yes. What you are proposing will be satisfactory. I shall observe the proceedings with much amusement. And now to other business. Plan Orange. My superiors are wishing to know that everything is in order.'

'Yes. Everything's in order at Reynolds Metal, Kaiser Bauxite and Alumina of Jamaica. But your stuff's plenty – what do they call it – volatile. Got to be replaced in the demolition chambers every five years. Hey,' there was a dry chuckle, 'I sure snickered when I saw that the how-do-it labels on the drums were in some of these African languages as well as English. Ready for the big black uprising, huh? You better warn me about The Day. I hold some pretty vulnerable stocks on Wall Street.'

'Then you will lose a lot of money,' said Mr Hendriks flatly. 'I shall not be told the date. I do not mind. I hold no stocks. You would be wise to keep your money in gold or diamonds or rare postage stamps. And now the next matter. It is of interest to my superiors to be able to place their hands on a very great quantity of narcotics. You have a source for the supply of ganja, or marijuana as we call it. You are now receiving your supplies in pound weight. I am asking whether you can stimulate your sources of supply to providing the weed by the hundredweight. It is suggested that you then run shipments to the Pedro Cays. My friends can arrange for collection from there.'

There was a brief silence. Scaramanga would be smoking his thin cheroot. He said, 'Yeah, I think we could swing that. But they've just put some big teeth into these ganja laws. Real rough jail sentences, see? So the goddam price has up and gone through the roof. The going price today is £16 an ounce. A hundredweight of the stuff could cost thousands of pounds. And it's darned bulky in those quantities. My fishing boat could probably only ship one hundredweight at a time. Anyway, where's it for? You'll be lucky to get those quantities ashore. A pound or two is difficult enough.'

'I am not being told the destinations. I assume it is for America. They are the largest consumers. Arrangements have been made to receive this and other consignments initially off the coast of Georgia. I am being told that this area is full of small islands and swamps and is already much favoured by smugglers. The money is of no importance. I have instructions to make an initial outlay of a million dollars, but at keen market prices. You will be receiving your usual ten per cent commission. Is it that you are interested?'

'I'm always interested in a hundred thousand dollars. I'll have to get in touch with my growers. They have their planta-tions in the Maroon country. That's in the centre of the island. This is going to take time. I can give you a quotation in about two weeks – a hundredweight of the stuff f.o.b. the Pedro Cays. Okay?'

'And a date? The Cays are very flat. This is not stuff to be left lying about, isn't it?'

'Sure. Sure. Now then. Any other business? Okay. Well, I've got something I'd like to bring up. This casino lark. Now, this is the picture. The government are tempted. They think it'll stimulate the tourist industry. But the Heavies – the boys who were kicked out of Havana, the Vegas machine, the Miami jokers, Chicago – the whole works, didn't take the measure of these people before they put the heat on. And they overplayed the slush fund approach – put too much money in the wrong pockets. Guess they should have employed a public relations outfit. Jamaica looks small on the map, and I guess the Syndicates thought they could hurry through a neat little operation like the Nassau job. But the Opposition party got wise, and the Church, and the old women, and there was talk of the Mafia taking over in Jamaica, the old "Cosa Nostra" and all that crap, and the spiel flopped. Remember we were offered an "in" coupla years back? That was when they saw it was a bust and wanted to unload their promotion expenses, coupla million bucks or so, on to The Group. You recall I advised against and gave my reasons. Okay. So we said no. But things have changed. Different party in power, bit of a tourist slump last year, and a certain Minister has been in touch with me. Says the climate's changed. Independence has come along and they've got out from behind the skirts of Aunty England. Want to show that Jamaica's with it. Got oomph and all that. So this friend of mine says he can get gambling off the pad here. He told me how and it makes sense. Before, I said stay out. Now I say come in. But it's going to cost money. Each of us'll have to chip in with a hundred thousand bucks to give local encouragement. Miami'll be the operators and get the franchise. The deal is that they'll put us in for five per cent – but off the top. Get me? On these figures, and they're not loaded, our juice should have been earned in eighteen months. After that it's gravy. Get the photo? But your, er, friends, don't seem too keen on these, er, capitalist enterprises. How do you figure it? Will they ante up? I don't want for us to go outside for the green. And, as from yesterday, we're missing a shareholder. Come to think of it, we've got to think of that too. Who we goin' to rope in as Number Six? We're short of a game for now.'

James Bond wiped his ear and the bottom of the glass with his handkerchief. It was almost unbearable. He had heard his own death sentence pronounced, the involvement of the K.G.B. with Scaramanga and the Caribbean spelled out, and such minor dividends as sabotage of the bauxite industry, massive drug smuggling into the States and gambling politics thrown in. It was a majestic haul in area Intelligence. He had the ball! Could he live to touch down with it? God, for a drink! He put his ear back to the hot base of the glass.

There was silence. When it came, the voice of Hendriks was cautious, indecisive. He obviously wanted to say 'I pass' – with the corollary, 'until I've talked to my Zentrale, isn't it?'

He said, 'Mister S. Is difficult pizzness, yes? My superiors are not disliking the profitable involvements but, as you will be knowing, they are most liking the pizzness that has the political objective. It was on these conditions that they instructed me to ally myself with your Group. The money, that is not the problem. But how am I to explain the political objective of opening casinos in Jamaica? This I am wondering.'

'It'll almost certainly lead to trouble. The locals'll want to play – they're terrific gamblers here. There'll be incidents. Coloured people'll be turned away from the doors for one reason or another. Then the Opposition party'll get hold of that and raise hell about colour bars and so on. With all the money flying about, the unions'll push wages through the roof. It can all add up to a fine stink. The atmosphere's too damn peaceful around here. This'll be a cheap way of raising plenty of hell. That's what your people want, isn't it? Give the islands the hot foot one after another?'

There was another brief silence. Mr Hendriks obviously didn't like the idea. He said so, but obliquely: 'What you are saying, Mister S., is very interesting. But is it not that these troubles you envisage will endanger our monies? However, I will report your inquiry and inform you at once. It is possible that my superiors will be sympathetic. Who can be telling? Now there is this question of a new Number Six. Are you having anyone in mind?'

'I think we want a good man from South America. We need a guy to oversee our operations in British Guiana. We oughta get smartened up in Venezuela. How come we never got further with that great scheme for blocking the Maracaibo Bar? Like robbing a blind man, given a suitable block ship. Just the threat of it would make the oil companies shell out – that's a joke by the way – and go on shelling by way of protection. Then, if this narcotics spiel is going to be important, we can't do without Mexico. How about Mr Arosio of Mexico City?'

'I am not knowing this gentleman.'

'Rosy? Oh, he's a great guy. Runs the Green Light Transportation System. Drugs and girls into L.A. Never been caught yet. Reliable operator. Got no affiliates. Your people'll know about him. Why not check with them and then we'll put it up to the others? They'll go along with our say-so.'

'Is good. And now, Mister S. Have you anything to report about your own employer? On his recent visit to Moscow, I understand that he expressed satisfaction with your efforts in this area. It is a matter for gratification that there should be such close co-operation between his subversive efforts and our own. Both our chiefs are expecting much in the future from our union with the Mafia. Myself I am doubting. Mr Gengerella is undoubtedly a valuable link, but it is my impression that these people are only being activated by money. What is it that you are thinking?'

'You've said it, Mr Hendriks. In the opinion of my chief, the Mafia's first and only consideration is the Mafia. It has always been so and it always will be so. My Mister C. is not expecting great results in the States. Even the Mafia can't buck the anti-Cuban feeling there. But he thinks we can achieve plenty in the Caribbean by giving them odd jobs to do. They can be very effective. It would certainly oil the wheels if your people would use the Mafia as a pipeline for this narcotics business. They'll turn your million-dollar investment into ten. They'll grab the nine out of it of course. But that's not peanuts, and it'll tie them in to you. Think you could arrange that? It'll give Leroy G. some good news to report when he gets home. As for Mister C., he seems to be going along all right. Flora was a body-blow but, largely thanks to the Americans leaning on Cuba the way they do, he's kept the country together. If the Americans once let up on their propaganda and needling and so forth, perhaps even make a friendly gesture or two, all the steam'll go out of the little man. I don't often see him. He leaves me alone. Likes to keep his nose clean, I guess. But I get all the co-operation I need from the D.S.S. Okay? Well let's go see if the folks are ready to move. It's eleven-thirty and the Bloody Bay Belle is due to be on her way at twelve. Guess it's going to be quite a fun day. Pity our Chiefs aren't going to be along to see the limey eye get his chips.'

'Ha!' said Mr Hendriks noncommittally.

James Bond moved away from the door. He heard Mr Scaramanga's pass key in the lock. He looked up and yawned.

Mr Scaramanga and Mr Hendriks looked down at him. Their expressions were vaguely interested and reflective. It was as if he were a bit of steak and they were wondering whether to have it done rare or medium rare.

13 .... HEAR THE TRAIN BLOW!

AT TWELVE o'clock they all assembled in the lobby. Scaramanga had added a broad-brimmed white Stetson to his immaculate tropical attire. He looked like the smartest plantation owner in the South. Mr Hendriks wore his usual stuffy suit, now topped with a grey Homburg. Bond thought that he should have grey suede gloves and an umbrella. The four hoods were wearing calypso shirts outside their slacks. Bond was pleased. If they were carrying guns in their waistbands, the shirts would hinder the draw. Cars were drawn up outside with Scaramanga's Thunderbird in the lead. Scaramanga walked up to the desk. Nick Nicholson was standing washing his hands in invisible soap and looking helpful. 'All set? Everything loaded on the train? Green Harbour been told? Okay, then. Where's that sidekick of yours, that man Travis? Haven't seen him around today.'

Nick Nicholson looked serious. 'He got an abscess in his tooth, sir. Real bad. Had to send him in to Sav' La Mar to have it out. He'll be okay by this afternoon.'

'Too bad. Dock him half a day's pay. No room for sleepers on this outfit. We're short-handed as it is. Should have had his snappers attended to before he took the job on. 'Kay?'

'Very good, Mr Scaramanga. I'll tell him.'

Mr Scaramanga turned to the waiting group. 'Okay, fellers. Now this is the spiel. We drive a mile down the road to the station. We get aboard this little train. Quite an outfit that. Feller by the name of Lucius Beebe had it copied for the Thunderbird company from the engine and rolling stock on the little old Denver, South Park and Pacific line. Okay. So we steam along this old cane-field line about twenty miles to Green Island Harbour. Plenty birds, bush rats, crocs in the rivers. Mebbe we get a little hunting. Have some fun with the hardware. All you guys got your guns with you? Fine, fine. Champagne lunch at Green Island and the girls and the music'll be there to keep us happy. After lunch we get aboard the *Thunder Bird*, big Chris-Craft, and take a cruise along to Lucea, that's a little township down the coast, and see if we can catch our dinner. Those that don't want to fish can play stud. Right? Then back here for drinks. Okay? Everyone satisfied? Any suggestions? Then let's go.'

Bond was told to get in the back of the car. They set off. Once again that offered neck! Crazy not to take him now! But it was open country with no cover and there were four guns riding behind. The odds simply weren't good enough. What was the plan for his removal? During the 'hunting' presumably. James Bond smiled grimly to himself. He was feeling happy. He wouldn't have been able to explain the emotion. It was a feeling of being keyed up, wound taut. It was the moment, after twenty passes, when you got a hand you could bet on – not necessarily win, but bet on. He had been after this man for over six weeks. Today, this morning perhaps, was to come the pay-off he had been ordered to bring about. It was win or lose. The odds? Foreknowledge was playing for him. He was more heavily forearmed than the enemy knew. But the enemy had the big battalions on their side. There were more of them. And, taking only Scaramanga, perhaps more talent. Weapons? Again leaving out the others, Scaramanga had the advantage. The long-barrelled Colt .45 would be a fraction slower on the draw, but its length of barrel would give it more accuracy than the Walther automatic. Rate of fire? The Walther should have the edge – and the first empty chamber of Scaramanga's gun, if it hadn't been discovered, would be an additional bonus. The steady hand? The cool brain? The sharpness of the lust to kill? How did they weigh up? Probably nothing to choose on the first two. Bond might be a shade trigger-happy – of necessity. That he must watch. He must damp down the fire in his belly. Get ice-cold. In the lust to kill, perhaps he was the strongest. Of course. He was fighting for his life. The other man was just amusing himself – providing sport for his friends, displaying his potency, showing off. That was good! That might be decisive! Bond said to himself that he must increase the other man's unawareness, his casual certitude, his lack of caution. He must be the P. G. Wodehouse Englishman, the limey of the cartoons. He must play easy to take. The adrenalin coursed into James Bond's bloodstream. His pulse rate began to run a fraction high. He felt it on his wrist. He breathed deeply and slowly to bring it down. He found that he was sitting forward, tensed. He sat back and tried to relax. All of his body relaxed except his right hand. This was in the control of someone else. Resting on his right thigh, it still twitched slightly from time to time like the paw of a sleeping dog chasing rabbits. He put it into his coat pocket and watched a turkey buzzard a thousand feet up, circling. He put himself into the mind of the 'John Crow', watching out for a squashed toad or a dead bush rat. The circling buzzard had found its offal. It came lower and lower. Bond wished it 'bon appétit'. The predator in him wished the scavenger a good meal.

He smiled at the comparison between them. They were both following a scent. The main difference was that the John Crow was a protected bird. No one would shoot back at it when it made its final dive. Amused by his thoughts, Bond's right hand came out of his pocket and lit a cigarette for him, quietly and obediently. It had stopped going off chasing rabbits on its own.

The station was a brilliant mock-up from the Colorado narrow-gauge era – a low building in faded clapboard ornamented with gingerbread along its eaves. Its name 'Thunder-bird Halt' was in old-style ornamental type, heavily seriffed. Advertisements proclaimed 'Chew Roseleaf Fine Cut Warranted Finest Virginia Leaf', 'Trains Stop for all Meals', 'No Checks Accepted'. The engine, gleaming in black and yellow varnish and polished brass, was a gem. It stood, panting quietly in the sunshine, a wisp of black smoke curling up from the tall stack behind the big brass headlight. The engine's name 'The Belle' was on a proud brass plate on the gleaming black barrel and its number, 'No. 1', on a similar plate below the headlight. There was one carriage, an open affair with padded foam-rubber seats and a daffodil Surrey roof of fringed canvas to keep off the sun, and then the brake van, also in black and yellow, with a resplendent gilt-armed chair behind the conventional wheel of the brake. It was a wonderful toy even down to the old-fashioned whistle which now gave a sharp admonitory blast.

Scaramanga was in ebullient form. 'Hear the train blow, folks! All aboard!' There was an anticlimax. To Bond's dismay he took out his golden pistol, pointed it at the sky and pressed the trigger. He hesitated only momentarily and fired again. The deep boom echoed back from the wall of the station and the stationmaster, resplendent in old-fashioned uniform, looked nervous. He pocketed the big silver turnip watch he had been holding and stood back obsequiously, the green flag now drooping at his side.

Scaramanga checked his gun. He looked thoughtfully at Bond and said, 'All right, my friend. Now then, you get up front with the driver.'

Bond smiled happily. 'Thanks. I've always wanted to do that since I was a child. What fun!'

'You've said it,' said Scaramanga. He turned to the others. 'And you, Mr Hendriks. In the first seat behind the coal-tender, please. Then Sam and Leroy. Then Hal and Louie. I'll be up back in the brake van. Good place to watch out for game. 'Kay?'

Everybody took their seats. The station-master had recovered his nerve and went through his ploy with the watch and the flag. The engine gave a triumphant hoot and, with a series of diminishing puffs, got under way and they bowled off along the three-foot gauge line that disappeared, as straight as an arrow, into a dancing shimmer of silver.

Bond read the speed gauge. It said twenty. For the first time he paid attention to the driver. He was a villainous-looking Rastafari in dirty khaki overalls with a sweat rag round his forehead. A cigarette drooped from between the thin moustache and the straggling beard. He smelled quite horrible. Bond said, 'My name's Mark Hazard. What's yours?'

'Rass, man! Ah doan talk wid buckra.'

The expression 'rass' is Jamaican for 'shove it'. 'Buckra' is a tough colloquialism for 'white man'.

Bond said equably, 'I thought part of your religion was to love thy neighbour.'

The Rasta gave the whistle halyard a long pull. When the shriek had died away, he simply said 'Sheeit', kicked the furnace door open and began shovelling coal.

Bond looked surreptitiously round the cabin. Yes. There it was! The long Jamaican cutlass, this one filed to an inch blade with a deadly point. It was on a rack by the man's hand. Was this the way he was supposed to go? Bond doubted it. Scaramanga would do the deed in a suitably dramatic fashion and one that would give him an alibi. Second executioner would be Hendriks. Bond looked back over the low coal-tender. Hendriks's eyes, bland and indifferent, met his. Bond shouted above the iron clang of the engine, 'Great fun, what?' Hendriks's eyes looked away and back again. Bond stooped so that he could see under the top of the Surrey. All the other four men were sitting motionless, their eyes also fixed on Bond. Bond waved a cheerful hand. There was no response. So they had been told! Bond was a spy in their midst and this was his last ride. In mobese, he was 'going to be hit'. It was an uncomfortable feeling having those ten enemy eyes watching him like ten gun barrels. Bond straightened himself. Now the top half of his body, like the iron 'man' in a pistol range, was above the roof of the Surrey and he was looking straight down the flat yellow surface to where Scaramanga sat on his solitary throne, perhaps twenty feet away, with all his body in full view. He also was looking down the little train at Bond – the last mourner in the funeral cortège behind the cadaver that was James Bond. Bond waved a cheery hand and turned back. He opened his coat and got a moment's reassurance from the cool butt of his gun. He felt in his trouser pocket. Three spare magazines. Ah, well! He'd take as many of them as he could with him. He flipped down the co-driver's seat and sat on it. No point in offering a target until he had to. The Rasta flicked his cigarette over the side and lit another. The engine was driving herself. He leant against the cabin wall and looked at nothing.

Bond had done his homework on the 1:50,000 Overseas Survey map that Mary had provided and he knew exactly the route the little cane line took. First there would be five miles of the cane fields between whose high green walls they were now travelling. Then came Middle River, followed by the vast expanse of swamplands, now being slowly reclaimed, but still shown on the map as 'The Great Morass'. Then would come Orange River leading into Orange Bay, and then more sugar and mixed forest and agricultural smallholdings until they came to the little hamlet of Green Island at the head of the excellent anchorage of Green Island Harbour.

A hundred yards ahead, a turkey buzzard rose from beside the line and, after a few heavy flaps, caught the inshore breeze and soared up and away. There came the boom of Scaramanga's gun. A feather drifted down from the great right-hand wing of the big bird. The turkey buzzard swerved and soared higher. A second shot rang out. The bird gave a jerk and began to tumble untidily down out of the sky. It jerked again as a third bullet hit it before it crashed into the cane. There was applause from under the yellow Surrey. Bond leant out and called to Scaramanga, 'That'll cost you five pounds unless you've squared the Rasta. That's the fine for killing a John Crow.'

A shot whistled past Bond's head. Scaramanga laughed. 'Sorry. Thought I saw a rat.' And then, 'Come on, Mr Hazard. Let's see some gun play from you. There's some cattle grazing by the line up there. See if you can hit a cow at ten paces.'

The hoods guffawed. Bond put his head out again. Scaramanga's gun was on his lap. Out of the corner of his eye he saw that Mr Hendriks, perhaps ten feet behind him, had his right hand in his coat pocket. Bond called, 'I never shoot game that I don't eat. If you'll eat the whole cow, I'll shoot it for you.'

The gun flashed and boomed as Bond jerked his head under cover of the coal-tender. Scaramanga laughed harshly. 'Watch your lip, limey, or you'll end up without it.' The hoods haw-hawed.

Beside Bond, the Rasta gave a curse. He pulled hard on the whistle lanyard. Bond looked down the line. Far ahead, across the rails, something pink showed. Still whistling, the driver pulled on a lever. Steam belched from the train's exhaust and the engine began to slow. Two shots rang out and the bullets clanged against the iron roof over his head. Scaramanga shouted angrily, 'Keep steam up, damn you to hell!'

The Rasta quickly pushed up the lever and the speed of the train gathered back to 20 m.p.h. He shrugged. He glanced at Bond. He licked his lips wetly. 'Dere's white trash across de line. Guess mebbe it's some frien' of de boss.'

Bond strained his eyes. Yes! It was a naked pink body with golden blonde hair! A girl's body!

Scaramanga's voice boomed against the wind. 'Folks. Jes' a little surprise for you all. Something from the good old Western movies. There's a girl on the line ahead. Tied across it. Take a look. And you know what? It's the girl friend of a certain man we've been hearing of called James Bond. Would you believe it? An' her name's Goodnight, Mary Goodnight. It sure is goodnight for her. If only that fellow Bond was aboard now, I guess we'd be hearing him holler for mercy.'

14 .... THE GREAT MORASS

JAMES BOND leaped for the accelerator lever and tore it downwards. The engine lost a head of steam but there was only a hundred yards to go and now the only thing that could save the girl
was the brakes under Scaramanga's control in the brake van. The
Rasta already had his cutlass in his hand. The flames from the
furnace glinted on the blade. He stood back like a cornered animal, his eyes red with ganja and fear of the gun in Bond's hand.
Nothing could save the girl now! Bond, knowing that Scaramanga
would expect him from the right side of the tender, leaped to the
left. Hendriks had his gun out. Before it could swivel, Bond put
a bullet between the man's cold eyes. The head jerked back. For
an instant, steel-capped back teeth showed in the gaping mouth.
Then the grey Homburg fell off and the dead head slumped. The
golden gun boomed twice. A bullet whanged round the cabin.
The Rasta screamed and fell to the ground, clutching at his throat.
His hand was still clenched round the whistle lanyard and the little train kept up its mournful howl of warning. Fifty yards to go!
The golden hair hung forlornly forward, obscuring the face. The

ropes on the wrists and ankles showed clearly. The breasts offered themselves to the screaming engine. Bond ground his teeth and shut his mind to the dreadful impact that would come any minute now. He leaped to the left again and got off three shots. He thought two of them had hit, but then something slammed a great blow into the muscle of his left shoulder and he spun across the cab and crashed to the iron floor, his face over the edge of the footplate. And it was from there, only inches away, that he saw the front wheels scrunch through the body on the line, saw the blonde head severed from the body, saw the china-blue eyes give him a last blank stare, saw the fragments of the showroom dummy disintegrate with a sharp crackling of plastic and the pink splinters shower down the embankment.

James Bond choked back the sickness that rose from his stomach into the back of his throat. He staggered to his feet, keeping low. He reached up for the accelerator lever and pushed it upwards. A pitched battle with the train at a standstill would put the odds even more against him. He hardly felt the pain in his shoulder. He edged round the right-hand side of the tender. Four guns boomed. He flung his head back under cover. Now the hoods were shooting, but wildly because of the interference of the Surrey top. But Bond had had time to see one glorious sight. In the brake van, Scaramanga had slid from his throne and was down on his knees, his head moving to and fro like a wounded animal. Where in hell had Bond hit him? And now what? How was he going to deal with the four hoods, just as badly obscured from him as he was from them?

Then a voice from the back of the train, it could only be from the brake van, Felix Leiter's voice, called out above the shriek of the engine's whistle, 'Okay, you four guys. Toss your guns over the side. Now! Quick!' There came the crack of a shot. 'I said quick! There's Mr Gengerella gone to meet his maker. Okay, then. And now hands behind your heads. That's better. Right. Okay, James. The battle's over. Are you okay? If so, show yourself. There's still the final curtain and we've got to move quick.'

Bond rose carefully. He could hardly believe it! Leiter must have been riding on the buffers behind the brake van. He wouldn't have been able to show himself earlier for fear of Bond's gunfire. Yes! There he was! His fair hair tousled by the wind, a long-barrelled pistol using his upraised steel hook as a rest, standing astride the now supine body of Scaramanga beside the brake wheel. Bond's shoulder had begun to hurt like hell. He shouted, with the anger of tremendous relief, 'God damn you, Leiter. Why in hell didn't you show up before? I might have got hurt.'

Leiter laughed. 'That'll be the day! Now listen, shamus. Get ready to jump. The longer you wait, the farther you've got to walk home. I'm going to stay with these guys for a while and hand them over to the law in Green Harbour.' He shook his head to show this was a lie. 'Now get goin'. It's The Morass. The landing'll be soft. Stinks a bit, but we'll give you an eau-de-Cologne spray when you get home. Right?'

The train ran over a small culvert and the song of the wheels changed to a deep boom. Bond looked ahead. In the distance was the spidery iron work of the Orange River bridge. The still shrieking train was losing steam. The gauge said 19 m.p.h. Bond looked down at the dead Rasta. In death, his face was as horrible as it had been in life. The bad teeth, sharpened from eating sugar cane from childhood, were bared in a frozen snarl. Bond took a quick glance under the Surrey. Hendriks's slumped body lolled with the movement of the train. The sweat of the day still shone on the doughy cheeks. Even as a corpse he didn't ask for sympathy. In the seat behind him, Leiter's bullet had torn through the back of Gengerella's head and removed most of his face. Next to him, and behind him, the three gangsters gazed up at James Bond with whipped eyes. They hadn't expected all this. This was to have been a holiday. The calypso shirts said so. Mr Scaramanga, the undefeated, the undefeatable, had said so. Until minutes before, his golden gun had backed up his word. Now, suddenly, everything was different. As the Arabs say when a great sheikh has gone, has removed his protection, 'Now there is no more shade!' They were covered with guns from the front and rear. The train stretched out its iron stride towards nowhere they had ever heard of before. The whistle moaned. The sun beat down. The dreadful stink of The Great Morass assailed their nostrils. This was abroad. This was bad news, really bad. The Tour Director had left them to fend for themselves. Two of them had been killed. Even their guns were gone. The tough faces, as white moons, gazed in supplication up at Bond. Louie Paradise's voice was cracked and dry with terror. 'A million bucks, Mister, if you get us out of this. Swear on my mother. A million.'

The faces of Sam Binion and Hal Garfinkel lit up. Here was hope! 'And a million.'

'And another! On my baby son's head!'

The voice of Felix Leiter bellowed angrily. There was a note of panic in it. 'Jump, damn you James! Jump!

James Bond stood up in the cabin, not listening to the voices supplicating from under the yellow Surrey. These men had wanted to watch him being murdered. They had been prepared to murder him themselves. How many dead men had each one of them got on his tally-sheet? Bond got down on the step of the cabin, chose his moment and threw himself clear of the clinker track and into the soft embraces of a stinking mangrove pool.

His explosion into the mud released the stench of hell. Great bubbles of marsh gas wobbled up to the surface and burst glutinously. A bird screeched and clattered off through the foliage. James Bond waded out on to the edge of the embankment. Now his shoulder was really hurting. He knelt down and was as sick as a cat.

When he raised his head it was to see Leiter hurl himself off the brake van, now a good two hundred yards away. He seemed to land clumsily. He didn't get up. And now, within yards of the long iron bridge over the sluggish river, another figure leaped from the train into a clump of mangrove. It was a tall, chocolate-clad figure. There was no doubt about it! It was Scaramanga! Bond cursed feebly. Why in hell hadn't Leiter put a finishing bullet through the man's head? Now there was unfinished business. The cards had only been reshuffled. The end game had still to be played!

The screaming progress of the driverless train changed to a roar as the track took to the trestles of the long bridge. Bond watched it vaguely, wondering when it would run out of steam. What would the three gangsters do now? Take to the hills? Get the train under control and go on to Green Harbour and try and take the *Thunder Bird* across to Cuba? Immediately the answer came! Half-way across the bridge, the engine suddenly reared up like a bucking stallion. At the same time there came a crash of thunder and a vast sheet of flame and the bridge buckled downwards in the centre like a bent leg. Chunks of torn iron sprayed upwards and sideways and there was a splintering crash as the main stanchions gave and slowly bowed down towards the water. Through the jagged gap, the beautiful Belle, a smashed toy, folded upon itself and, with a giant splintering of iron and woodwork and a volcano of spray and steam, thundered into the river.

A deafening silence fell. Somewhere behind Bond, a wakened tree frog tinkled uncertainly. Four white egrets flew down and over the wreck, their necks outstretched inquisitively. In the distance, black dots materialized high up in the sky and circled lazily closer. The sixth sense of the turkey buzzards had told them that the distant explosion was disaster – something that might yield a meal. The sun hammered down on the silver rails and, a few yards away from where Bond lay, a group of yellow butterflies danced in the shimmer. Bond got slowly to his feet and, parting the butterflies, began walking slowly but purposefully up the line towards the bridge. First Felix Leiter and then after the big one that had got away.

Leiter lay in the stinking mud. His left leg was at a hideous angle. Bond went down to him, his finger to his lips. He knelt beside him and said softly, 'Nothing much I can do for now, pal. I'll give you a bullet to bite on and get you into some shade. There'll be people coming before long. Got to get on after that bastard. He's somewhere up there by the bridge. What made you think he was dead?'

Leiter groaned, more in anger with himself than from the pain. 'There was blood all over the place.' The voice was a halting whisper between clenched teeth. 'His shirt was soaked in it. Eyes closed. Thought if he wasn't cold he'd go with the others on the bridge.' He smiled faintly. 'How did you dig the River Kwai stunt? Go off all right?'

Bond raised a thumb. 'Fourth of July. The crocs'll be sitting down to table right now. But that damned dummy! Gave me a nasty turn. Did you put her there?'

'Sure. Sorry, boy. Mr S. told me to. Made an excuse to spike the bridge this morning. No idea your girl friend was a blonde or that you'd fall for the spiel.'

'Bloody silly of me, I suppose. Thought he'd got hold of her last night. Anyway, come on. Here's your bullet. Bite the lead. The story-books say it helps. This is going to hurt, but I must haul you under cover and out of the sun.' Bond got his hands under Leiter's armpits and, as gently as he could, dragged him to a dry patch under a big mangrove bush above swamp level. The sweat of pain poured down Leiter's face. Bond propped him up against the roots. Leiter gave a groan and his head fell back. Bond looked thoughtfully down at him. A faint was probably the best thing that could have happened. He took Leiter's gun out of his waistband and put it beside his left, and only, hand. Bond still might get into much trouble. If he did, Scaramanga would come after Felix.

Bond crept off along the line of mangroves towards the bridge. For the time being he would have to keep more or less in the open. He prayed that, nearer the river, the swamp would yield to drier land so that he could work down towards the sea and then cut back towards the river and hope to pick up the man's tracks.

It was 1.30 and the sun was high. James Bond was hungry and very thirsty and his shoulder wound throbbed with his pulse. The wound was beginning to give him a fever. One dreams all day as well as all night, and now, as he stalked his prey, he found, quizzically, that much of his mind was taken up with visualizing the champagne buffet waiting for them all, the living and the dead, at Green Harbour. For the moment, he indulged himself. The buffet would be laid out under the trees, as he saw it, adjoining the terminal station, which would probably be on the same lines as Thunderbird Halt. There would be long trestle tables, spotless tablecloths, rows of glasses and plates and cutlery and great dishes of cold lobster salad, cold meat cuts, and mounds of fruit – pineapple and such – to make the décor look Jamaican and exotic. There might be a hot dish, he thought. Something like roast stuffed sucking-pig with rice and peas – too hot for the day, decided Bond, but a feast for most of Green Harbour when the rich 'tourists' had departed. And there would be drink! Champagne in frosted silver coolers, rum punches, Tom Collinses, whisky sours, and, of course, great beakers of iced water that would only have been poured when the train whistled its approach to the gay little station. Bond could see it all. Every detail of it under the shade of the great ficus trees. The white-gloved, uniformed coloured waiters enticing him to take more and more; beyond, the dancing waters of the harbour, in the background the hypnotic throb of the calypso band, the soft, enticing eyes of the girls. And, ruling, ordering all, the tall, fine figure of the gracious host, a thin cigar between his teeth, the wide white Stetson tilted low over his brow, offering Bond just one more goblet of iced champagne.

James Bond stumbled over a mangrove root, threw out his right hand for support from the bush, missed, tripped again and fell heavily. He lay for a moment, measuring the noise he must have made. It wouldn't have been much. The inshore wind from the sea was feathering the swamp. A hundred yards away the river added its undertone of sluggish turbulence. There were cricket and bird noises. Bond got to his knees and then to his feet. What in hell had he been thinking of? Come on, you bloody fool! There's work to be done! He shook his head to clear it. Gracious host! God damn it! He was on his way to kill the gracious host! Goblets of iced champagne? That'd be the day! He shook his head angrily. He took several very deep slow breaths. He knew the symptoms. This was nothing worse than acute nervous exhaustion with – he gave himself that amount of grace – a small fever added. All he had to do was to keep his mind and his eyes in focus. For God's sake no more day-dreaming! With a new sharpened resolve he kicked the mirages out of his mind and looked to his geography.

There were perhaps a hundred yards to go to the bridge. On Bond's left, the mangroves were sparser and the black mud was dry and cracked. But there were still soft patches. Bond put up the collar of his coat to hide the white shirt. He covered another twenty yards beside the rail and then struck off left into the man-groves. He found that if he kept close to the roots of the mangroves the going wasn't too bad. At least there were no dry twigs or leaves to crack and rustle. He tried to keep as nearly as possible parallel with the river, but thick patches of bushes made him make small detours and he had to estimate his direction by the dryness of the mud and the slight rise of the land towards the river bank. His ears were pricked like an animal's for the smallest sound. His eyes strained into the greenery ahead. Now the mud was pitted with the burrows of land crabs and there were occasional remnants of their shells, victims of big birds or mongoose. For the first time, mosquitoes and sand-flies began to attack him. He could not slap them off but only dab at them softly with his handkerchief that was soon soaked with the blood they had sucked from him and wringing with the white man's sweat that attracted them.

Bond estimated that he had penetrated two hundred yards into the swamp when he heard the single, controlled cough.

15 .... CRAB-MEAT

THE COUGH sounded about twenty yards away, towards the river. Bond dropped to one knee, his senses questing like the antennae of an insect. He waited five minutes. When the cough was not repeated, he crept forwards on hands and knees, his gun gripped between his teeth.

In a small clearing of dried, cracked black mud, he saw the man. He stopped in his tracks, trying to calm his breathing.

Scaramanga was lying stretched out, his back supported by a clump of sprawling mangrove roots. His hat and his high stock had gone and the whole of the right-hand side of his suit was black with blood upon which insects crawled and feasted. But the eyes in the controlled face were still very much alive. They swept the clearing at regular intervals, questing. Scaramanga's hands rested on the roots beside him. There was no sign of a gun.

Scaramanga's face suddenly pointed, like a retriever's, and the roving scrutiny held steady. Bond could not see what had caught his attention, but then a patch of the dappled shadow at the edge of the clearing moved and a large snake, beautifully diamonded in dark and pale brown, zigzagged purposefully across the black mud towards the man.

Bond watched, fascinated. He guessed it was a boa of the Epicrates family, attracted by the smell of blood. It was perhaps five feet long and quite harmless to man. Bond wondered if Scaramanga would know this. He was immediately put out of his doubt. Scaramanga's expression had not changed, but his right hand crept softly down his trouser leg, gently pulled up the cuff and removed a thin, stiletto-style knife from the side of his short Texan boot. Then he waited, the knife held ready across his stomach, not clenched in his fist, but pointed in the flick-knife fashion. The snake paused for a moment a few yards from the man and raised its head high to give him a final inspection. The forked tongue licked out inquisitively, again and again, then, still with its head held above the ground, it moved slowly forward.

Not a muscle moved in Scaramanga's face. Only the eyes were dead steady, watchful slits. The snake came into the shadow of his trouser leg and moved slowly up towards the glistening shirt. Suddenly the tongue of steel that lay across Scaramanga's stomach came to life and leaped. It transfixed the head of the snake exactly in the centre of the brain and pierced through it, pinning it to the ground and holding it there while the powerful body thrashed wildly, seeking a grip on the mangrove roots, on Scaramanga's arm. But immediately, when it had a grip, its convulsions released its coils which flailed off in another direction.

The death struggles diminished and finally ceased altogether. The snake lay motionless. Scaramanga was careful. He ran his hand down the full length of the snake. Only the tip of the tail lashed briefly. Scaramanga extracted the knife from the head of the snake, cut off its head with a single hard stroke and threw it, after reflection, accurately towards a crab hole. He waited, watching, to see if a crab would come out and take it. None did. The thud of the arrival of the snake's head would have kept any crab underground for many minutes, however enticing the scent of what had made the thud.

James Bond, kneeling in the bush, watched all this, every nuance of it, with the most careful attention. Each one of Scaramanga's actions, every fleeting expression on his face, had been an index of the man's awareness, of his aliveness. The whole episode of the snake was as revealing as a temperature chart or a lie-detector. In Bond's judgement, Mr Scaramanga, for all his blood-letting and internal injuries, was still very much alive. He was still a most formidable and dangerous man.

Scaramanga, his task satisfactorily completed, minutely shifted his position, and, once again, foot by foot, made his penetrating examination of the surrounding bush.

As Scaramanga's gaze swept by him without a flicker, Bond blessed the darkness of his suit – a black patch of shadow among so many others. In the sharp blacks and whites from the midday sun, Bond was well camouflaged.

Satisfied, Scaramanga picked up the limp body of the snake, laid it across his stomach and carefully slit it down its underside as far as the anal vent. Then he scoured it and carefully etched the skin away from the red-veined flesh with the precise flicks and cuts of a surgeon. Every scrap of unwanted reptile he threw towards crab holes and, with each throw, a flicker of annoyance crossed the granite face that no one would come and pick up the crumbs from the rich man's table. When the meal was ready, he once again scanned the bush and then, very carefully, coughed and spat into his hand. He examined the results and flung his hand sideways. On the black ground, the sputum made a bright pink scrawl. The cough didn't seem to hurt him or cause him much effort. Bond guessed that his bullet had hit Scaramanga in the right chest and had missed a lung by a fraction. There was haemorrhage and Scaramanga was a hospital case, but the blood-soaked shirt was not telling the whole truth.

Satisfied with his inspection of his surroundings, Scaramanga bit into the body of the snake and was at once, like a dog with its meal, absorbed by his hunger and thirst for the blood and juices of the snake.

Bond had the impression that, if he now came forward from his hiding-place, Scaramanga, like a dog, would bare his teeth in a furious snarl. He got quietly up from his knees, took out his gun and, his eyes watching Scaramanga's hands, strolled out into the centre of the little clearing.

Bond was mistaken. Scaramanga did not snarl. He barely looked up from the cut-off length of snake in his two hands and, his mouth full of meat, said, 'You've been a long while coming. Care to share my meal?'

'No thanks. I prefer my snake grilled with hot butter sauce. Just keep on eating. I like to see both hands occupied.'

Scaramanga sneered. He gestured at his blood-stained shirt. 'Frightened of a dying man? You limeys come pretty soft.'

'The dying man handled that snake quite efficiently. Got any more weapons on you?' As Scaramanga moved to undo his coat, 'Steady! No quick movements. Just show your belt, armpits, pat the thighs inside and out. I'd do it myself only I don't want what the snake got. And while you're about it, just toss the knife into the trees. Toss. No throwing, if you don't mind. My trigger-finger's been getting a bit edgy today. Seems to want to go about its business on its own. Wouldn't like it to take over. Yet, that is.'

Scaramanga, with a flick of his wrist, tossed the knife into the air. The sliver of steel spun like a wheel in the sunshine. Bond had to step aside. The knife pierced the mud where Bond had been standing and stood upright. Scaramanga gave a harsh laugh. The laugh turned into a cough. The gaunt face contorted painfully. Too painfully? Scaramanga spat red, but not all that red. There could be only slight haemorrhage. Perhaps a broken rib or two. Scaramanga could be out of hospital in a couple of weeks. Scaramanga put down his piece of snake and did exactly as Bond had told him, all the while watching Bond's face with his usual cold, arrogant stare. He finished and picked up the piece of snake and began gnawing it. He looked up. 'Satisfied?'

'Sufficiently.' Bond squatted down on his heels. He held his gun loosely, aiming somewhere half-way between the two of them. 'Now then, let's talk. 'Fraid you haven't got too much time, Scaramanga. This is the end of the road. You've killed too many of my friends. I have the licence to kill you and I am going to kill you. But I'll make it quick. Not like Margesson. Remember him? You put a shot through both of his knees and both of his elbows. Then you made him crawl and kiss your boots. You were foolish enough to boast about it to your friends in Cuba. It got back to us. As a matter of interest, how many men have you killed in your life?'

'With you, it'll make the round fifty.' Scaramanga had gnawed the last segment of backbone clean. He tossed it towards Bond. 'Eat that, scum, and get on with your business. You won't get any secrets out of me, if that's your spiel. An' don't forget. I've been shot at by experts an' I'm still alive. Mebbe not precisely kicking but I've never heard of a limey who'd shoot a defenceless man who's badly wounded. They ain't got the guts. We'll just sit here, chewing the fat, until the rescue team comes. Then I'll be glad to go for trial. What'll they get me for eh?'

'Well, just for a start, there's that nice Mr Rotkopf with one of your famous silver bullets in his head in the river back of the hotel.'

'That'll match with the nice Mr Hendriks with one of your bullets somewhere behind his face. Mebbe we'll serve a bit of time together. That'd be nice, wouldn't it? They say the jail at Spanish Town has all the comforts. How about it, limey? That's where you'll be found with a shiv in your back in the sack-sewing department. An' by the same token, how d'you know about Rotkopf?'

'Your bug was bugged. Seems you're a bit accident-prone these days, Scaramanga. You hired the wrong security men. Both your managers were from the C.I.A. The tape'll be on the way to Washington by now. That's got the murder of Ross on it too. See what I mean? You've got it coming from every which way.'

'Tape isn't evidence in an American court. But I see what you mean, shamus. Mistakes seem to have got made. So okay,' Scaramanga made an expansive gesture of the right hand. 'Take a million bucks and call it quits?'

'I was offered three million on the train.'

'I'll double that.'

'No. Sorry.' Bond got to his feet. The left hand behind his back was clenched with the horror of what he was about to do. He forced himself to think of what the broken body of Margesson must have looked like, of the others that this man had killed, of the ones he would kill afresh if Bond weakened. This man was probably the most efficient one-man death-dealer in the world. James Bond had him. He had been instructed to take him. He must take him – lying down wounded, or in any other position. Bond assumed casualness, tried to make himself the enemy's cold equal. 'Any messages for anyone, Scaramanga? Any instructions? Anyone you want looking after? I'll take care of it if it's personal. I'll keep it to myself.'

Scaramanga laughed his harsh laugh, but carefully. This time the laugh didn't turn into the red cough. 'Quite the little English gentleman! Just like I spelled it out. S'pose you wouldn't like to hand me your gun and leave me to myself for five minutes like in the books? Well, you're right, boyo! I'd crawl after you and blast the back of your head off.' The eyes still bored into Bond's with the arrogant superiority, the cold superman quality that had made him the greatest pro gunman in the world – no drinks, no drugs – the impersonal trigger man who killed for money and, by the way he sometimes did it, for the kicks.

Bond examined him carefully. How could Scaramanga fail to break when he was going to die in minutes? Was there some last trick the man was going to spring? Some hidden weapon? But the man just lay there, apparently relaxed, propped up against the mangrove roots, his chest heaving rhythmically, the granite of his face not crumbling even minutely in defeat. On his forehead, there was not as much sweat as there was on Bond's. Scaramanga lay in dappled black shadow. For ten minutes, James Bond had stood in the middle of the clearing in blazing sunshine. Suddenly he felt the vitality oozing out through his feet into the black mud. And his resolve was going with it. He said, and he heard his voice ring out harshly, 'All right, Scaramanga, this is it.' He lifted his gun and held it in the two-handed grip of the target man. 'I'm going to make it as quick as I can.'

Scaramanga held up a hand. For the first time his face showed emotion. 'Okay, feller.' The voice, amazingly, supplicated. 'I'm a Catholic, see? Jes' let me say my last prayer. Okay? Won't take long, then you can blaze away. Every man's got to die some time. You're a fine guy as guys go. It's the luck of the game. If my bullet had been an inch, mebbe two inches, to the right, it'd be you that's dead in place of me. Right? Can I say my prayer, Mister?'

James Bond lowered his gun. He would give the man a few minutes. He knew he couldn't give him more. Pain and heat and hunger and thirst. It wouldn't be long before he lay down himself, right there on the hard cracked mud, just to rest. If someone wanted to kill him, they could. He said, and the words came out slowly, tiredly, 'Go ahead, Scaramanga. One minute only.'

'Thanks, pal.' Scaramanga's hand went up to his face and covered his eyes. There came a drone of Latin which went on and on. Bond stood there in the sunshine, his gun lowered, watching Scaramanga, but at the same time not watching him, the edge of his focus dulled by the pain and the heat and the hypnotic litany that came from behind the shuttered face and the horror of what Bond was going to have to do – in one minute, perhaps two.

The fingers of Scaramanga's right hand crawled imperceptibly sideways across his face, inch by inch, centimetre by centimetre. They got to his ear and stopped. The drone of the Latin prayer never altered its slow, lulling tempo.

And then the hand leaped behind the head and the tiny golden Derringer roared and James Bond spun round as if he had taken a right to the jaw and crashed to the ground.

At once Scaramanga was on his feet and moving forward like a swift cat. He snatched up the discarded knife and held it forward like a tongue of silver flame.

But James Bond twisted like a dying animal on the ground and the iron in his hand cracked viciously again and again – five times, and then fell out of his hand on to the black earth as his gun-hand went to the right side of his belly and stayed there, clutching at the terrible pain.

The big man stood for a moment and looked up at the deep blue sky. His fingers opened in a spasm and let go the knife. His pierced heart stuttered and limped and stopped. He crashed flat back and lay, his arms flung wide, as if someone had thrown him away.

After a while, the land crabs came out of their holes and began nosing at the scraps of the snake. The bigger offal could wait until the night.

16 .... THE WRAP-UP

THE EXTREMELY smart policeman from the wrecking squad
on the railway came down the river bank at the normal, digni-
fied gait of a Jamaican constable on his beat. No Jamaican policeman ever breaks into a run. He has been taught that this lacks
authority. Felix Leiter, now put under with morphine by the doctor, had said that a good man was after a bad man in the swamp
and that there might be shooting. Felix Leiter wasn't more explicit
than that, but, when he said he was from the F.B.I. – a legitimate
euphemism – in Washington, the policeman tried to get some of
the wrecking squad to come with him and, when he failed, sauntered cautiously off on his own, his baton swinging with assumed
jauntiness.

The boom of the guns and the explosion of screeching marsh
birds gave him an approximate fix. He had been born not far away,
at Negril, and, as a boy, he had often used his gins and his sling-
shot in these marshes. They held no fears for him. When he came
to the approximate point on the river bank, he turned left into the
mangrove and, conscious that his black-and-blue uniform was

desperately conspicuous, stalked cautiously from clump to clump into the morass. He was protected by nothing but his nightstick and the knowledge that to kill a policeman was a capital offence without the option. He only hoped that the good man and the bad man knew this too.

With all the birds gone, there was dead silence. The constable noticed that the tracks of bush rats and other small animals were running past him on a course that converged with his target area. Then he heard the rattling scuttle of the crabs and, in a moment, from behind a thick mangrove clump, he saw the glint of Scaramanga's shirt. He watched and listened. There was no movement and no sound. He strolled, with dignity, into the middle of the clearing, looked at the two bodies and the guns and took out his nickel police whistle and blew three long blasts. Then he sat down in the shade of a bush, took out his report pad, licked his pencil and began writing in a laborious hand.

A week later, James Bond regained consciousness. He was in a green-shaded room. He was under water. The slowly revolving fan in the ceiling was the screw of a ship that was about to run him down. He swam for his life. But it was no good. He was tied down, anchored to the bottom of the sea. He screamed at the top of his lungs. To the nurse at the end of the bed it was the whisper of a moan. At once she was beside him. She put a cool hand on his forehead. While she took his pulse, James Bond looked up at her with unfocused eyes. So this was what a mermaid looked like! He muttered 'You're pretty,' and gratefully swam back down into her arms.

The nurse wrote ninety-five on his sheet and telephoned down to the ward sister. She looked in the dim mirror and tidied her hair in preparation for the R.M.O. in charge of this apparently Very Important Patient.

The Resident Medical Officer, a young Jamaican graduate from Edinburgh, arrived with the matron, a kindly dragon on loan from King Edward VII's. He heard the nurse's report. He went over to the bed and gently lifted Bond's eyelids. He slipped a thermometer under Bond's armpit and held Bond's pulse in one hand and a pocket chronometer in the other and there was silence in the little room. Outside, the traffic tore up and down a Kingston road.

The doctor released Bond's pulse and slipped the chronometer back into the trouser pocket under the white smock. He wrote figures on the chart. The nurse held the door open and the three people went out into the corridor. The doctor talked to the matron. The nurse was allowed to listen. 'He's going to be all right. Temperature well down. Pulse a little fast but that may have been the result of his waking. Reduce the antibiotics. I'll talk to the floor sister about that later. Keep on with the intravenous feeding. Dr Macdonald will be up later to attend to the dressings. He'll be waking again. If he asks for something to drink, give him fruit juice. He should be on soft foods soon. Miracle really. Missed the abdominal viscera. Didn't even shave a kidney. Muscle only. That bullet was dipped in enough poison to kill a horse. Thank God that man at Sav' La Mar recognized the symptoms of snake venom and gave him those massive anti-snake bite injections. Remind me to write to him, matron. He saved the man's life. Now then, no visitors of course, for at least another week. You can tell the police and the High Commissioner's Office that he's on the mend. I don't know who he is, but apparently London keep on worrying us about him. Something to do with the Ministry of Defence. From now on, put them and all other inquiries through to the High Commissioner's Office. They seem to think they're in charge of him.' He paused. 'By the way, how's his friend getting on in Number Twelve? The one the American Ambassador and

Washington have been on about. He's not on my list, but he keeps on asking to see this Mr Bond.'

'Compound fracture of the tibia,' said the matron. 'No complications.' She smiled. 'Except that he's a bit fresh with the nurses. He should be walking with a stick in ten days. He's already seen the police. I suppose it's all to do with that story in the *Gleaner* about those American tourists being killed when the bridge collapsed near Green Island Harbour. But the Commissioner's handling it all personally. The story in the *Gleaner's* very vague.'

The doctor smiled. 'Nobody tells me anything. Just as well. I haven't got the time to listen to them. Well, thank you, matron. I must get along. Multiple crash at Halfway Tree. The ambulances'll be here any minute.' He hurried away. The matron went about her business. The nurse, excited by all this high-level talk, went softly back into the green-shaded room, tidied the sheet over the naked right shoulder of her patient where the doctor had pulled it down, and went back to her chair at the end of the bed and her copy of *Ebony*.

Ten days later, the little room was crowded. James Bond, propped up among extra pillows, was amused by the galaxy of officialdom that had been assembled. On his left was the Commissioner of Police, resplendent in his black uniform with silver insignia. On his right was a Judge of the Supreme Court in full regalia accompanied by a deferential clerk. A massive figure, to whom Felix Leiter, on crutches, was fairly respectful, had been introduced as 'Colonel Bannister' from Washington. Head of Station C, a quiet civil servant called Alec Hill, who had been flown out from London, stood near the door and kept his appraising eyes unwaveringly on Bond. Mary Goodnight, who was to take notes of the proceedings but also, on the matron's strict instructions, watch for any sign of fatigue in James Bond and have absolute authority to close the meeting if he showed strain, sat demurely beside the bed with a shorthand pad on her knees. But James Bond felt no strain. He was delighted to see all these people and know that at last he was back in the great world again. The only matters that worried him were that he had not been allowed to see Felix Leiter before the meeting to agree their stories and that he had been rather curtly advised by the High Commissioner's Office that legal representation would not be necessary.

The Police Commissioner cleared his throat. He said, 'Commander Bond, our meeting here today is largely a formality, but it is held on the Prime Minister's instructions and with your doctor's approval. There are many rumours running around the island and abroad and Sir Alexander Bustamante is most anxious to have them dispelled for the sake of justice and of the island's good name. So this meeting is in the nature of a judicial inquiry having Prime Ministerial status. We very much hope that, if the conclusions of the meeting are satisfactory, there need be no more legal proceedings whatever. You understand?'

'Yes,' said Bond, who didn't.

'Now,' the Commissioner spoke weightily. 'The facts as ascertained are as follows. Recently there took place at the Thunderbird Hotel in the Parish of Westmoreland a meeting of what can only be described as foreign gangsters of outstanding notoriety, including representatives of the Soviet Secret Service, the Mafia, and the Cuban Secret Police. The objects of this meeting were, inter alia, sabotage of Jamaican installations in the cane industry, stimulation of illicit ganja-growing in the island and purchase of the crop for export, the bribery of a high Jamaican official with the object of installing gangster-run gambling in the island and sundry other malfeasances deleterious to law and order in Jamaica and to her international standing. Am I correct, Commander?'

'Yes,' said Bond, this time with a clear conscience.

'Now.' The Commissioner spoke with even greater emphasis. 'The intentions of this subversive group became known to the Criminal Investigation Department of the Jamaican Police and the facts of the proposed assembly were placed before the Prime Minister in person by myself. Naturally the greatest secrecy was observed. A decision then had to be reached as to how this meeting was to be kept under surveillance and penetrated so that its intentions might be learned. Since friendly nations, including Britain and the United States, were involved, secret conversations took place with the representatives of the Ministry of Defence in Britain and of the Central Intelligence Agency in the United States. As a result, expert personnel in the shape of yourself, Mr Nicholson and Mr Leiter were generously made available, at no cost to the Jamaican Government, to assist in unveiling these secret machinations against Jamaica held on Jamaican soil.' The Commissioner paused and looked round the room to see if he had stated the position correctly. Bond had noticed that Felix Leiter nodded his head vigorously with the others, but, in his case, in Bond's direction.

Bond smiled. He had at last got the message. He also nodded his agreement.

'Accordingly,' continued the Commissioner, 'and working throughout under the closest liaison and direction of the Jamaican C.I.D., Messrs Bond, Nicholson and Leiter carried out their duties in exemplary fashion. The true intentions of the gangsters were unveiled, but alas, in the process, the identity of at least one of the Jamaica-controlled agents was discovered and a battle royal took place during the course of which the following enemy agents – here there will be a list – were killed, thanks to the superior gunfire of Commander Bond and Mr Leiter, and the following – another list – by the destruction by Mr Leiter's ingenious use of explosive of the Orange River Bridge on the Lucea–Green Island Harbour railway, now converted for tourist use. Unfortunately, two of the Jamaica-controlled agents received severe wounds from which they are now recovering in the Memorial Hospital. It remains to mention the names of Constable Percival Sampson of the Negril Constabulary who was first on the scene of the final battlefield, and Dr Lister Smith of Savannah La Mar who rendered vital first aid to Commander Bond and Mr Leiter. On the instructions of the Prime Minister, Sir Alexander Bustamante, a judicial inquiry was held this day at the bedside of Commander Bond and in the presence of Mr Felix Leiter to confirm the above facts. These, in the presence of Justice Morris Cargill of the Supreme Court, are now and hereby confirmed.'

The Commissioner was obviously delighted with his rendering of all this rigmarole. He beamed at Bond. 'It only remains', he handed Bond a sealed packet, a similar one to Felix Leiter and one to Colonel Bannister, 'to confer on Commander Bond of Great Britain, Mr Felix Leiter of the United States and, in absentia, Mr Nicholas Nicholson of the United States, the immediate award of the Jamaican Police Medal for gallant and meritorious services to the Independent State of Jamaica.'

There was muted applause. Mary Goodnight went on clapping after the others had stopped. She suddenly realized the fact, blushed furiously and stopped.

James Bond and Felix Leiter made stammered acknowledgments. Justice Cargill rose to his feet and, in solemn tones, asked Bond and Leiter in turn, 'Is this a true and correct account of what occurred between the given dates?'

'Yes, indeed,' said Bond.

'I'll say it is, Your Honour,' said Felix Leiter fervently.

The Judge bowed. All except Bond rose and bowed. Bond just bowed. 'In that case, I declare this inquiry closed.' The bewigged figure turned to Miss Goodnight. 'If you will be kind enough to obtain all the signatures, duly witnessed, and send them round to my chambers? Thank you so much.' He paused and smiled. 'And the carbon, if you don't mind?'

'Certainly, my lord.' Mary Goodnight glanced at Bond. 'And now, if you will forgive me, I think the patient needs a rest. Matron was most insistent …'

Goodbyes were said. Bond called Leiter back. Mary Goodnight smelled private secrets. She admonished, 'Now, only a minute!' and went out and closed the door.

Leiter leant over the end of the bed. He wore his most quizzical smile. He said, 'Well, I'll be goddamned, James. That was the neatest wrap-up job I've ever lied my head off at. Everything clean as a whistle and we've even collected a piece of lettuce.'

Talking starts with the stomach muscles. Bond's wounds were beginning to ache. He smiled, not showing the pain. Leiter was due to leave that afternoon. Bond didn't want to say goodbye to him. Bond treasured his men friends and Felix Leiter was a great slice of his past. He said, 'Scaramanga was quite a guy. He should have been taken alive. Maybe Tiffy really did put the hex on him with Mother Edna. They don't come like that often.'

Leiter was unsympathetic. 'That's the way you limeys talk about Rommel and Dönitz and Guderian. Let alone Napoleon. Once you've beaten them, you make heroes out of them. Don't make sense to me. In my book, an enemy's an enemy. Care to have Scaramanga back? Now, in this room, with his famous golden gun on you – the long one or the short one? Standing where I am? One bets you a thousand you wouldn't. Don't be a jerk, James. You did a good job. Pest control. It's got to be done by someone. Going back to it when you're off the orange juice?' Felix Leiter jeered at him. 'Of course you are, lamebrain. It's what you were put into the world for. Pest control, like I said. All you got to figure is how to control it better. The pests'll always be there. God made dogs. He

also made their fleas. Don't let it worry your tiny mind. Right?'
Leiter had seen the sweat on James Bond's forehead. He limped
towards the door and opened it. He raised his hand briefly. The
two men had never shaken hands in their lives. Leiter looked into
the corridor. He said, 'Okay, Miss Goodnight. Tell matron to take
him off the danger list. And tell him to keep away from me for a
week or two. Every time I see him a piece of me gets broken off.
I don't fancy myself as The Vanishing Man.' Again he raised his
only hand in Bond's direction and limped out.

Bond shouted, 'Wait, you bastard!' But, by the time Leiter had
limped back into the room, Bond, no effort left in him to fire off
the volley of four-letter words that were his only answer to his
friend, had lapsed into unconsciousness.

Mary Goodnight shooed the remorseful Leiter out of the
room and ran off down the corridor to the floor sister.

17 .... ENDIT

A WEEK later, James Bond was sitting up in a chair, a towel round his waist, reading Allen Dulles on *The Craft of Intelligence* and cursing his fate. The hospital had worked miracles on him, the nurses were sweet, particularly the one he called 'The Mermaid', but he wanted to be off and away. He glanced at his watch. Four o'clock. Visiting time. Mary Goodnight would soon be there and he would be able to let off his pent-up steam on her. Unjust perhaps, but he had already tongue-lashed everyone in range in the hospital and, if she got into the field of fire, that was just too bad!

Mary Goodnight came through the door. Despite the Jamaican heat, she was looking fresh as a rose. Damn her! She was carrying what looked like a typewriter. Bond recognized it as the Triple-X deciphering machine. Now what?

Bond grunted surly answers to her inquiries after his health. He said, 'What in hell's that for?'

'It's an "Eyes Only". Personal from M.,' she said excitedly. 'About thirty groups.'

'Thirty groups! Doesn't the old bastard know I've only got one arm that's working? Come on, Mary. You get cracking. If it sounds really hot, I'll take over.'

Mary Goodnight looked shocked. 'Eyes Only' was a top-sacred prefix. But Bond's jaw was jutting out dangerously. Today was not a day for argument. She sat on the edge of the bed, opened the machine and took a cable form out of her bag. She laid her shorthand book beside the machine, scratched the back of her head with her pencil to help work out the setting for the day – a complicated sum involving the date and the hour of dispatch of the cable – adjusted the setting on the central cylinder and began cranking the handle. After each completed word had appeared in the little oblong window at the base of the machine, she recorded it in her book.

James Bond watched her expression. She was pleased. After a few minutes she read out: 'M. PERSONAL FOR 007 EYES ONLY STOP YOUR REPORT AND DITTO FROM TOP FRIENDS [a euphemism for the C.I.A.] RECEIVED STOP YOU HAVE DONE WELL AND EXECUTED AYE DIFFICULT AND HAZARDOUS OPERATION TO MY ENTIRE REPEAT ENTIRE SATISFACTION STOP TRUST YOUR HEALTH UNIMPAIRED [Bond gave an angry snort] STOP WHEN WILL YOU BE REPORTING FOR FURTHER DUTY QUERY.'

Mary Goodnight smiled delightedly. 'I've never seen him be so complimentary! Have you, James? That repeat of ENTIRE! It's tremendous!' She looked hopefully for a lifting of the black clouds from Bond's face.

In fact Bond was secretly delighted, but he certainly wasn't going to show it to Mary Goodnight. Today she was one of the wardresses confining him, tying him down. He said grudgingly, 'Not bad for the old man. But all he wants is to get me back to that bloody desk. Anyway, it's a lot of jazz so far. What comes next?'

He turned the pages of his book, pretending as the little machine whirred and clicked not to be interested.

'Oh, James!' Mary Goodnight exploded with excitement. 'Wait! I'm almost finished. It's tremendous!'

'I know,' commented Bond sourly. 'Free luncheon vouchers every second Friday. Key to M.'s personal lavatory. New suit to replace the one that's somehow got full of holes.' But he kept his eyes fixed on the flitting fingers, infected by Mary Goodnight's excitement. What in hell was she getting so steamed up about? And all on his behalf! He examined her with approval. Perched there, immaculate in her white tussore shirt and tight beige skirt, one neat foot curled round the other in concentration, the golden face under the shortish fair hair incandescent with pleasure, she was, thought Bond, a girl to have around always. As a secretary? As what? Mary Goodnight turned, her eyes shining, and the question went, as it had gone for weeks, without an answer.

'Now, just listen to this, James.' She shook the notebook at him. 'And for heaven's sake stop looking so curmudgeonly.'

Bond smiled at the word. 'All right, Mary. Go ahead. Empty the Christmas stocking on the floor. Hope it's not going to bust any stitches.' He put his book down on his lap.

Mary Goodnight's face became portentous. She said seriously, 'Just listen to this!' She read very carefully: 'IN VIEW OF THE OUTSTANDING NATURE OF THE SERVICES REFERRED TO ABOVE AND THEIR ASSISTANCE TO THE ALLIED CAUSE COMMA WHICH IS PERHAPS MORE SIGNIFICANT THAN YOU IMAGINE COMMA THE PRIME MINISTER PROPOSES TO RECOMMEND TO HER MAJESTY QUEEN ELIZABETH THE IMMEDIATE GRANT OF A KNIGHTHOOD STOP THIS TO TAKE THE FORM OF THE ADDITION OF A KATIE AS PREFIX TO YOUR CHARLIE MICHAEL GEORGE. [James Bond uttered a defensive, embarrassed laugh. 'Good old cypherines. They wouldn't think of just putting KCMG – much too easy! Go

ahead, Mary. This is good!'] IT IS COMMON PRACTICE TO INQUIRE
OF PROPOSED RECIPIENT WHETHER HE ACCEPTS THIS HIGH HON-
OUR BEFORE HER MAJESTY PUTS HER SEAL UPON IT STOP WRIT-
TEN LETTER SHOULD FOLLOW YOUR CABLED CONFIRMATION OF
ACCEPTANCE PARAGRAPH THIS AWARD NATURALLY HAS MY SUP-
PORT AND ENTIRE APPROVAL AND EYE SEND YOU MY PERSONAL
CONGRATULATIONS ENDIT MAILEDFIST.'

James Bond again hid himself behind the throw-away line.
'Why in hell does he always have to sign himself "Mailedfist" for
"M."? There's a perfectly good English word "Em". It's a measure
used by printers. But of course it's not dashing enough for the
Chief. He's a romantic at heart like all the silly bastards who get
mixed up with the Service.'

Mary Goodnight lowered her eyelashes. She knew that
Bond's reflex concealed his pleasure – a pleasure he wouldn't for
the life of him have displayed. Who wouldn't be pleased, proud?
She put on a businesslike expression. 'Well, would you like me to
draft something for you to send? I can be back with it at six and
I know they'll let me in. I can check up on the right sort of for-
mula with the High Commissioner's staff. I know it begins with "I
present my humble duty to Her Majesty". I've had to help with the
Jamaica honours at New Year and her birthday. Everyone seems
to want to know the form.'

James Bond wiped his forehead with his handkerchief. Of
course he was pleased! But above all pleased with M.'s commen-
dation. The rest, he knew, was not in his stars. He had never been
a public figure and he did not wish to become one. He had no
prejudice against letters after one's name, or before it. But there
was one thing above all he treasured. His privacy. His anonym-
ity. To become a public person, a person, in the snobbish world
of England, of any country, who would be called upon to open
things, lay foundation stones, make after-dinner speeches,

brought the sweat to his armpits. 'James Bond'! No middle name. No hyphen. A quiet, dull, anonymous name. Certainly he was a Commander in the Special Branch of the R.N.V.R., but he rarely used the rank. His C.M.G. likewise. He wore it perhaps once a year, together with his two rows of 'lettuce', because there was a dinner for the 'Old Boys' – the fraternity of ex-Secret Service men that went under the name of 'The Twin Snakes Club' – a grisly reunion held in the banqueting hall at Blades that gave enormous pleasure to a lot of people who had been brave and resourceful in their day but now had old men's and old women's diseases and talked about dusty triumphs and tragedies which, since they would never be recorded in the history books, must be told again that night, over the Cockburn '12, when 'The Queen' had been drunk, to some next-door neighbour such as James Bond who was only interested in what was going to happen tomorrow. That was when he wore his 'lettuce' and the C.M.G. below his black tie – to give pleasure and reassurance to the 'Old Children' at their annual party. For the rest of the year, until May polished them up for the occasion, the medals gathered dust in some secret repository where May kept them.

So now James Bond said to Mary Goodnight, avoiding her eyes, 'Mary, this is an order. Take down what follows and send it tonight. Right? Begins, quote MAILEDFIST EYES ONLY [Bond interjected, I might have said PROMONEYPENNY. When did M. last touch a cypher machine?] YOUR [Put in the number, Mary] ACKNOWLEDGED AND GREATLY APPRECIATED STOP AM INFORMED BY HOSPITAL AUTHORITIES THAT EYE SHALL BE RETURNED LONDONWARDS DUTIABLE IN ONE MONTH STOP REFERRING YOUR REFERENCE TO AYE HIGH HONOUR EYE BEG YOU PRESENT MY HUMBLE DUTY TO HER MAJESTY AND REQUEST THAT EYE MAY BE PERMITTED COMMA IN ALL HUMILITY COMMA TO DECLINE THE SIGNAL FAVOUR HER MAJESTY IS GRACIOUS ENOUGH TO PROPOSE

TO CONFER UPON HER HUMBLE AND OBEDIENT SERVANT BRACKET
TO MAILEDFIST PLEASE PUT THIS IN THE APPROPRIATE WORDS
TO THE PRIME MINISTER STOP MY PRINCIPAL REASON IS THAT
EYE DONT WANT TO PAY MORE AT HOTELS AND RESTAURANTS
BRACKET.'

Mary Goodnight broke in, horrified. 'James. The rest is your
business, but you really can't say that last bit.'

Bond nodded. 'I was only trying it on you, Mary. All right,
let's start again at the last stop. Right, EYE AM A SCOTTISH PEAS-
ANT AND EYE WILL ALWAYS FEEL AT HOME BEING A SCOTTISH
PEASANT AND EYE KNOW COMMA SIR COMMA THAT YOU WILL
UNDERSTAND MY PREFERENCE AND THAT EYE CAN COUNT ON
YOUR INDULGENCE BRACKET LETTER CONFIRMING FOLLOWS
IMMEDIATELY ENDIT OHOHSEVEN.'

Mary Goodnight closed her book with a snap. She shook her
head. The golden hair danced angrily. 'Well really, James! Are you
sure you don't want to sleep on it? I knew you were in a bad mood
today. You may have changed your mind by tomorrow. Don't
you want to go to Buckingham Palace and see the Queen and the
Duke of Edinburgh and kneel and have your shoulder touched
with a sword and the Queen to say "Arise, Sir Knight" or whatever
it is she does say?'

Bond smiled. 'I'd like all those things. The romantic streak
of the S.I.S. – and of the Scot, for the matter of that. I just refuse
to call myself Sir James Bond. I'd laugh at myself every time I
looked in the mirror to shave. It's just not my line, Mary. The
thought makes me positively shudder. I know M.'ll understand.
He thinks much the same way about these things as I do. Trouble
was, he had to more or less inherit his K with the job. Anyway,
there it is and I shan't change my mind so you can buzz that off
and I'll write M. a letter of confirmation this evening. Any other
business?'

'Well there is one thing, James.' Mary Goodnight looked down her pretty nose. 'Matron says you can leave at the end of the week, but that there's got to be another three weeks' convalescence. Had you got any plans where to go? You have to be in reach of the hospital.'

'No ideas. What do you suggest?'

'Well, er, I've got this little villa up by Mona dam, James.' Her voice hurried. 'It's got quite a nice spare room looking out over Kingston harbour. And it's cool up there. And if you don't mind sharing a bathroom.' She blushed. 'I'm afraid there's no chaperone, but you know, in Jamaica, people don't mind that sort of thing.'

'What sort of thing?' said Bond, teasing her.

'Don't be silly, James. You know, unmarried couples sharing the same house and so on.'

'Oh, that sort of thing! Sounds pretty dashing to me. By the way, is your bedroom decorated in pink, with white jalousies, and do you sleep under a mosquito net?'

She looked surprised. 'Yes. How did you know?' When he didn't answer, she hurried on. 'And James, it's not far from the Liguanea Club and you can go there and play bridge, and golf when you get better. There'll be plenty of people for you to talk to. And then of course I can cook and sew buttons on for you and so on.'

Of all the doom-fraught graffiti a woman can write on the wall, those are the most insidious, the most deadly.

James Bond, in the full possession of his senses, with his eyes wide open, his feet flat on the linoleum floor, stuck his head blithely between the mink-lined jaws of the trap. He said, and meant it, 'Goodnight. You're an angel.'

At the same time, he knew, deep down, that love from Mary Goodnight, or from any other woman, was not enough for him. It would be like taking 'a room with a view'. For James Bond, the same view would always pall.

ABOUT THE AUTHOR

Courtesy of the Cecil Beaton Studio
Archive at Sotheby's

IAN FLEMING was born in London on May 28, 1908. He was educated at Eton College and later spent a formative period studying languages in Europe. His first job was with Reuters News Agency where a Moscow posting gave him firsthand experience with what would become his literary *bête noire*—the Soviet Union. During World War II he served as Assistant to the Director of Naval Intelligence and played a key role in Allied espionage operations.

After the war he worked as foreign manager of the *Sunday Times*, a job that allowed him to spend two months each year in Jamaica. Here, in 1952, at his home "Goldeneye," he wrote a book called *Casino Royale*—and James Bond was born. The first print run sold out within a month. For the next twelve years Fleming produced a novel a year featuring Special Agent 007, the most famous spy of the century. His travels, interests, and wartime experience lent authority to everything he wrote. Raymond Chandler described him as "the most forceful and driving writer of thrillers in England." Sales soared when President Kennedy named the fifth title, *From Russia With Love*, one of his favorite books. The Bond novels have sold more than one hundred million copies worldwide, boosted by the hugely successful film franchise that began in 1962 with the release of *Dr No*.

He married Anne Rothermere in 1952. His story about a magical car, written in 1961 for their only son, Caspar, went on to become the well-loved novel and film *Chitty Chitty Bang Bang*.

Fleming died of heart failure on August 12, 1964, at the age of fifty-six.

www.ianfleming.com